BOOK LOVERS'
EDINBURGH

For Chris

BOOK LOVERS' EDINBURGH

A GUIDE AND COMPANION

ALLAN FOSTER

Copyright © Allan Foster 2018
All rights reserved
The moral right of the author has been asserted

First published in 2005 by Mainstream Publishing
as *The Literary Traveller in Edinburgh*
Revised and updated in 2018
and published by Book Lovers' Press
under the title *Book Lovers' Edinburgh*

No part of this book may be reproduced or transmitted in any form or by any other means without permission in writing from the publisher, except by a reviewer who wishes to quote brief passages in connection with a review written for insertion in a magazine, newspaper or broadcast

The author has tried to clear all copyright permissions, but where this has not been possible and amendments are required, the publisher will be pleased to make any necessary arrangements at the earliest opportunity

Typeset in Minion Pro

CONTENTS

Old Town 8
Canongate 80
Holyrood 108
Calton 116

Southside 126
Mayfield 186
Sciennes 188
Marchmont 190
The Grange 192
Bruntsfield 194
Morningside 200
Craiglockhart 210

Greenside 216
Pilrig 230

West End 232
New Town 248
Stockbridge 302
Comely Bank 304

Dean Village 308
Canonmills 314
Inverleith 316

Colinton 318
Swanston 324
Pentland Hills 328

Leith 330
Portobello 334

Corstorphine 338
Turnhouse 340

Lasswade 344
Glencorse 348
Penicuik 350
Roslin 354
South Queensferry 358
Appendices 360
Index 372

PROLOGUE

Treat this book like a treasure map that tells ye whaur tae howk. Then tak yer hurdies on a puckle dander roond this windflaucht city. Sometimes yer shovel will turn up gold, occasionally a wee bit shite, but when yer lookin for literati, who knows whaur yer finger-nebbs will alight. A guid guidebook shouldnae tell ye ony mair than ye want tae know or huv time tae absorb, so I hope this book leaves ye gaggin fur a wee keek mair. And mony a keek lasted mony a man a' his days. The journey, of course, niver ends, but the treasure is there fur the takin.

Allan Foster

OLD TOWN

EDINBURGH CASTLE

It is hardly necessary to say much about this Castle, which everybody has seen; on which account, doubtless, nobody has ever yet thought fit to describe it – at least that I am aware. Be this as it may, I have no intention of describing it...
George Borrow, *Lavengro* (1851)

It may project a Colditz-like visage, but history has proved Edinburgh Castle about as impregnable as a child's piggy-bank. It never controlled any strategic north–south route and invading armies often just gave it a wide berth, fighting Scotland's decisive battles under the shadow of the much more tactically positioned Stirling Castle, 30 miles to the north-west. Much of the Scottish nobility shunned its refuge, preferring the delights of Holyrood, and according to Midlothian-born novelist Margaret Oliphant (1828–97), the room where Mary, Queen of Scots gave birth to the future James VI of Scotland and I of England 'would scarcely be occupied, save under protest, by a housemaid in our days'. Today, the Castle is one of the UK's most visited attractions, but if it's just the spectacular view you're after, nearby Calton Hill offers similar vistas at no charge. The old Parliament Hall, on the south side of the

Left: The south facing visage of Edinburgh Castle
Right: George Borrow

Grand Parade, was used for royal banquets as well as for meetings of Parliament. It was here in 1440 that the Earl of Douglas and his younger brother were invited to dine as guests of the King, ten-year-old James II, by his Regents Sir Alexander Livingston and Sir William Crichton. The House of Douglas was seen as a threat to the Regency and the invitation was a trap, described dramatically by Sir Walter Scott in *Tales of a Grandfather* (1828–30):

> Of a sudden, the scene began to change. At an entertainment which was served up to the Earl and his brother, the head of a black bull was placed on the table. The Douglases knew this, according to a custom which prevailed in Scotland, to be the sign of death, and leaped from the table in great dismay. But they were seized by armed men who entered the apartment. They underwent a mock trial, in which all the insolences of their ancestors were charged against them, and were condemned to immediate execution. The young King wept and implored Livingston and Crichton to show mercy to the young noblemen, but in vain. These cruel men only reproved him for weeping at the death of those whom they called his enemies. The brothers were led out to the court of the Castle, and beheaded without delay.

'The Vaults' were used as a prison for French soldiers during the Napoleonic Wars, a period which Robert Louis Stevenson used as the setting for *St Ives* (1897), in which he relates the adventures of the Vicomte de Saint-Yves:

> It was in the month of May 1813 that I was so unlucky as to fall at last into the hands of the enemy … Into the Castle of Edinburgh, standing in the midst of that city on the summit of an extraordinary rock, I was cast with several hundred fellow-sufferers …

English writer George Borrow (1803–81) lived within the Castle walls as a boy when his soldier father was posted there. The famous landmark duly features in his autobiographical novel *Lavengro* (1851). 'To scale the rock was merely child's play for the Edinbro' callants [young boys],' he recalled. Once, he casually remarked to a friend while seated at the rock's summit that the story of William Wallace was 'full of lies'. To this, his friend retorted, 'Ye had better sae naething agin Willie Wallace, Geordie, for if ye do, De'il hae me, if I dinna tumble ye doon the craig.'

Novelist Eric Linklater (1899-1974) was billeted at the Castle during The First World War after he was badly wounded at Ypres. He featured Edinburgh Castle in *The Impregnable Women* (1938), his modern version of Aristophanes' *Lysistrata*, and describes it in his 1934 novel, *Magnus Merriman*, as 'Scotland's castle, Queen Mary's castle and the castle of fifty thousand annual visitors who walk through it with rain on their boots and bewilderment in their hearts'.

SEE ALSO: Sir Walter Scott, Swanston Cottage, Margaret Oliphant.

FURTHER READING: M.D. Armstrong, *George Borrow* (Haskell House, 1982); M. Parnell, *Eric Linklater: A Critical Biography* (John Murray, 1984).

Edinburgh Castle viewed from West Princes Street Gardens

BOOK LOVERS' EDINBURGH

CASTLE HILL
Ramsay Garden
Ramsay Lodge
Home of Allan Ramsay (1686–1758)
Poet, bookseller, publisher and creator
of Britain's first lending library

When these good old Bards wrote, we had not yet made Use of imported Trimming.
Allan Ramsay, from the preface of *The Evergreen* (1724), a collection of Scots poems written before 1600

Allan Ramsay was the precursor of Robert Fergusson and Robert Burns in helping to reawaken and develop an interest in the vernacular tradition of Scottish song and verse, and, in so doing, inspired their genius. Like Fergusson and Burns, he enjoyed the camaraderie of the tavern, the bawdy song, the brothel and the language of the common people. He was a poet who became a bookseller and publisher, but probably more importantly, he

OLD TOWN

was also a great propagandist who did much to rejuvenate the Scots language.

He was born in Leadhills, Lanarkshire, on 15 October 1686. His father, who died shortly after his birth, was factor to the Earl of Hopetoun. In 1701, Ramsay was apprenticed to an Edinburgh wig-maker, and in 1710 opened his own premises in the Grassmarket. He was inspired to write verse when he became a member of the Easy Club, a literary and political drinking club he helped found in 1712. He became the Club Laureate in 1715 and began publishing his own work in broadsheets. His reputation as

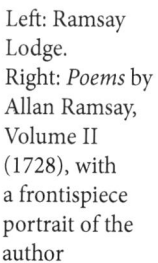
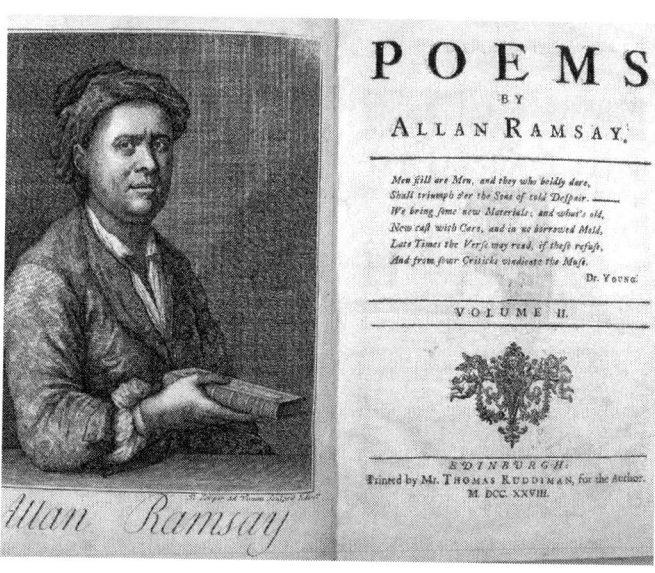

Left: Ramsay Lodge.
Right: *Poems* by Allan Ramsay, Volume II (1728), with a frontispiece portrait of the author

a poet began to grow and, in 1718, the master wig-maker metamorphosed into a bookseller and converted his premises into a bookshop. Four years later, he moved from the Grassmarket to a shop in the Luckenbooths 'alongside St Giles' Church', where his window looked onto the City Cross. It was from this building, in 1728, that Ramsay created the first lending library in Britain, wonderfully described by the God-fearing Reverend Robert Wodrow as a place where 'All the villainous, profane, and obscene

books and plays, as printed in London, are got down by Allan Ramsay and lent out, for an easy price, to young boys, servant weemen of the better sort, and gentlemen.'
He published the first collection of his own poems in 1721 and, in 1723, he published *The Tea-Table Miscellany*, collections of eighteenth-century songs and ballads, and, in 1724, *The Evergreen*, containing the works of Scotland's late medieval poets, including Dunbar and Henryson. In 1725, while living and trading in Niddry's Wynd (now Niddry Street) he produced his dramatic pastoral *The Gentle Shepherd*. Ramsay founded Edinburgh's first theatre in 1736 in Carrubber's Close, off the High Street, but this was soon closed down following the Licensing Act of 1737, which banned theatrical performances outside the City of London. Ramsay's wrath penned many a satirical verse to the Court of Session on this subject, which not only humiliated him, but 'cost him dearly':

> Shall London have its houses twa,
> And we be doomed to nane ava?
> Is our metropolis ance the place
> Where lang-syne dwelt the royal race
> Of Fergus, this gait dwindled doun
> To the level o' a clachan toun?
> While thus she suffers the desertion
> Of a maist rational diversion.

In 1755, he retired from his business to the house he had built on the slopes of Castle Hill. Known affectionately as 'the goosepie' because of its octagonal shape, he lived out the rest of his life there with his wife. He died on 7 January 1758 and is buried in an unmarked grave in Greyfriars Kirkyard. A plaque was erected in his memory on the south wall of Greyfriars Kirk during the nineteenth century. On Ramsay's death, his house passed to his son, Allan, the famous portrait painter. Other occupants over the years

OLD TOWN

have included poet and essayist Anne Grant (1755–1838) and novelist John Galt (1779–1839).

SEE ALSO: Greyfriars Kirkyard, Robert Fergusson, Robert Burns, William Dunbar.

FURTHER INFORMATION: Ramsay Garden is situated near the top of the Royal Mile below Edinburgh Castle. Ramsay Lodge was the first notable building to be erected on the site, which today houses some of the most expensive and desirable properties in the city.

FURTHER READING: J.B. Martin, *Allan Ramsay: A Study of his Life and Works* (Greenwood Press, 1973).

Allan Ramsay's statue in West Princes Street Gardens on the corner of The Mound and Princes Street

JAMES COURT
Site of the residence of James Boswell (1740-95), where Dr Johnson lodged prior to their tour of the Hebrides in 1773

Servile and impertinent, shallow and pedantic, a bigot and a sot, bloated with family pride, and eternally blustering about the dignity of a born gentleman, yet stooping to be a talebearer, and eavesdropper, a common butt in the taverns of London ... Everything which another man would have hidden, everything the publication of which would have made another man hang himself, was matter of exaltation to his weak and diseased mind.
Lord Macaulay (1800-59) on Boswell

James Boswell, a 'weak and diseased mind'

The American literary critic Edmund Wilson (1895-1972) once described Boswell as 'a vain and pushing artist', and he was probably right. He certainly comes across as extremely persistent and an ardent social climber. He also picked up prostitutes, contracted gonorrhoea, was the father of an illegitimate child, had prolonged bouts of drunkenness and was unfaithful to his wife. In spite of these apparent shortcomings, however, Boswell's inherently perspicacious nature and his intimate knowledge of Johnson have clearly combined to produce a biographical masterpiece in his *Life of Samuel Johnson*, which has never been equalled.

Boswell was born in Edinburgh in 1740, the eldest son of Lord Auchinleck, a lawyer who came from a family of wealthy Ayrshire landowners. He was educated at a private academy in Edinburgh and by private tutors, later studying law at Edinburgh, Glasgow and Utrecht. His ambitions began leaning towards literature, politics and the theatre, but it was as an advocate that he practised for most of his life, which left him feeling 'sadly low-spirited, indolent, listless and gloomy'. While in Europe, he skilfully effected meetings with Voltaire, Rousseau and the Corsican hero Pasquale Paoli, which inspired him to write his *Account of Corsica* (1768), his first significant work. In 1769, he married his cousin, Margaret Montgomerie, a long-suffering woman who endured his infidelities until her death, leaving Boswell with six children and a guilt complex.

He first met Dr Johnson (1709–84) on his second visit to London, on 16 May 1763, at Tom Davies' bookshop in Russell Street, and from then on cemented his friendship with him on his all-too-infrequent visits to London. On 14 August 1773, Dr Johnson arrived in Edinburgh to begin his famous tour of the Hebrides with Boswell, and it was at Boswell's townhouse at 501 on the western half of James Court (destroyed, unfortunately, by fire in 1857, but later rebuilt) that he entertained Johnson that Saturday evening:

> My wife had tea ready for him, which it is well known he delighted to drink at all hours, particularly when sitting up late. He shewed much complacency upon finding that the mistress of the house was so attentive to his singular habit; and as no man could be more polite when he chose to be so, his address to her was most courteous and engaging; and his conversation soon charmed her into a forgetfulness of his external appearance. We sat till near two in the morning, having chatted a good while after my wife left us. She had insisted, that to shew all respect to the Sage, she would give up her

own bed-chamber to him, and take a worse. This I cannot but gratefully mention, as one of a thousand obligations which I owe her, since the great obligation of her being pleased to accept of me as her husband.

On Wednesday, 18 August 1773, Boswell and Johnson set out from James Court on their celebrated tour of Scotland and the Hebrides, returning to Edinburgh 83 days later on Tuesday, 9 November. Johnson was 63 years old and Boswell 32. 'I mentioned our design to Voltaire,' wrote Boswell. 'He looked at me as if I had talked of going to the North Pole ...' They each kept a journal, and while Johnson was busy cynically scrutinising Scotland, Boswell was busy scrutinising and recording Johnson. 'We came too late,' wrote Johnson, 'to see what we expected.'

In 1784, when Boswell was 44, Johnson died. Two years later, Boswell was called to the English Bar and moved to London with his wife and children, but his practice was unsuccessful. He was also unsuccessful in his pursuit of a political career, and he eventually began to write his *Life of Samuel Johnson*, 'perhaps now the only concern of any consequence' that he would 'ever have in this world'. While he was writing his *Life*, other biographies of Johnson were being published, and his greatest fear must have been that the public, having gorged on Johnson, would finally say enough was enough – and Boswell's was stretching to two volumes at a cost of two guineas. It was finally published in 1791, and its reception, recorded Boswell, was 'very favourable'. Forty years later, in 1831, Thomas Macaulay declared it the best biography ever written, and Thomas Carlyle, writing in *Fraser's* magazine in 1832, described it as a book 'beyond any other product of the eighteenth century ... It was as if the curtains of the past were drawn aside, and we looked into a country ... which had seemed forever hidden from our eyes ... Wondrously given back to us, there once more it lay. There it still lies.'

Boswell, however, had always been well aware of his talents, writing in his journal for 20 January 1763, 'I think there is a blossom about me of something more distinguished than the generality of mankind.'

SEE ALSO: Dr Johnson, David Hume, St Giles.

FURTHER READING: I. Finlayson, *The Moth and the Candle: Life of James Boswell* (Constable, 1984); G. Turnbull (ed.), *The Yale Editions of the Private Papers of James Boswell* (Edinburgh Uni. Press, 2004); D. Hankins and J. Caudle (eds), *The General Correspondence of James Boswell, 1757-63* (Edinburgh Uni. Press, 2004).

The 1756 portrait of Johnson by Sir Joshua Reynolds just after publication of Johnson's famous Dictionary, and as it appeared in an engraving on the frontispiece to Boswell's *Life of Johnson*

RIDDLE'S COURT
Former home of David Hume (1711-76)
Philosopher, historian
and political thinker

A man who has so much conceit as to tell all mankind that they have bubbled for ages, and he is the wise man who sees better than they – a man who has so little scrupulosity as to venture to oppose those principles which have been thought necessary to human happiness – is he to be surprised if another man comes and laughs at him?
Dr Johnson on David Hume

Dr Johnson's reaction to Hume was typical for his time. As a celebrated atheist, sceptic, believer in civil liberties, opponent of 'divine right' and a political thinker who greatly influenced European thought, it's not surprising that many thought that David Hume was in league with the Devil. Even the binge drinking, whoring and gonorrhoea-ridden James Boswell thought his character might be besmirched by associating with Hume, commenting, 'I was not clear that it was right in me to keep company with him.' German philosopher Immanuel Kant, however, was not so blinkered, reporting in the *Prolegomena* that Hume 'first interrupted my dogmatic slumber', and Jeremy Bentham said Hume 'caused the scales to fall' from his eyes. Charles Darwin considered him a central influence, and history now rightfully ranks Hume as one of the great men of genius in eighteenth-century Edinburgh.
Born in Edinburgh in 1711, Hume spent his childhood at Ninewells, his family's estate near Chirnside in the Scottish Borders. When he was 12, he attended Edinburgh University but did not graduate. He later studied law and was briefly employed as a clerk for a Bristol sugar importer before entering the Jesuit College at La Flèche in 1734, where for three years he read French and other European

OLD TOWN

David Hume, after a portrait by Allan Ramsay, 1766

literature. It was here, between 1734 and 1737, that he drafted his first and most important work, *A Treatise of Human Nature*, which he published anonymously in 1739. Its hostile reception prompted Hume to describe it as falling 'dead-born from the press'. He produced two, more popular, volumes of *Essays Moral and Political* in 1741 and 1742. He applied for the chair of moral philosophy at Edinburgh in 1744, but his religious scepticism ruled against him. For the next seven or eight years, he held various posts as tutor, secretary and minor diplomat, returning to Edinburgh in 1751 to take up a post as librarian to the Faculty of Advocates.

Hume's first permanent Edinburgh home was at Riddel's Land (now Riddle's Court), 322 High Street, 'in the first court reached on entering the close, and it is approached by a projecting turret stair'. Hume described his household as 'consisting of a head, viz. myself, and two inferior members – a maid and a cat. My sister has since joined me, and keeps me company.' It was in this house that Hume wrote his *Political Discourses* (1752) and started on his monumental *History of England* (5 volumes, 1754–62). In 1753, he moved to Jack's Land, now renumbered 229 Canongate, where he lived for nine years, and where he completed his *History*, a work which became a bestseller and at last made him financially independent. From 1763 to 1765 he acted as secretary to the British ambassador in Paris, where he was fêted by the French court. He befriended Rousseau and returned to London with him in 1766, but they later quarrelled bitterly. In 1767, he became undersecretary of state for the Northern Department, returning to Scotland in 1768, where he lived out the rest of his life as a man of letters at his house on a corner of St Andrew Square – a then-unnamed street. One day, his maid informed him that someone had chalked 'St David Street' on the wall. 'Never mind, lassie, mony a waur man has been made a saint o' before.'

David Hume died aged 65 of intestinal cancer on 25 August 1776, and is buried in Old Calton Burial Ground, Waterloo Place.

SEE ALSO: Old Calton Burial Ground, Pilrig House, Dr Johnson, James Boswell, Old College.

FURTHER INFORMATION: During the 1960s, the southern edge of George Square was demolished to make way for the new campus of Edinburgh University. The tall tower built to the east of the library was named David Hume Tower, and a better example of an architectural monstrosity will not be found anywhere. Robert Garioch immortalised the tower in his poem 'A Wee Local Scandal'. A statue of David Hume was erected in 1997 on the corner of Bank Street and the High Street by the Saltire Society to mark its 60th anniversary. Due to the statue's low height, Hume's head can often be seen sporting a jaunty traffic cone.

OLD TOWN

Riddle's Court

FURTHER READING: R. Graham, *The Great Infidel* (Tuckwell Press, 2005); A.J. Ayer, *Hume* (Oxford, 1980); P. Jones, *Hume's Sentiments* (Edinburgh Uni. Press, 1982).

LADY STAIR'S CLOSE

SITE OF BAXTER'S CLOSE
Lodgings of Robert Burns (1759-96) on his first visit to Edinburgh during the winter of 1786-7

Men and women quite suddenly realised that here lay one who was the poet of the country - perhaps of mankind - as none had been before, because none before had combined so many human weaknesses with so great an ardour of living and so generous a warmth of admission. Certainly none had ever possessed a racier gift of expression for his own people. Catherine Carswell on the death of Burns, in *The Life of Robert Burns* (1930)

Robert Burns is without doubt the most celebrated of Scottish poets. He left for posterity a volume of work which, written in his native tongue and championing the common man, has contributed significantly to Scottish cultural identity. Following the success of the first edition of his poems in July 1786, the famous Kilmarnock edition of *Poems, Chiefly in the Scottish Dialect*, Burns was eager to print a second edition as soon as possible, but the Kilmarnock printer insisted on full payment in advance. Unable to pay, he was persuaded to try for a second edition in Edinburgh.

And so the 'ploughman poet' set out from Ayrshire for his first visit to the metropolis on a borrowed horse, arriving on the evening of 28 November 1786. After stabling his horse in the Grassmarket, he made his way to nearby Baxter's Close, off the Lawnmarket, where he shared lodgings with his old friend John Richmond, from Mauchline, employed at this time as a clerk in a law office. Richmond's

OLD TOWN

An engraving of Robert Burns after Alexander Naysmith's portrait of 1787

room, which he rented for three shillings a week, consisted of 'a deal table, a sanded floor and a chaff bed', and was conveniently situated below a brothel.

One of the first things Burns did after his arrival was to search out poet Robert Fergusson's neglected grave in Canongate Kirkyard and set the wheels in motion for a simple memorial stone to be erected over his unmarked grave. He also visited the Castle and the Palace, stood in reverence outside Allan Ramsay's house and climbed up Arthur's Seat with all the ardour of a typical tourist; but he had come to Edinburgh for much more than sightseeing.

In his pocket, he carried a sheaf of introductory letters from his Masonic brothers back in Ayrshire and, within a week, doors opened and his star began to rise. The Earl of

Glencairn was particularly helpful, and Professor Dugald Stewart was instrumental in getting the Kilmarnock edition favourably reviewed by Henry Mackenzie in The Lounger, a magazine published by William Creech, who was to become the publisher of the second edition of Burns's poems, the Edinburgh edition, in April 1787. Glencairn took out a subscription of 24 copies and persuaded the Caledonian Hunt to take 100 copies, which earned them the book's dedication. The Edinburgh edition was heavily oversubscribed, and, after a second and third print run, 3,000 copies were eventually printed. This edition had 22 new poems, including the 'Address to a Haggis', and the copyright was sold to Creech for 100 guineas.

Burns was 28 years old, just under 6 ft tall, well built with a slight stoop from years at the plough, and with the twinkle in his eyes of a Don Juan. Dressed in his famous blue coat, buff waistcoat, buckskin breeches and high boots, with neck and cuffs trimmed with lace, Robert Burns the ploughman poet had arrived.

Everybody who was anybody made a point of meeting this latest vogue of the city's salons and drawing rooms and Burns initially enjoyed being the focus of so much fame and attention. It wasn't long, however, before he began to feel like a prize pig brought from his pen for the amusement of the party guests. He wrote to a friend:

> I am willing to believe that my abilities deserved a better fate than the veriest shades of life; but to be dragged forth, with all my imperfections on my head, to the full glare of learned and polite observations, is what, I am afraid, I shall have bitter reason to repent.

Eventually, the novelty of the ploughman poet wore off for the city's literati and Burns became something of an embarrassment, with Dugald Stewart commenting, 'his conduct and manners had become so degraded that

OLD TOWN

decent persons could hardly take any notice of him'.

To be fair to Burns, he had probably had enough of the airs and graces of genteel Edinburgh and was reaching out for what he enjoyed best – drinking wine, wooing lassies and singing a bawdy song.

Although Burns had become disillusioned with the trappings of fame, he did achieve what he came to Edinburgh for: a second edition of his poems. He also befriended the printer of his book, William Smellie, who in turn introduced him to his famous drinking club, the Crochallan Fencibles. James Johnson approached Burns to help him with the lyrics of the second volume of his book, *Scots Musical Museum*, a collection of songs, many of which were eventually written by Burns and occupied him until the end of his life.

On 5 May 1787, Burns left Edinburgh on horseback for a tour of the Scottish Borders with his law-student friend and fellow Mason Bob Ainslie. One person Burns didn't meet in Edinburgh was James Boswell, who was visiting London at the time. History would have been the better for a description of the immortal bard from the pen of Boswell. One wonders what he would have made of Burns.

SEE ALSO: Anchor Close, St James Square, Buccleuch Street, Burns Monument, Canongate Kilwinning Lodge, White Hart Inn, St Giles, William Smellie, William Creech, The Writers' Museum, Sciennes Hill House, Robert Fergusson, Clarinda, Jean Lorimer, Henry Mackenzie, The Pear Tree pub.

FURTHER INFORMATION: Baxter's Close, which was demolished in 1798 during the construction of Bank Street, would have been on the east side of Lady Stair's Close. The area is now part of a large, open square which, in the eighteenth century, would have been cramped with the squalor of tenement buildings.

FURTHER READING: C. Carswell, *The Life of Robert Burns* (1930); D. Daiches, *Robert Burns* (Saltire, 1994).

BOOK LOVERS' EDINBURGH

THE WRITERS' MUSEUM
Dedicated to the life and works of Robert Burns, Sir Walter Scott and Robert Louis Stevenson

There's muckle lyin yont the Tay that's mair to me nor life. Violet Jacob (1863–1946). Quotation inscribed in stone in the Makars' Court

There is an argument for building a new and more spacious writers' museum for Edinburgh that would do full justice to its vast literary heritage, but trading the small and rather stuffy Lady Stair's House for a prizewinning architect's steel and glass vision would be literally losing the plot. Edinburgh's literary past is historically welded to the cramped, rabbit-warren ghetto of the Old Town, and it seems only fitting that a museum dedicated to three of its biggest hitters should be located here. Lady Stair's Close was the chief thoroughfare for foot passengers from the Old Town to the New Town prior to the opening of Bank Street. Today it is a spacious square, but in the eighteenth century this area was packed cheek by jowl with tenements, including the adjacent Baxter's Close, where Robert Burns lodged in the winter of 1786–7. Outside the museum is the Makars' Court, where Scottish writers, from the fourteenth-century poet John Barbour to Sorley Maclean, are celebrated with inscriptions carved into stones. The house, which has had many owners, was built in 1622 for local merchant Sir William Gray, but its most memorable occupant was the Dowager Countess of Stair, who presided over Edinburgh's fashionable society and, as the Viscountess Primrose, inspired Scott's story 'My Aunt Margaret's Mirror'.

The museum is on three floors. Artefacts connected to Stevenson on display include: various photographs and

paintings; the 'Davos' printing press on which he and Lloyd Osbourne produced *Moral Emblems* and *The Graver and the Pen*; a first edition of *A Child's Garden of Verses* (1885); letters to W.E. Henley and Alison Cunningham; a 1908 edition of *An Inland Voyage*; a copy of George Borrow's *The Bible in Spain*, which Stevenson took with him on his *Travels with a Donkey*; a wineglass and plate used at Vailima, the Stevensons' home in Samoa; riding boots used in Samoa; and also a cabinet made by the infamous

BOOK LOVERS' EDINBURGH

Deacon Brodie, which sat in young Louis's bedroom.

The Scott collection includes: his wallet; walking sticks; a brass face-plate and latch from 39 North Castle Street; a letter claiming exemption from the Army Reserve; a lock of Scott's hair; first editions of *Waverley*, *The Antiquary* and *The Vision of Don Roderick*; and a rocking horse with one foot-rest higher than the other to accommodate his right leg, disabled through poliomyelitis contracted when he was about 18 months old.

The Robert Burns collection includes: a lock of Jean Armour's hair; her gloves and umbrella; an account and receipt sent to Burns for the erection of a headstone on Robert Fergusson's unmarked grave; drawings and poetry by Clarinda; and a round carved oak table, made from the rafters of the Crochallan Fencibles' club rooms in Anchor Close.

SEE ALSO: Robert Burns, Sir Walter Scott, Robert Louis Stevenson, Clarinda, Robert Fergusson, William Smellie, The Edinburgh Book Lovers' Tour.

Detail from the carved stone lintel over the museum entrance dated 1622, with the initals of Sir William Gray, the city merchant who built the house, and his wife Geida Smith. Lady Stair purchased the house in c.1719 whereupon the close and the building acquired her name.

OLD TOWN

THE EDINBURGH BOOK LOVERS' TOUR
Dan Lentell, Features Editor for Edinburgh49, reviews the Tour:

'Don't expect a crowd.' As I pick my way towards the Writers' Museum I can't help wondering if Allan Foster hasn't rather overdone things in the modesty department. En route to the rendezvous I pass assorted aldermen, literary luminaries and even the odd duke (it's a truism of getting older that policemen and dukes all start looking younger). But it turns out that the gathered multitude isn't in Lady Stair's Close to join The Edinburgh Book Lovers' Tour.

My host explains that a memorial is being unveiled to Gavin Douglas (1474–1522) (no? – me neither) the priest, poet and statesman who translated *The Aeneid* into Middle Scots. Presumably paint dried faster at the turn of the sixteenth century, thus offering less spectacle, so this is how they spent their time. Douglas is the 37th writer to be commemorated with an inscribed flagstone – handy for that direct form of criticism alluded to in Byron's lament for Castlereagh. I will not find anything good to say about the flagstone commemorations until the organisers cease to shun McGonagall.

I have an awful lot good to say about Foster's approach to guiding, starting with the way he rides out the noisy intrusion into his routine by the horde of newly fledged Douglas groupies. The weather is on our side but even so Foster's laconic embrace acts like an umbrella on our small party, shielding we few from the outside elements. It's an odd thing taking a walking tour through one's own regular haunts – unsettling, almost. That is until you remember how much fun you will have over the coming months lecturing anyone fortunate enough to be in company with you on the Southside's glorious (and not so glorious) literary heritage. Foster is not short of an opinion or three but he is better than most (present author included) at separating his commentary from reportage.

Our route takes us from the Writers' Museum, across the Royal Mile to Parliament Square, down Barrie's Close, along the Cowgate to the Old Infirmary, up Drummond Street through the Potterrow Port and via George Square, before concluding beside Greyfriars.

Along the way we are treated to a grand narrative, illustrated with dozens of facts trivial and otherwise. My two companions are a journalist and English professor from daaahn sauff and Newfoundland respectively. I enjoy chatting to them as we pass from point to point. This is not such familiar geography for them but then they have sailed to Treasure Island, peered under morgue sheets with Rebus, played Quidditch with Potter and gazed upon the gently rolling eyes induced by Scott's best romantic vistas. This rain-soaked ground we Edinbuggers bustle about on is holy. It slowly dawns on me how much we are taking for granted. It's not just the sack of Robert Louis Stevenson's beloved Rutherford's Bar by pirates of the Caribbean. Nor how little bronze or marble denotes the untended springs of creativity sacred to Clio, Calliope, Melpomene and their sisters. It's the sinking feeling that we are not much better than the historically illiterate residents of Worcester who met Messrs Adams and Jefferson with such bemused incomprehension and contempt.

Scott was derided in his own life for writing popular trash unworthy of a gentleman of letters. Despite huge sales and an even larger intellectual impact (especially, much to the regret of Mark Twain, in the American South) the true identity of 'The Author of Waverley' was kept an open secret in case it sullied Scott's true reputation as a provincial lawyer. Foster does not avoid questions of taste when discussing Edinburgh's literary present but does identify them as secondary and somewhat unbecoming. Foster is not crippled by paroxysms of grief, as is one former literary editor of the North Britischer newspaper of my acquaintance, when he thinks of the work McCall Smith, Rowling and Rankin could be writing – what matters is that they are writing (and, incidentally, are being read by millions).

For the visitor this must surely be the best tour available. For the resident, The Edinburgh Book Lovers' Tour is a masterclass in presenting our city to visitors. Unlike the former literary editor and his discredited vintage of print pundits there is nothing in Foster cringing or apologetic. The plaque to Rowling just above eye level across from Old College is treated with as much deference as are those to Stevenson or McGonagall across the way. Knowledgeable and in the know, he must navigate the tour by all the names he drops, Foster is informed and informative. Lyrically laconic but also hugely welcoming. A civic ambassador extraordinaire.

Statue of Gavin Douglas at the west door of St Giles' Cathedral, Edinburgh

FURTHER INFORMATION: The Edinburgh Book Lovers' Tour is a guided walking tour visiting the sites and haunts of Edinburgh's literary legends: Robert Burns, Sir Walter Scott, Robert Louis Stevenson, Sir Arthur Conan Doyle, J.M. Barrie, Alexander McCall Smith, Ian Rankin, J.K. Rowling and others in the company of Allan Foster, author of *Book Lovers' Edinburgh*. The tour departs from outside The Writers' Museum throughout the year. For further details visit edinburghbooktour.com

BRODIE'S CLOSE
Site of Deacon Brodie's house
A notorious burglar who fascinated and inspired Robert Louis Stevenson

Do you see this table, Walter? He made it while he was yet a 'prentice. I remember how I used to sit and watch him at his work. It would be grand, I thought, to be able to do as he did, and handle edge-tools without cutting my fingers, and getting my ears pulled for a meddlesome minx!
From *Deacon Brodie, or, The Double Life* (1880), by RLS and W.E. Henley

William Brodie entered Stevenson's imagination, and no doubt his nightmares, from a very early age. His bedroom at Heriot Row – which was furnished with items of furniture made by Brodie – was where his nurse Cummy, 'with her vivid Scotch imagination' (recalled Stevenson's wife), had told him endless tales about the rogue.
Brodie was a cabinet-maker and respected member of the Town Council, but after hours he whored, gambled, boozed and supported two mistresses and numerous children. He financed his expensive lifestyle with nocturnal robberies, often carried out on his customers using door keys copied while working in their houses. His last armed robbery was at the excise office in Chessels Court, on the Canongate, where the authorities caught his gang in the act. Brodie escaped to Holland, but was later captured. He was hanged at the Tolbooth on a gallows of his own design in 1788, and is buried in an unmarked grave in the kirkyard of the former Buccleuch Parish Church.
Stevenson wrote a play about this unsavoury character with his friend W.E. Henley in 1880. They wrote three more plays together, but neither were dramatists, and the plays are rarely read, let alone performed, today.

OLD TOWN

To say that Deacon Brodie inspired *The Strange Case of Dr Jekyll and Mr Hyde* would be stretching it, but it was probably one of many ingredients which seeped into Stevenson's 'fine bogey tale' about the division of good and evil in man. Stevenson wrote the story, which came to him in a dream, when he was seriously ill with a 'hectic fever' and on a six-day cocaine bender, at his house in Bournemouth in 1885. The first draft of the story was written in three days, but after Stevenson's wife criticised him for missing the point, i.e. missing the allegory, he burned the manuscript and rewrote the story as we know it today. Although it is set in London, it was Edinburgh that inspired many of the landscapes. The story became a bestseller in Britain and America and the adjectival expression 'Jekyll and Hyde' is now part of the English language.

Hanging sign for Deacon Brodie's Tavern, with Brodie holding keys copied for his next unlawful entry. The pub is directly across the street from Brodie's Close

SEE ALSO: Howard Place, Inverleith Terrace, Heriot Row, Pilrig House, Colinton Manse, Swanston Cottage, Baxter's Place, Glencorse Kirk, Rutherford's Howff, New Calton Cemetery, Old Calton Burial Ground, St Giles, Hawes Inn, Rullion Green, W.E. Henley, Alison Cunningham, Henderson's School, *Kidnapped* Statue, RLS Club, Museum of Scotland, George Mackenzie, Martyrs' Monument, Old College, Parliament Hall, Holyrood Park, Royal College of Surgeons' Museum, R.M. Ballantyne, RLS Memorial, Edinburgh Castle.

FURTHER INFORMATION: A cabinet made by Deacon Brodie, which was in Stevenson's childhood bedroom, can be seen at The Writers' Museum, Lady Stair's Close.

FURTHER READING: J. Herdman, *The Double in Nineteenth-Century Fiction* (Palgrave, 1990); W. Veeder & G. Hirsch (eds), *Dr Jekyll and Mr Hyde after One Hundred Years* (University of Chicago Press, 1988).

THE HEART OF MIDLOTHIAN
The Old Tolbooth Prison
featured in Walter Scott's 1818 novel

The Heart of Midlothian was the nickname of the Old Tolbooth Prison, which was situated close to the northwest corner of St Giles'. Built in the early fifteenth century, it served over the years as a town hall, a customs office, a Parliament and a Court of Session. An eighteenth-century visitor to the prison described it as having 'no ventilation, water nor privy: filth was thrown into a hole at the foot of the stair, leading to a drain so completely choked as to serve no other purpose but filling the gaol with a disagreeable stench'. The Heart of Midlothian was also the name of the prison's punishment cell: a 9-ft square, ironplated oak chest, built into a stone wall and sealed by a heavy iron door. When the prison was demolished in 1817, Walter Scott acquired the door of the punishment cell and added it to his collection of relics at Abbotsford, his Borders retreat.

OLD TOWN

Captain Porteous was imprisoned in the Old Tolbooth after he was sentenced to death for ordering the City Guard to open fire on a stone-throwing crowd after a public hanging in the Grassmarket in 1736. He was later reprieved, but an enraged Edinburgh mob dispensed its own justice, storming the Tolbooth and hanging him from a dyer's pole. Scott recounted the events of that night in his novel *The Heart of Midlothian* (for a full account, see Grave of Captain Porteous, Greyfriars Kirkyard). Dorothy Dunnett imprisoned her romantic hero, Francis Crawford of Lymond, in the Old Tolbooth in her very first historical novel, *The Game of Kings*, published in 1961. The site of the prison today is marked by inlaid brass sets, and a heartshaped motif sunk into the cobbles, near the statue of the Seventh Duke of Queensberry. As befits the memory of such an obnoxious place, the passing public traditionally embellish the cobbled motif with generous gobbets of spit, although the reasoning behind the gesture for most daily gob-droppers has long been forgotten.

Left: An engraving of the Old Tolbooth from a watercolour by Sir Daniel Wilson
Right: The Heart of Midlothian motif

SEE ALSO: Birthplace of W.S., childhood home of W.S., townhouse of W.S., Lasswade Cottage, Parliament Hall, Greyfriars Kirkyard, Scott Monument, Holyrood Park, St John's Churchyard, The Writers' Museum, High School, Old College, Sciennes Hill House, Assembly Rooms, J.G. Lockhart, Portobello Sands, Canongate Kirkyard, Dorothy Dunnett.

FURTHER INFORMATION: In 1813, an Act of Parliament proposed the building of a new prison, and Calton Jail opened in 1817 on Regent Road, the year the Old Tolbooth was demolished. Although the new prison had a modern interior, the exterior was in a fake-Gothic style inspired by the Waverley novels. The turrets of the old governor's house can still be seen in the southeast corner of the Old Calton Burial Ground, Waterloo Place.

PARLIAMENT SQUARE
Parliament Hall
Where advocates Walter Scott and Robert Louis Stevenson perambulated in conference with their clients

I walk about Parliament House five forenoons a week, in wig and gown; I have either a five- or six-mile walk, or an hour or two hard skating on the rink, every afternoon, without fail.
RLS, letter to Sidney Colvin (1875)

Although Scott and Stevenson both qualified as advocates, their law careers were very different. Stevenson passed his Bar exams in July 1875 and was given the enormous sum of £1,000 from his father to launch his legal career. He ceremoniously put up a brass plaque at 17 Heriot Row, but shortly afterwards he retired from the law, by which time the money was all spent. Financial insecurity never appeared on his horizon as his father bankrolled him well into his writing career. Earning a living as a lawyer was never seriously considered.

Scott remained a lawyer all his days. In 1792, he qualified as an advocate, became principal clerk to the Court of Session in 1806 and remained sheriff-deputy of Selkirkshire until his death in 1832. His first novel, *Waverley*, was published in 1814, but novel-writing at that time was viewed as a lowly form of literature – certainly not something a principal clerk to the Court of Session should be involved with – and Scott sensibly published anonymously. Also, Scott liked being a part of the Establishment, and a career in the legal world ensured he remained part of it.

The courts are housed in old Parliament House, a seventeenth-century building fronted by a nineteenth-century facade in Parliament Square, home of the Scottish Parliament between 1639 and the Act of Union in 1707 and now part of the High Court complex. The building comprises Parliament Hall and the Inner and Outer Houses. Advocates still promenade and strut around Parliament Hall today, just as Scott and Stevenson would have done, but not waiting to be hired; more likely taking a break from court, or in conference with a client. Under the gilded oak hammerbeam roof of the Great Hall stands a statue of Scott, surrounded by portraits of legal worthies over the centuries, lit by the huge Great South Window depicting James V founding the College of Justice.

Parliament Hall. Where RLS walked about 'five forenoons a week, in wig and gown'

SEE ALSO: Sir Walter Scott, Robert Louis Stevenson, Quintin Jardine, National Library of Scotland.

FURTHER INFORMATION: Parliament Hall is open to the public. Admission free. RLS's advocate's thesis is in the National Library of Scotland. In Scotland an advocate is the lawyer who presents a case in court on someone else's behalf. In England they are known as barristers.

HIGH STREET
St Giles' Cathedral
The High Kirk of Edinburgh

Come, let me see what was once a church!
Dr Johnson in Boswell's *Journal of a Tour to the Hebrides* (1785)

A church has stood on this site at the centre of the Old Town since before AD 854. Over 1,000 years later, St Giles', reputedly named after a French saint who supported the Auld Alliance between Scotland and France, still stands unyielding, having survived numerous reincarnations, renovations, burnings, riots, the doctrines of John Knox and the stinging criticisms of Dr Johnson and Robert Louis Stevenson, the latter remarking, in 1878, on its latest renovation in *Edinburgh: Picturesque Notes*:

> The church itself, if it were not for the spire, would be unrecognisable; the Krames are all gone, not a shop is left to shelter in its buttresses; and zealous magistrates and a misguided architect have shorn the design of manhood, and left it poor, naked, and pitifully pretentious.

Boswell thought it 'shamefully dirty' (an ironic comment coming from someone Dr Johnson could smell in the dark! – see Canongate, Boyd's Entry), but considering St Giles' has been used over the years as a prison, police office and general storeroom, its past state of degradation is not surprising. Today it stands solitary and detached, but until fairly recently in history it was cramped by encroaching tenements, the Old Tolbooth Prison and the Luckenbooths shopping arcade – seven timber-fronted tenements of six storeys clamped to its north wall. The clutter and filth of its past have now disappeared, but even in the twentieth century, in Muriel Spark's *The Prime of Miss Jean Brodie*,

OLD TOWN

The crown spire of St Giles'

BOOK LOVERS' EDINBURGH

David Hume's statue on the corner of Bank St. and Lawnmarket, with St Giles' in the distance

the haunting presence of 'its tattered bloodstained banners of the past' sent a chill through Jean Brodie's pupil Sandy, who 'had not been there, and did not want to go'. St Giles' first minister after the Reformation in 1560 was John Knox (*c*.1513-72), a theologian who has been branded by history as a joyless, narrow-minded bigot. Rightly or wrongly, anyone who writes a tract entitled 'The First Blast of the Trumpet Against the Monstrous Regiment of Women' has to take what's coming to them. Nobody, however, can deny Knox's place as the father of the Protestant Reformation in Scotland, which replaced the Catholic Church with the Presbyterian Church of Scotland, founded on Calvinist principles. His *Historie of the Reformation of the Church of Scotland* was first printed in 1587. The poet Edwin Muir wrote a biography of Knox, but when writing it came to dislike Knox intensely, understanding 'why every Scottish writer since the beginning of the eighteenth century had detested him: Hume, Boswell, Burns, Scott, Hogg, Stevenson; everyone except Carlyle, who, like Knox, admired power'. Dr Johnson described Knox as one of the 'ruffians of the Reformation' and Boswell relates in his *Journal of a Tour to the Hebrides* that he 'happened to ask where Knox was buried'. Dr Johnson burst out, 'I hope in the highway. I have been looking at his reformations.' Dr Johnson almost got his wish. Knox was buried in St Giles' Churchyard, which once stretched from its southern wall down to the Cowgate. Today it has been completely built over, and John Knox now lies under asphalt, at the rear of St Giles', near the statue of Charles II. Sixteenth-century soldier of fortune Francis Crawford of Lymond fought a duel with the truly evil Sir Graham Reid Malett on the steps of St Giles' altar in Dorothy Dunnett's historical novel *The Disorderly Knights* (1966), where the Kirk's 'long, white tapers pricked to life with their small flame the dim treasures of jewels and paintings, of silver-gilt and delicate, hand-sewn fabric'.

Jenny Geddes, who kept a greengrocer's stall outside the Tron Kirk, is famous in the history of St Giles' for chucking a stool at the Dean of Edinburgh when he began reading from an English prayer book in 1637 (part of Charles I's policy of imposing Episcopalianism in Scotland, which, for many, reeked of Catholicism). 'Villain! Dost thou say Mass at ma lug?' screamed Jenny at the pulpit. The Dean made a hasty retreat, followed by a volley of stones outside in the street, and the rioting that ensued led eventually to the signing of the National Covenant.

To view St Giles' many literary memorials, enter through the main west entrance and walk anticlockwise round its walls.

Robert Burns (1759–96)
On entering, turn full circle to view the centre stained-glass window installed in the west gable celebrating 'Robert Burns, poet of humanity'.

Robert Louis Stevenson (1850–94)
About 20 paces from the entrance, over on the right, is the Moray Aisle, where a memorial to Robert Louis Stevenson can be seen. In 1887, RLS and his family were in New York, where the American sculptor Augustus Saint-Gaudens started work on a medallion of RLS, sculpted from sittings at St Stephen's Hotel from 23 September. The medallion was not completed until five years later, and ended up on display in the hall at Vailima, the Stevensons' home in Samoa. In a letter to Saint-Gaudens, written in July 1894, RLS describes the medallion's arrival at Vailima:

> This is to tell you that the medallion has been at last triumphantly transported up the hill and placed over my smoking-room mantelpiece. It is considered by everyone a first-rate but flattering portrait. We have it in a very good light which brings out the artistic merits of the god-like sculptor to great advantage. As for my opinion, I believe it to be a speaking likeness and not flattering at all, possibly a little the reverse.

Stevenson was ill at the time of the first sittings and in bed draped with blankets, as early sketches revealed, but when Saint-Gaudens was working on the finer details in the spring of 1888, when RLS's health had much improved, the sculptor transformed the sickbed to a couch and the blankets to a travelling rug.

An enlarged copy was erected at St Giles' in 1904 based on the original medallion, which featured RLS with newspaper, cigarette and ivy border. For the enlarged memorial, however, what was considered a more 'timeless' image was created: the cigarette became a pen and a decorative border of heather and hibiscus, intertwining Scotland and Samoa, was included. Personally, I can't think of a more representative image of RLS than of his lying in bed covered in blankets smoking endless fags. Why the substituted pen should make him more 'timeless' is beyond me, and I can't help feeling he's been sanitised for posterity. 'It's no like him!' commented his old nurse Cummy; but his wife, Fanny, claimed it was her favourite image of her husband.

Margaret Oliphant (1828–97)

Along the wall from RLS, beneath the window, to the right of a door, is a gold-reliefed plaque in memory of Margaret Oliphant. Novelist, essayist, biographer and historian, Oliphant wrote over 100 books, but is best remembered for her *Chronicles of Carlingford* series (1863–76), which earned her the sobriquet 'a feminist Trollope'. Born in Wallyford, she married her artist cousin Francis Oliphant and was early widowed. Left with debts and three young children to bring up, she was forced to write for an income. From her house in Fettes Row, her pen poured out a prolific flow of work, distinguishing her as Edinburgh's first full-time woman of letters. She formed a close relationship with Edinburgh publisher Blackwood and *Blackwood's Magazine*, writing their history in *Annals of a Publishing House* (1897). A memorial service was held for her in 1908 at St Giles', during which she was described in an address as 'the greatest Scottish female writer since Mrs Ferrier'.

Robert Fergusson (1750–74)

To Oliphant's left is a memorial plaque to the witty and earthy poetic genius Robert Fergusson, whom Burns acknowledged as his 'elder brother in misfortune, by far my elder brother in the muse'. Fergusson died aged only 24, in the public asylum, which stood behind the building that is now the Bedlam Theatre in Forrest Road.

BOOK LOVERS' EDINBURGH

Gavin Douglas (*c*.1474–1522)
Opposite the organ gallery, to the right of the green choir stalls, is a memorial plaque to Scottish poet and prelate Gavin Douglas, who, from 1501 to 1514, was Provost of St Giles'. He is best remembered for his Scottish vernacular translation of *The Aeneid* (*Eneados, with prologues*, 1553) and his allegorical poem *The Palice of Honour* (*c*.1501). Through the influence of Queen Margaret Tudor, he became Bishop of Dunkeld in 1515, an affiliation which later caused him to be imprisoned in Edinburgh Castle. In 1521, he was found guilty of treason and exiled to England, where he died of the plague.

Walter Chepman (1473–1538)
To the left of the organ gallery is the Chepman Aisle, last resting place of Walter Chepman, who, with master printer Androw Myllar, set up Edinburgh's first printing press in 1507. Chepman was a local merchant and clerk to the King's secretary, who was granted a Royal patent to procure a printing press. They operated from the Cowgate, at the foot of Blackfriars Wynd, with equipment imported from France, where Myllar had trained as a printer. Little of their work survives today, although four copies of their original *Aberdeen Breviary* still exist.

Marquess of Montrose (1612–50)
Also in the Chepman Aisle lies one of the great romantic figures of Scottish history, James Graham, Marquess of Montrose: poet, soldier, Calvinist, Royalist and one of the first to put his name to the National Covenant in support of Presbyterianism in 1638. He later defected to the King, but was eventually betrayed and hanged at the Cross in the High Street on 21 May 1650. His body was quartered and displayed at the gates of Stirling, Glasgow, Perth and Aberdeen. His trunk was buried on the Burgh Muir and his head fixed to a spike on the

OLD TOWN

Tolbooth. Eleven years later, Charles II ordered that his remains be gathered and buried in St Giles' Cathedral. On the anniversary of his death, his tomb is often bedecked with flowers from admirers around the world. During his imprisonment, he wrote the following poem:

> Let them bestow on ev'ry airt a limb;
> Open all my veins, that I may swim
> To thee my Saviour, in that crimson lake;
> Then place my pur-boil'd head upon a stake;
> Scatter my ashes, throw them in the air;
> Lord (since Thou know'st where all these atoms are)
> I'm hopeful, once Thou'lt recollect my dust,
> And confident Thou'lt raise me with the just

The tomb of the Marquess of Montrose

Robert Stevenson Memorial Window
A stained-glass window in memory of RLS's grandfather, Robert Stevenson (1772–1850), by James Ballantyne, 1873, can be seen at the n. east corner (top left) of the Cathedral.

William Chambers (1800–83)
In the first aisle after the gift shop lies the tomb of William Chambers. The brothers William and Robert Chambers

(1802–71) were born into a mill-owning family in Peebles who hit hard times after their charitable father reputedly issued cloth on credit to French prisoners of war to make themselves clothes during the war with Napoleon. After the war, they returned to France promising to repay their benefactor, but they never did, and the family was ruined. William became apprenticed to an Edinburgh bookseller, and shortly afterwards his younger brother Robert set up as a bookseller on Leith Walk. When William's apprenticeship came to an end, he went into partnership with his brother. They purchased a small handpress and in 1824 printed and published Robert's *Traditions of Edinburgh*. In 1832, they began publishing *The Chambers' Journal*, a weekly magazine, the circulation of which reached 84,000 copies within a few years. *Chambers' Encyclopaedia* followed in 1859, published in 520 parts between 1859 and 1868. Educational publishing made both brothers extremely wealthy and their many philanthropic gestures included funding the restoration of St Giles'. William was Lord Provost of Edinburgh twice.

James Dalrymple, 1st Viscount Stair (1619–95)
On the archway of the next aisle, the St Eloi Aisle, is a plaque to the memory of Viscount Stair, whose place in Scottish literary history was secured when the marriage of his daughter, Janet Dalrymple, inspired Sir Walter Scott's *The Bride of Lammermoor* (1819), a love story set against political intrigues following the aftermath of the Civil War. Scott wrote the novel during a period of illness when suffering from excruciating stomach cramps. Too ill to correct the proofs, he was heavily drugged, and reputedly had no recollection of writing it, describing it as 'monstrous, gross and grotesque'.

SEE ALSO: Robert Louis Stevenson, Sir Walter Scott, James Boswell, Dr Johnson, Robert Burns, Robert Fergusson, Robert Stevenson, Dorothy Dunnett, William Blackwood.

OLD TOWN

FURTHER READING: E.J. Cowan, *Montrose: For Covenant and King* (Weidenfeld & Nicolson, 1977); J. Buchan, *Montrose* (House of Stratus, 2001); M. Oliphant and Mrs H. Coghill (ed.), *Autobiography and Letters of Mrs Margaret Oliphant* (1899); J. Ridley, *John Knox* (Oxford Uni. Press, 1968).

The west facing facade and main entrance of St Giles'

BOOK LOVERS' EDINBURGH

ADVOCATE'S CLOSE
Site of the first appearance of Bob Skinner, Quintin Jardine's maverick detective

As a city, Edinburgh is a two-faced bitch.
Quintin Jardine, *Skinner's Rules* (1993)

Frequently referred to as Edinburgh's most famous crime writer after Ian Rankin, Quintin Jardine can rattle out a novel in four months, although his personal record for a book is five weeks. Devoted fans can usually rely on the appearance of two books a year – proof that crime writing may be formulaic, but at least its adherents don't kick their heels for long.

Quintin Jardine

An only child, Jardine was born in Motherwell to parents who were both teachers. Educated at Glasgow High School for Boys, he started his working life as a junior reporter on the *Motherwell Times* and later the *Daily Record*. After a stint as a government press officer, he joined the Scottish Tories as their senior press officer in 1980. In 1985 he set up his own public-relations firm, and in 1997 he defected from the Tories to join the SNP. Jardine began writing in his mid-40s after reading a trashy novel while on holiday. 'I can do better than that,' he thought. Sounds like a cliché, but the result was *Skinner's Rules*, published in 1993, which introduced the unorthodox Edinburgh cop Bob Skinner, a character for whom lovers of the genre seem to have an inexhaustible appetite. Almost equally popular are his books about Oz Blackstone, a private investigator turned Hollywood movie star.

Bob Skinner made his first appearance at the mouth of Advocate's Close, opposite St Giles', and has subsequently appeared at many city locations, including: his base at police headquarters in Fettes Avenue; Murrayfield Stadium in the climax of *Stay of Execution*; the Crown Jewel Chamber at Edinburgh Castle in *Festival*; gunplay breaks out in Parliament Hall at the end of *Autographs in the Rain*; Skinner foils a bomb plot at the Edinburgh International Conference Centre in *Thursday Legends*; and the tropical section of the big greenhouse at the Royal Botanic Gardens is where Skinner had a fight almost to the death with Big Lenny Plenderleith.

Today, Quintin Jardine divides his time between his house in Gullane and his retreat in Catalonia, where he does much of his writing. His spin-doctor days are now history, but in a radio interview he was asked the question, 'You were a Tory press officer; what made you want to write fiction?'

46–54 CANDLEMAKER ROW
Site of the Harrow Inn, periodic residence of James Hogg, the Ettrick Shepherd (1770–1835)

Pray, who wishes to know anything about his [Hogg's] life? Who indeed cares a single farthing whether he be at this blessed moment dead or alive? Only picture yourself a stout country lout with a bushel of hair on his shoulders that had not been raked for months, enveloped in a coarse plaid impregnated with tobacco, with a prodigious mouthful of immeasurable tusks, and a dialect that sets all conjecture at defiance …
John Wilson (Christopher North)
'Noctes Ambrosianae', *Blackwood's Magazine*

James Hogg was a distinct oddity in the Edinburgh literary world of the early nineteenth century. A Border poet with a shepherd's plaid slung across his shoulders, his crudeness and outspokenness sent shockwaves through the salons of the city's literati. Initially, they were charmed and reverential, but eventually they tired of him and often ridiculed him as the novelty of the artistic bumpkin wore thin. A similar reception had greeted the 'ploughman poet' Robert Burns a generation earlier. But Hogg was no transient performing seal for New Town drawing rooms and dining clubs. He evolved into a major writer who was admired by Byron and André Gide, and has influenced Scottish writers from Robert Louis Stevenson to Muriel Spark. In 1824, he wrote

The Ettrick Shepherd, 1819

one of the masterpieces of Scottish literature: *The Private Memoirs and Confessions of a Justified Sinner*.

Hogg was born the second of four sons in 1770 in the parish of Ettrick in the Scottish Borders. When he was six years old, his father, an impoverished farmer, became bankrupt and he was forced to leave school. Most of his childhood was spent working on farms and, in his mid-teens, he became a shepherd and taught himself to write and play the fiddle. From his mother, he had learned the oral tradition of ballads and Borders folklore. His mother had inherited these songs and stories from her father, the legendary Will o' Phaup, reputed to have been the last man to converse with the fairies. Soon, Hogg was composing his own songs and verses, publishing his first poem in *The Scots Magazine* in 1793, and in 1801 publishing *Scottish Pastorals*, a small volume of poems. The locals dubbed him 'Jamie the Poeter'.

In the summer of 1802, he first met Walter Scott while working as a shepherd for Scott's friend William Laidlaw when Scott, the newly appointed Sheriff of Selkirk, was scouring the countryside for the disappearing ballads of the Borders. Hogg, with the help of his mother, aided Scott in his search, and the two contemporaries began a lifelong, if sometimes traumatic, friendship.

When Scott's *The Minstrelsy of the Scottish Border* was published in 1802, they came in for severe criticism from Hogg's mother Margaret: 'There was never ane o' my sangs prentit till ye prentit them yoursel', and ye have spoilt them awthegither. They were made for singin' and no' for readin', but ye have broken the charm now, an' they'll never be sung mair.'

In 1810, after his attempts at farming failed, Hogg moved to Edinburgh to try to earn his living as a writer. Scott's assistance to his friend was invaluable, but he eventually achieved fame with the publication of his long poem, *The Queen's Wake*, completed in Deanhaugh Street in 1813,

BOOK LOVERS' EDINBURGH

Left: James Hogg, by Sir John Watson Gordon (1830)
Right: Frontispiece reproduction of the 1824 first edition of *The Private Memoirs and Confessions of a Justified Sinner*

and in 1815 *The Pilgrims of the Sun* was published. He edited the short-lived literary magazine *The Spy*, and many of his stories and poems were published in *Blackwood's Magazine*, in which he first used his now famous sobriquet: the Ettrick Shepherd. He was often caricatured by *Blackwood's* in John Wilson's (Christopher North's) 'Noctes Ambrosianae' as an unsophisticated 'boozing buffoon', a portrayal often accentuated and exploited by Hogg, who played up his celebrity image.

He is best remembered today for his novel *The Private Memoirs and Confessions of a Justified Sinner*. Originally published anonymously, because, Hogg explained, 'it being a story replete with horrors, after I had written it,

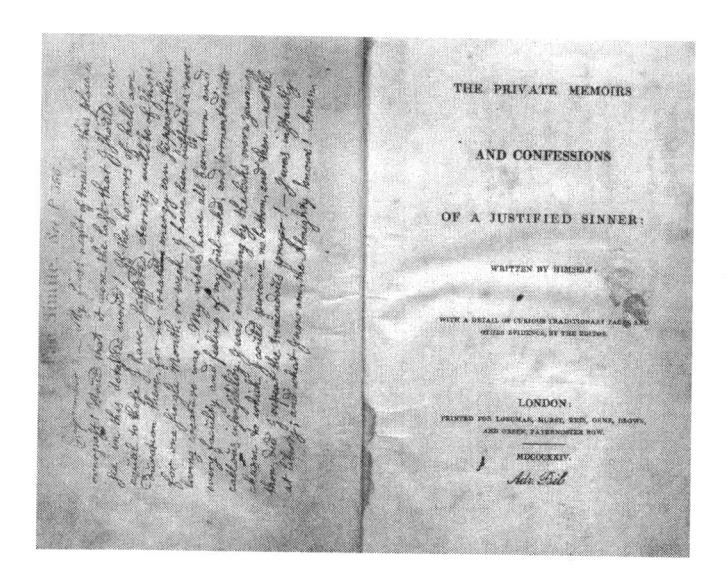

I durst not venture to put my name to it.' A more likely explanation may be that he didn't want to cause offence to Calvinist Edinburgh.

He lived for five years in Edinburgh at various addresses, including The Harrow Inn. In 1815, the Duke of Buccleuch granted him a rent-free farm at Altrive (now Edinhope) in Yarrow, where he lived for the rest of his life. In 1820, he married Margaret Phillips, a pious woman from a Nithsdale farming family, with whom he had five children. He died on 21 November 1835, from 'what the country folks call black jaundice' (probably liver failure) and is buried in Ettrick Kirkyard. At his funeral, most of the Edinburgh literati were conspicuous by their absence, except for the towering figure of John Wilson, who wept for his departed friend.

SEE ALSO: Holyrood Park, Sir Walter Scott, John Wilson, *Blackwood's Magazine*.

FURTHER READING: W. Elliot, *The James Hogg Trail* (Scottish Borders Tourist Board, 2001); K. Miller, *Electric Shepherd* (Faber, 2003); N. Parr, *James Hogg at Home* (D.S. Mack, 1980); W. Elliot, *The New Minstrelsy of the Scottish Border 1805–2005* (Deerpark Press, 2006).

1 GREYFRIARS PLACE
Greyfriars Kirkyard

They finally arrived at the burial-place of the Singleside family. This was a square enclosure in the Greyfriars churchyard, guarded on one side by a veteran angel, without a nose and having only one wing, who had the merit of having maintained his post for a century ... Here then, amid the deep black fat loam into which her ancestors were now resolved, they deposited the body of Mrs Margaret Bertram; and, like soldiers returning from a military funeral, the nearest relations who might be interested in the settlements of the lady, urged the dogcattle of the hackney coaches to all the speed of which they were capable, in order to put an end to further suspense on that interesting topic.
Sir Walter Scott, *Guy Mannering* (1815)

Greyfriars Kirkyard. Described by Eleanor Atkinson as 'that old garden of souls'

OLD TOWN

Greyfriars takes its name from a pre-Reformation Franciscan convent (the grey friars) that stood nearby. In 1562, Mary, Queen of Scots granted the land to the town council for use as a burial ground, and the church, which dates from 1620, became the first church built in Edinburgh after the Reformation. On 28 February 1638, its place in Scottish history was assured when Presbyterians, opposing the Episcopal faith introduced by Charles I, swore to uphold their forms of worship in a National Covenant which was presented and signed in front of the pulpit (an original copy is displayed in the Visitor Centre). From 1650 to 1653, Cromwell used Greyfriars as a barracks during his invasion of Scotland. Little of the original church survives, because in the early eighteenth century the town council stored its gunpowder in a nearby tower which blew up in 1718, taking most of the church with it. Misfortune struck again in 1845 when fire gutted the church. Burial records were not kept until 1658, making the exact location of many graves impossible to determine.

Greyfriars Bobby, canine paragon of virtue

As a burial place of the great, the good and the bloodcurdlingly infamous, Greyfriars has no equal in the city, but most visitors arrive at this historic kirkyard seeking the grave of a man whose life was unremarkable and would have passed unnoticed had he not been the master of a little dog. The story of Greyfriars Bobby, the faithful Skye terrier who reputedly kept a vigil for 14 years on his master's grave, is well known, but is there any truth in it, or was it all just a cosy myth fuelled by mawkish books and a Walt Disney movie? Eleanor Atkinson was the American author of the bestselling novel *Greyfriars Bobby*, published in 1912, but she never visited Edinburgh, let alone Scotland, and she wrote the novel on the other side of the Atlantic.

BOOK LOVERS' EDINBURGH

Left: Bobby's statue, erected opposite the Kirkyard gates in 1873. Funded by Baroness Burdett-Coutts Right: Eleanor Atkinson

They could not see the little dog, but they knew he was there. They knew now that he would still be there when they could see him no more — his body a part of the soil, his memory a part of all that was held dear and imperishable in that old garden of souls. They could go up to the lodge and look at his famous collar, and they would have his image in bronze on the fountain. And sometime, when the mysterious door opened for them, they might see Bobby again, a sonsie doggie running on the green pastures and beside the still waters, at the heels of his shepherd master ...
Eleanor Atkinson, from *Greyfriars Bobby*

Born Eleanor Stackhouse in Indiana in 1863, she worked as a schoolmistress in Indianapolis before joining the *Chicago Tribune* as an investigative reporter. Writing under the pseudonym Nora Marks, she took undercover jobs and infiltrated the seamier side of life, which included investigating baby-farming scams, divorce sharks and the Salvation Army, and posing as a beggar. In 1891 she married Chicago editor, Francis Atkinson, and together they published *The Little Chronicle*, a children's newspaper for which Atkinson wrote much of the content. In 1903 she published her first novel, *Mamzelle Fifine*, which launched her style of transforming incidents from history into appealing stories for young readers. Her two best-known novels are *Greyfriars Bobby*, and *Johnny Appleseed* (1915). The rest are now forgotten potboilers. In 1942, at Rockland State Hospital, Orangetown, New York, Atkinson died. She was 3,000 miles away from the Edinburgh she had never visited, and the dog she had never known. The myth she created, however, is still very much alive and kicking.

Grave of Duncan Ban MacIntyre (1724–1812)

> My blessing with the foxes dwell,
> For that they hunt the sheep so well.
> Ill fare the sheep, a grey-fac'd nation
> That swept our hills with desolation.
> Duncan Ban MacIntyre, 'Song to the Foxes'

Although regarded as one of the great Gaelic poets, Donnchadh Bàn Mac an t-Saoir never learned to read or write, but with the help of his extensive memory and the pen of his friend, Revd Donald MacNicol, Minister of Lismore, his verses are preserved for posterity. Born in Glen Orchy, he worked there as a forester and gamekeeper, and his love of the countryside inspired his verse. His poems included satires, love songs and drinking songs, but he will be best remembered for his poems about the Argyll–Perthshire border, namely 'Moladh Beinn Dobhrain' ('The Praise of Ben Doran'), which describes his love of deer and deer-hunting, and 'Oran Coire a Cheathaich' ('The Song of Misty Corrie'). He moved to Edinburgh in 1767, where he became a member of the City Guard and served in the Breadalbane Fencibles. MacIntyre and his wife, together with some of his children and grandchildren, are buried in the churchyard.

From the main entrance, follow the path round the right-hand side of the church and take the second (cobbled) path on the right. Near its end, over on the left, stands the large obelisk marking MacIntyre's grave.

Grave of George Buchanan (*c*.1506–82)
Scholar, poet, dramatist and historian

Best known for his Latin history of Scotland, *Rerum scoticarum historia* (20 volumes, 1582) and *De juri regniapud Scotos* (1579), his decrial of the divine right of monarchs, Buchanan was born near Killearn in Stirlingshire and studied at Paris and St Andrews universities.

George Buchanan's bronze-headed memorial

In 1537, he became tutor to one of the illegitimate sons of James V, but later fled the country after he was charged with heresy on the publication of his poem, 'Franciscanus', in which he satirised the Franciscans. He ended up teaching in Bordeaux, where Montaigne was one of his pupils, and where he wrote his Latin tragedies, *Jeptha* and *Baptistes*. In 1547, he was arrested and imprisoned as a suspected heretic by the Inquisition, but managed to return to Scotland in 1561, now purporting to be a Protestant, where he was appointed Classical tutor to the teenage Mary, Queen of Scots. He later charged her with complicity in the murder of Lord Darnley in the pamphlet 'Ane Detectioun of the Duings of Mary Quene' (1571). His appointments in later life included moderator of the General Assembly of Scotland, keeper of the Privy Seal of Scotland and tutor to the four-year-old King James VI of Scotland (1570–8). He died in an Edinburgh lodging house in 1582 shortly after completing his monumental, but alas unreliable, 20-volume work on the history of Scotland.

From the main entrance, follow the path round the right-hand side of the church. When you reach the end of the building, Buchanan's bronze-headed memorial can be seen in front of you between the trees.

SEE ALSO: Mary, Queen of Scots.

FURTHER READING: I.D. McFarlane, *Buchanan* (Duckworth, 1981).

Where Walter Scott fell in love with Williamina Stuart-Belsches

> Much have I owed thy strains on life's long way,
> Through secret woes the world has never known,
> When on the weary night dawn'd wearier day,
> And bitterer was the grief devour'd alone,
> That I o'erlive such woes, Enchantress! is thine own.

An allusion to Scott's lost love, Williamina Stuart-Belsches, from the envoi of *The Lady of the Lake* (1810)

One rainy Sunday in 1790 at Greyfriars Kirkyard, while Scott was still a teenager, he offered his umbrella to a 14-year-old girl called Williamina and fell instantly in love with her. She was a well-born heiress, the daughter of Sir John Stuart-Belsches, who owned an estate at Fettercairn in Kincardineshire, and Lady Jane, daughter of the Earl of Leven and Melville. They courted and corresponded; Scott felt encouraged, but to support a wife of Williamina's social standing was far beyond his means. In the winter of 1795, Williamina met William Forbes, heir to a banking family, and the following autumn they announced their plans to marry. The jilted Scott was devastated and carried with him the pain of losing Williamina for the rest of his life. Williamina died at the age of 34 in 1810.

The agony he suffered during this doomed courtship surfaced later in some of his works, namely in the thwarted passions of Wilfred Wycliffe for Matilda in *Rokeby* (1812), the Master of Ravenswood for Lucy Ashton in *The Bride of Lammermoor* (1819) and Darsie Latimer for 'Greenmantle' in *Redgauntlet* (1824).

In September 1797, while touring the Lake District, he was introduced to 27-year-old, French-born Charlotte Carpenter at a ball. Within three weeks of meeting her, Scott proposed, and they were married a few months later on Christmas Eve. Twelve years later, he described his marriage in a letter to Lady Abercorn as 'something short of love in all its forms, which I suspect people feel once in all their lives; folk who have been nearly drowned in bathing rarely venturing a second time out of their depth'.

SEE ALSO: Sir Walter Scott.

Grave of Walter Scott (1729–99)
Father of Sir Walter Scott

The grave of Scott's father, a former elder of Greyfriars Kirk, is marked by a bedraggled pink granite slab and, compared to his son's Gothic extravaganza down on Princes Street, the elder Scott's memory seems somewhat neglected. His roots were in the Scottish Borders and on his mother's side he was descended from the Haliburtons of Newmains, who passed on to the Scott family the hereditary right of burial in Dryburgh Abbey, where his famous son now lies. He moved to Edinburgh as a young man to study law, and was studious and successful, becoming senior partner in the firm he was apprenticed to, and later a Writer to the Signet. A strict Calvinist with a deep interest in theology, his son described him as 'uncommonly handsome'. In April 1758, he married Anne Rutherford, with whom he had twelve children, six of whom died in infancy. Scott

OLD TOWN

penned an affectionate portrait of his father, whom he caricatured in *Redgauntlet* (1824) as Saunders Fairford. From the main entrance, follow the path round the right-hand side of the church until you are standing in front of the archway in the Flodden Wall. Walter Scott's grave is to your left.

SEE ALSO: Grave of Anne Rutherford, Birthplace of Sir Walter Scott, Childhood home of Sir Walter Scott.

Grave of Captain Porteous (d. 1736)
The man responsible for the Porteous Riots, featured in Walter Scott's *The Heart of Midlothian*

> And thou, great god of Aqua Vitæ!
> Wha sways the empire of this city,
> When fou we're sometimes capernoity,
> Be thou prepar'd
> To hedge us frae that black banditti,
> The City-Guard.
> Robert Fergusson (1750–74), from 'The Daft Days'

John Porteous, the son of an Edinburgh tailor, served in the army and then joined the City Guard – Fergusson's famous 'black banditti'. History does not record Porteous as a credit to his office, but a man who frequently exceeded the bounds of his commission, dishing out excessive cruelty to his prisoners.

BOOK LOVERS' EDINBURGH

In 1736, two smugglers, Robertson and Wilson, were convicted and sentenced to death. The handcuffed Robertson escaped during a church service, but Wilson was later conducted from the Old Tolbooth Prison (nicknamed The Heart of Midlothian) in the High Street to temporary gallows in the Grassmarket by 50 of the City Guard commanded by Porteous, who was said by a witness to be 'heated by wine'. When the hangman proceeded to cut down Wilson's body, hails of stones were thrown from the crowd. Porteous ordered the Guard to 'fire and be damned'. Nine of the crowd were left dead and many were wounded. Porteous was subsequently arrested and sentenced to death. Here the tragic story should have ended, but Caroline, the Queen Regent, ordered Porteous's reprieve, and the citizens of Edinburgh were outraged.

On the evening of 7 September 1736, a large mob entered the city, crying out, 'All those who dare avenge innocent blood, let them come here.' The mob stormed the Old Tolbooth, dragged Porteous from his cell and hanged him from a nearby dyer's pole. This and other such incidents became known as the Porteous Riots and were immortalised by Walter Scott in *The Heart of Midlothian* in 1818:

> 'Away with him – away with him!' was the general cry. 'Why do you trifle away time in making a gallows? – that dyester's pole is good enough for the homocide.' The unhappy man was forced to his fate with remorseless rapidity. Butler, separated from him by the press,

OLD TOWN

> escaped the last horrors. Unnoticed by those who had hitherto detained him as a prisoner, he fled from the fatal spot without caring in what direction his course lay. A loud shout proclaimed the stern delight with which the agents of this deed regarded its completion. Butler, then, at the opening into the low street called the Cowgate, cast back a terrified glance, and, by the red and dusky light of the torches, he could discern a figure waving and struggling as it hung suspended above the heads of the multitude, and could even observe men striking it with their Lochaber-axes and partisans. The sight was of a nature to double his horror and to add wings to his flight.

From the main entrance, follow the path round the right-hand side of the church. Take the path to the right just before the archway in the Flodden Wall. Porteous's grave is behind the third tree on your left.

SEE ALSO: The Heart of Midlothian, Holyrood Park, Sir Walter Scott, Robert Fergusson.

FURTHER READING: Alexander Carlyle's *Autobiography* (Thoemmes Press, 1991) relates an eyewitness account of the execution of Wilson.

Grave of William Creech (1745–1815)
Bookseller, publisher and Lord Provost of Edinburgh

> [Robert Burns was] coming up Leith Walk brandishing a sapling and with much violence in his face and manner. When asked what was the matter, Burns replied, 'I am going to smash that Shite, Creech.'
> Related to John Grierson

William Creech was a bookseller and publisher who had his premises in the Luckenbooths (locked booths), a rabbit-warren of six timber-fronted tenements on six floors, connected to the Old Tolbooth by St Giles'. Creech's ground-floor shop, known as 'Creech's Land', was described by Lord Monboddo as 'the natural resort of lawyers, authors and all sorts of literary idlers'. He founded the famous Speculative Society while studying at Edinburgh University, and his house, known as Creech's Levee, in Craig's Close, off Cockburn Street, was the setting for his regular literary salons. The second edition of Burns's poems, the Edinburgh edition, was published by William Creech in 1787; he had it printed at William Smellie's printing works in Anchor Close, off the High Street. Burns rashly sold the copyright to him for one hundred guineas 'to be payable on demand', but getting money out of Creech was an art in itself, and Burns had to wait over six months to be paid. Creech was also responsible for commissioning Alexander Naysmith (free of charge) to paint his famous portrait of Burns, which today adorns thousands of trinkets.

From the main entrance, follow the path round the right-hand side of the church. Walk through the archway in the Flodden Wall. Take the last path on your right before the gates. The grave of William Creech is behind the third tree on the left.

SEE ALSO: Robert Burns, William Smellie.

Grave of William Smellie (1740–1795)
Printer, editor, antiquary, naturalist and founder of the Crochallan Fencibles

> His uncomb'd, hoary locks, wild-staring, thatch'd;
> A head for thought profound and clear, unmatch'd;
> Yet tho' his caustic wit was biting rude,
> His heart was warm, benevolent and good.
> Robert Burns, 'The Poet's Progress'

Described by his friend Robert Burns as 'that old Veteran in Genius, Wit and Bawdry', William Smellie was a man of many talents. The son of a stonemason, he left school aged 12 to become an apprentice printer. In 1763, he married a Miss Robertson, with whom he had 13 children, many of whom died in infancy. In 1765, he set up his own printing house and, with Andrew Bell and Colin MacFarquhar, produced the first edition of the *Encyclopaedia Britannica* (1768–71), much of it reputedly written by himself.

William Smellie

He also wrote *A Philosophy of Natural History* and was a founder member of the Society of Antiquities in 1780. He printed the works of Robert Fergusson, Adam Smith, Adam Ferguson and later the second edition of Burns's poems, the Edinburgh edition, in 1787. Smellie was not your average, run-of-the-mill printer, but a talented editor and writer. He also liked to drink, debate and sing a bawdy song or two, which led to his founding the renowned drinking club, the Crochallan Fencibles, at Dawney Douglas's Tavern. Dawney liked to sing Gaelic songs and Smellie took the name of one of them, Crodh Challein (Colin's Cattle), for the first half of the club's name, and Fencibles from the city's much-derided volunteer corps of militia. Its members included Adam Smith, Adam Ferguson, Henry Mackenzie and Robert Burns. Smellie introduced Burns to the club during his first visit to Edinburgh in 1787, and the ploughman poet would have needed no excuse to join in the revelry after a hard day selling himself in the salons of Edinburgh society. It was at Dawney Douglas's Tavern that Burns delivered for the first time his 'Address to a Haggis' – Fair fa' your honest, sonsie face, Great chieftain o' the puddin-race! – now an almost religious rite at every traditional Burns supper. The Crochallan Fencibles also inspired many of the bawdy lyrics of Burns's *The Merry Muses of Caledonia*, verse far removed from the tea parties of the literati:

> There's no a lass in a' the land,
> Can fuck sae weel as I can;
> Louse down your breeks, lug out your wand,
> Hae ye nae mind to try, man ...
> From 'Ellibanks'

From the main entrance, take the path on your left, following it around the perimeter wall. At the end of the path, two large gated tombs face you. Smellie's grave is to the right of these tombs.

SEE ALSO: William Smellie, Robert Burns, William Creech, Adam Smith, Henry Mackenzie, Robert Fergusson, The Writers' Museum.

FURTHER INFORMATION: The site of Smellie's printing house, including the room where Burns used to sit and correct his proofs, and Dawney Douglas's Tavern, was in Anchor Close, off the High Street. Stools from Smellie's printing house can be seen at The Writers' Museum, Lady Stair's Close.

Grave of Henry Mackenzie (1745–1831)
Novelist and essayist known as 'the Scottish Addison'

The son of an Edinburgh physician, Henry Mackenzie was educated at the Royal High School and, after studying law at Edinburgh University, earned his living as a lawyer. He is best remembered for his novel *The Man of Feeling*, published anonymously in 1771, which, although criticised for its overabundant sentimentality, was hugely popular in its day and was one of Burns's 'bosom favourites'. Mackenzie edited two literary periodicals, *The Mirror* and *The Lounger*, and it was in the latter that he gave early recognition to Burns, writing in 1786, 'Though I am far from meaning to compare our rustic bard to Shakespeare, yet whoever will read his lighter and more humorous poems ... will perceive with what uncommon penetration and sagacity this Heaven-taught ploughman, from his humble and unlettered station, has looked upon men and manners.'

And so the myth of the 'ploughman poet' was born. On the negative side, Mackenzie has been criticised for brokering the deal between Burns and his publisher, William Creech, when he advised Burns to part with his copyright for a hundred guineas. Robert Fergusson parodied Mackenzie, who was never a great lover of work written in Scots, in his poem 'The Sow of Feeling'. Mackenzie's other novels include *The Man of the World* (1773) and *Julia de Roubigné* (1777). He also wrote a play, *The Prince of Tunis* (1773). Mackenzie died at his house at 6 Heriot Row, but immortality was assured when his friend and fellow romantic, Sir Walter Scott, dedicated *Waverley* to 'Our Scottish Addison, Henry Mackenzie'.

From the main entrance, take the path round the right-hand side of the church. Turn down the second path (cobbled) on your right, then take the second path on your left. Mackenzie's grave is in the middle of the terrace wall.

SEE ALSO: Robert Burns, William Creech.

FURTHER READING: H.W. Thompson, *A Scottish Man of Feeling* (1931).

The Martyrs' Monument

Halt passenger take heed what thou dost see, This tomb doth shew for what some men did die ...
Inscription on the Martyrs' Monument

BOOK LOVERS' EDINBURGH

At the northern end of the Kirkyard stands the Martyrs' Monument, erected in 1706 and commemorating some of the 18,000 Covenanters who died for their faith. The Covenanters raised an army in 1639 to defend their Presbyterian faith against the Episcopalianism of

Charles I, but were eventually defeated by the Duke of Monmouth's army at Bothwell Bridge in June 1679. About a thousand Covenanters were imprisoned in Greyfriars Yard for months with no shelter and scant food. Those who signed a bond were freed, but many refused and were transported to slavery in the Colonies. Ironically, near the southern wall stands the mausoleum of the King's Advocate Sir George Mackenzie (1636–91), known as 'Bluidy Mackenzie', the hanging judge, for his vigorous persecution of the Covenanters.

Robert Louis Stevenson was captivated by the Covenanters. His old nurse, Cummy, fed him tales of the martyrs when he was a boy. His mother grew up in Colinton Manse beside the kirkyard where the army of the Covenant bivouacked. As a teenager at Swanston, he was almost within sight of Rullion Green, where 900 bedraggled Covenanters were defeated by 3,000 regular troops of General Sir Thomas Dalyell in 1666, a battle which inspired him to write his pamphlet 'The Pentland Rising', published anonymously in 1866 when he was only 16 years old.

In *Edinburgh: Picturesque Notes* (1878), RLS devotes a chapter to Greyfriars, where he pours out his feelings for the martyrs:

> Down in the corner farthest from Sir George [Mackenzie], there stands a monument dedicated, in uncouth Covenanting verse, to all who lost their lives in that contention. There is no moorsman shot in a snow shower beside Irongray or Co'monell; there is not one of the two hundred who were drowned off the Orkneys; nor so much as a poor, over-driven, Covenanting slave in the American plantations; but can lay claim to a share in that memorial, and, if such things interest just men among the shades, can boast he has a monument on earth as well as Julius Caesar or the Pharaohs. Where they may all lie, I know not. Far-scattered bones, indeed!

From the main entrance, take the first path on your right. The Martyrs' Monument is at the end of the path on the right, beside a hedge.

SEE ALSO: Robert Louis Stevenson, Sir George Mackenzie.

Tomb of Sir George Mackenzie (1636–91)
Also known as 'Bluidy Mackenzie', the hanging judge

> *When a man's soul is certainly in hell, his body will scarce lie quiet in a tomb however costly; some time*

> *or other the door must open, and the reprobate come forth in the abhorred garments of the grave.*
> Robert Louis Stevenson

Although a prolific writer of works of fiction, politics, history and law, Mackenzie is best remembered today as a ruthless and brutal persecutor of the Covenanters. Born in Dundee, he was the son of the 2nd Earl of Seaforth. He studied at St Andrews, Aberdeen and Bourges, was called to the Scottish Bar in 1659 and became MP for Ross-shire in 1669. In 1677, he was appointed Lord Advocate and in 1682 he founded the Advocates Library (now the National Library of Scotland).

His mausoleum has been associated throughout history with hauntings and poltergeist activity, and in *Edinburgh: Picturesque Notes* (1878) Stevenson grimly recalls 'the reprobate' Mackenzie:

> Behind the church is the haunted mausoleum of Sir George Mackenzie: Bloody Mackenzie, Lord Advocate in the Covenanting troubles and author of some pleasing sentiments on toleration. Here, in the last century, an old Heriot's Hospital boy once harboured from the pursuit of the police. The Hospital is next door to Greyfriars – a courtly building among lawns, where, on Founder's Day, you may see a multitude of children playing Kiss-in-the-Ring and Round the Mulberry-bush. Thus, when the fugitive had managed to conceal himself in the tomb, his old schoolmates had a hundred opportunities to bring him food; and there he lay in safety till a ship was found to smuggle him abroad. But his must have been indeed a hard heart of brass, to lie all day and night alone with the dead persecutor; and other lads were far from emulating him in courage. When a man's soul is certainly in hell, his body will scarce lie quiet in a tomb however costly; some time or other the

OLD TOWN

door must open, and the reprobate come forth in the abhorred garments of the grave. It was thought a high piece of prowess to knock at the Lord Advocate's mausoleum and challenge him to appear. 'Bluidy Mackenzie, come oot if ye daur!' sang the foolhardy urchins. But Sir George had other affairs on hand; and the author of an essay on toleration continues to sleep peacefully among the many whom he so intolerantly helped to slay.

From the main entrance, take the first path on your left around the perimeter wall. Mackenzie's tomb is the large circular structure against the wall.

SEE ALSO: Robert Louis Stevenson, Martyrs' Monument.

Tomb of Sir George Mackenzie

BOOK LOVERS' EDINBURGH

25 FORREST ROAD
Sandy Bell's
Watering hole of Hamish Henderson
Poet, songwriter and guardian
of Scottish folk heritage

*Roch the wind in the clear day's dawin
Blaws the cloods heelster-gowdie ow'r the bay,
But there's mair nor a roch wind blawin
Through the great glen o' the warld the day.
It's a thocht that will gar oor rottans
- A' they rogues that gang gallus, fresh and gay –
Tak the road, and seek ither loanins
For their ill ploys, tae sport and play*

*Nae mair will the bonnie callants
Mairch tae war when oor braggarts crousely craw,
Nor wee weans frae pit-heid and clachan
Mourn the ships sailin' doon the Broomielaw
Broken faimlies in lands we've herriet,
Will curse Scotland the Brave nae mair, nae mair;
Black and white, ane til ither mairret,
Mak the vile barracks o' their maisters bare.*

*So come all ye at hame wi' Freedom,
Never heed whit the hoodies croak for doom.
In your hoose a' the bairns o' Adam
Can find breid, barley-bree and painted room.
When MacLean meets wi's freens in Springburn
A' the roses and geans will turn tae bloom,
And a black boy frae yont Nyanga
Dings the fell gallows o' the burghers doon.*

Hamish Henderson, 'Freedom Come-All-Ye' (1960)

Immortalised as 'Sunday Balls in Fairest Redd' in Sydney Goodsir Smith's *Carotid Cornucopius* (1947), this pub remains very much as it has always been: a no-frills, no-tat,

OLD TOWN

Hamish recording Alec Stewart in the 1950s. The Stewarts of Blair were one of the most respected singing families, discovered working in the berry fields of Blairgowrie.

no-nonsense, good old Scottish drinking den. Close to the University, its clientele consists of academics, students, locals, folk enthusiasts and well oiled fiddlers. Sandy Bell's was also the favourite haunt of the late Hamish Henderson (1919–2002), the father of the Scottish folk revival.

'At the age of seven,' he once recalled, 'I asked my mother about a song she was singing. We had a book of songs in the house. I asked her where that song was in the book. She said, "Some of the songs we sing are not in books." That started me off as a folklorist and collector.'

Born in Blairgowrie and educated at Cambridge University, where he studied languages, he served as an intelligence officer in North Africa during the Second World War. After the war, he acted as a 'native guide' to the American folklorist Alan Lomax on his visit to Scotland in 1951 and lived for long periods with the travelling people of Scotland, collecting songs, classical ballads and stories passed along 'the carrying stream'.

'I remember in 1955 in the berry fields of Blairgowrie, picking berries and recording songs,' he said. 'Collecting in the berry fields was a wee bit like holding a tin under the Niagara Falls.'

BOOK LOVERS' EDINBURGH

In the early '50s, he joined the newly founded School of Scottish Studies at Edinburgh University, immersing himself in the Scottish folk tradition and building up a huge archive of songs on tape. His greatest discovery, he always maintained, was the singer Jeannie Robertson, described by A.L. Lloyd as 'a singer, sweet and heroic'. His own works included his collection of verse, *Elegies for the Dead in Cyrenaica* (1948), *Ballads of World War Two* (1947), *Alias MacAlias* (1992), *Armstrong Nose* (1996) and various translations of the modern Italian poets Eugenio Montale, Alfonso Gatto, Salvatore Quasimodo and Giuseppe Ungaretti. Many of his songs have passed into the folk tradition, but the two songs he will be best remembered for are 'The John Maclean March', a tribute to the Red Clydesider John Maclean, and 'Freedom Come-All-Ye', a heart-rending plea for a world free from injustice and English imperialism, often referred to as Scotland's unofficial national anthem. A veteran of many Aldermaston and Faslane marches, Henderson was a tireless campaigner for CND and the Anti-Apartheid Movement. He believed he was the target of two assassination attempts by the South African security services, and in 1983 he publicly refused an OBE award in protest at the Thatcher government's nuclear arms policy – a defiant act for which Radio Scotland listeners voted him 'Scot of the Year'. Hamish Henderson died on 9 March 2002 in an Edinburgh nursing home, aged 82. The friendly atmosphere of 'Sunday Balls in Fairest Redd' is a fitting memorial to this man who dedicated his life to the survival of the Scots folk tradition and believed bursting into song was an essential ingredient of life.

FURTHER READING: E. Bort (ed.), *Borne on the Carrying Stream: The Legacy of Hamish Henderson* (Grace Note, 2012); T. Neat, *Hamish Henderson* (Polygon, 2 volumes, 2009).

Hamish Henderson and faithful friend.
Photo - Ian Mackenzie

GUTHRIE STREET
Formerly College Wynd
Birthplace of Sir Walter Scott (1771-1832)

Walter Scott (or 'Wattie' as he was known) was born on 15 August 1771, the ninth child of Anne Rutherford, daughter of a former professor of medicine at Edinburgh University, and Walter Scott, a solicitor and Writer to the Signet, a solicitor entitled to use the King's signet, the private seal of the Scottish King. The house of his birth, along with others, was demolished to make room for the northern frontage of Old College (then known as the new College). It was situated at the top of College Wynd, near Chambers Street, and stood in the corner of a small courtyard. It was a typical dark, overcrowded and airless Old Town tenement; a warren of flats where people lived amid the stink of refuse and bad sanitation; a place where sunlight and fresh air rarely ventured. Six of the Scotts' children had died in infancy behind the walls of this cramped slum, and shortly after Wattie's birth, in 1772, the Scotts wisely moved to the clean air and leafy outlook of newly built George Square.

SEE ALSO: Childhood home of W.S., townhouse of W.S., Lasswade Cottage, Parliament Hall, The Heart of Midlothian, Greyfriars Kirkyard, Scott Monument, Holyrood Park, St John's Churchyard, The Writers' Museum, High School, Old College, Sciennes Hill House, Assembly Rooms, J.G. Lockhart, Portobello Sands, Canongate Kirkyard.

FURTHER INFORMATION: A plaque high up on the eastern wall where Guthrie Street meets Chambers Street commemorates Scott's birthplace. College Wynd was originally named the Wynd of the Blessed Virgin-in-the-Fields as the tall, gabled house at the top was built on the site of Kirk-o'-Field, where Lord Darnley was murdered in 1567. Irish playwright, novelist and poet Oliver Goldsmith (1730-74) is believed to have lived in College Wynd around 1750 while studying medicine at the University; he left without taking a degree.

OLD TOWN

CANONGATE

BOYD'S ENTRY
Site of Boyd's Inn, at which Dr Johnson arrived in Edinburgh in 1773

Oats. A grain, which in England is generally given to horses, but in Scotland supports the people.
Dr Johnson, *A Dictionary of the English Language* (1755)

On Saturday, 14 August 1773, James Boswell received a note at his house at 501 James Court, off the Lawnmarket, that Dr Samuel Johnson had arrived at Boyd's Inn (now demolished), at the head of the Canongate. Johnson had come to Edinburgh to begin his tour of Scotland and the Hebrides with his friend James Boswell, a journey which would eventually produce two classic works of travel literature: Johnson's *A Journey to the Western Islands of Scotland* (1775) and Boswell's *Journal of a Tour to the Hebrides* (1785). 'Late that evening ... I went to him directly,' Boswell wrote.

> He embraced me cordially; and I exulted in the thought, that I now had him actually in Caledonia ... the Doctor had unluckily had a bad specimen of Scottish cleanliness. He then drank no fermented liquor. He asked to have his lemonade made sweeter; upon which the waiter, with his greasy fingers, lifted a lump of sugar, and put it into it. The Doctor, in indignation, threw it out of the window ... He was to do me the honour to lodge under my roof ... Mr Johnson and I walked arm in arm up the High Street, to my house in James

CANONGATE

Court: it was a dusky night: I could not prevent his being assailed by the evening effluvia of Edinburgh. I heard a late baronet, of some distinction in the political world, observe, that 'walking the streets of Edinburgh at night was pretty perilous, and a good deal odoriferous'. The peril is much abated, by the care which the magistrates have taken to enforce the city laws against throwing foul water from the windows; but, from the structure of the houses in the Old Town, which consist of many stories, in each of which a different family lives, and there being no covered sewers, the odour still continues. A zealous Scotsman would have wished Mr Johnson to be without one of his five senses upon this occasion. As we marched slowly along, he grumbled in my ear, 'I smell you in the dark!' But he acknowledged that the breadth of the street, and the loftiness of the buildings on each side, made a noble appearance.

SEE ALSO: James Boswell, David Hume, St Giles.

FURTHER INFORMATION: A plaque can be seen commemorating Dr Johnson's visit at the junction of Boyd's Entry and St Mary's Street.

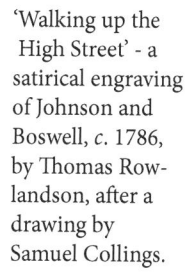

'Walking up the High Street' - a satirical engraving of Johnson and Boswell, c. 1786, by Thomas Rowlandson, after a drawing by Samuel Collings.

OLD PLAYHOUSE CLOSE
Site of the Playhouse Theatre (1747–69)

Whaur's yer Wullie Shakespeare noo?
Shouted from the audience on the first night of *Douglas*

The powerful tragedy called *Douglas* was first performed at the Playhouse Theatre on 14 December 1756 and was a brilliant success. It was written by John Home (1722–1808), a Church of Scotland minister at Athelstaneford in East Lothian, but Home ended up paying a heavy price for its triumph as the play gave such offence to the Edinburgh Presbytery that he was forced to resign from the ministry. Home's play, although rarely performed today, was influential in its day because it was instrumental in breaking down the belief of the Church that all drama was immoral, which eventually led to the licensing of Edinburgh's Theatre Royal in 1767 in Shakespeare Square at the east end of Princes Street.

John Home was born in a house in Quality Street (now Maritime Street), Leith, and educated at Edinburgh University. He fought on the government side in the 1745 Jacobite Rebellion and was captured after the Battle of Falkirk and imprisoned in Doune Castle, from where he escaped using the age-old trick of tying his blankets together to form a rope. He became a minister in 1747, and after his enforced resignation in 1757, he became tutor to the Prince of Wales (later George III).

After the success of *Douglas* in Edinburgh, David Garrick decided to produce it on the London stage. Garrick also produced Home's next play, *The Siege of Aquileia* in 1760. Other works of Home's include *The Fatal Discovery* (1769), *Alonzo* (1773), *Alfred* (1778) and *A History of the Rebellion of 1745* (1802). John Home is buried in the graveyard of South Leith Parish Church, Henderson Street, Leith.

CANONGATE

FURTHER INFORMATION: Old Playhouse Close is situated opposite New Street. A plaque marks the site of John Home's birthplace at 28 Maritime Street, Leith.

FURTHER READING: H. Mackenzie, *An Account of the Life and Writings of John Home* (1822).

22 ST JOHN STREET
Lodgings of Tobias Smollett (1721–71)
Historian and writer
of picaresque comic novels

The city [of Edinburgh] stands upon two hills ... which with all its defects, may very well pass for the capital of a moderate kingdom.
Tobias Smollett, *The Expedition of Humphry Clinker* (1771)

Although born on a farm in Dumbartonshire, and educated at Glasgow University, Smollett was never really considered 'Scotland's own', partly because he lived most of his life in London and later moved abroad for his health. Where Robert Louis Stevenson turned exile into legend, Smollett was probably too anglicised, too caustic, too prejudiced and too out of touch with his roots for many Scottish people to really identify with him.

Tobias Smollett

He was a surgeon's mate in the Royal Navy and later practised in London, but his main calling and career was as a man of letters. It was his picaresque novels which brought him fame, namely *Roderick Random* (1748), *Peregrine Pickle* (1751) and *The Expedition of Humphry Clinker* (1771). In 1753, he edited the *Critical Review*, but his criticism was so savage it led to his imprisonment for libel in 1760. He was a noted historian, writing his *History of England* (three volumes, 1757–8), and another major achievement was his translation of Cervantes' *Don Quixote* into English in 1755.

During the summer of 1766, he stayed with his sister, Mrs

Telfer, who occupied the second flat of 182 Canongate (now renumbered 22 St John Street) above the pend (vaulted entrance), and it was here he wrote part of his last and most popular novel, *The Expedition of Humphry Clinker*. Written during the last two years of his life, the story is told by its characters through a series of letters on a journey encompassing Wales, London and Scotland, where Edinburgh disgusts them by its filth.

For health reasons, his last years were spent abroad, and he died in Livorno, Italy. Shortly before his death he visited his mother at St John Street, confiding to her that he was ill and did not have long to live. To this, she replied, 'We'll no' be very long pairted onie way. If you gang first, I'll be close on your heels. If I lead the way, you'll no' be far ahint me.'

SEE ALSO: Holyrood Palace.

FURTHER READING: L.M. Knapp, *Doctor of Men and Manners* (1940); G.M. Kahrl, *Tobias Smollett: Traveller-Novelist* (1945).

The pend, St John Street

23 ST JOHN STREET
Hall of the Canongate Kilwinning Lodge of Freemasons
Visited by Robert Burns in 1787

> Ther's mony a badge that's unco braw;
> Wi' ribbon, tape and lace on;
> Let kings an' princes wear them a' –
> Gie me the Master's apron!
>
> The honest craftsman's apron,
> The jolly Freemason's apron,
> Be he at hame, or roam afar,
> Before his touch fa's bolt and bar,
> The gates of fortune fly ajar,
> Gin he but wears the apron!
>
> For wealth and honour, pride and power
> Are crumbling stanes to base on;
> Fraternity suld rule the hour,
> And ilka worthy Mason!
> Each Free Accepted Mason,
> Each Ancient Crafted Mason.
>
> Then, brithers, let a halesome sang
> Arise your friendly ranks alang!
> Guidwives and bairnies blithely sing
> To the ancient badge wi' the apron string
> That is worn by the Master Mason!
>
> Robert Burns, 'The Master's Apron'

Burns became a Freemason when he was 23, in 1781, when he was initiated into the Lodge St David at Tarbolton in Ayrshire. Five years later, he visited Edinburgh for the first

CANONGATE

time in an attempt to secure enough patronage to publish a second edition of his poems. He carried with him letters of introduction from his Masonic contacts in Ayrshire, which opened many doors for him and were instrumental in assuring his success.

On 1 February 1787, he made his only recorded visit to the Canongate Kilwinning Lodge. He was later reputedly made their Poet Laureate, an office which was held by James Hogg, the Ettrick Shepherd, in 1835.

Hall of the Canongate Kilwinning Lodge of Freemasons

SEE ALSO: Anchor Close, St James Square, Buccleuch Street, Burns Monument, St Giles, William Smellie, William Creech, The Writers' Museum, Sciennes Hill House, Robert Fergusson, Clarinda/Agnes McLehose, Jean Lorimer, Henry Mackenzie, Thomas Blacklock.

152 CANONGATE
Canongate Kirkyard

Left: Canongate Kirkyard
Right: Grave of Adam Smith

The original Canongate Kirk was located at the now ruined Abbey of the Holy Rood, adjacent to the Palace of Holyroodhouse. King James VII (James II of England) appropriated the Abbey church for use as a Chapel of the Order of the Thistles and built the present church for parishioners as a replacement in 1690.

Grave of Adam Smith (1723–90)
Philosopher and economist

> With the greater part of rich people, the chief enjoyment of riches consists in the parade of riches, which in their eyes is never so complete as when they appear to possess those decisive marks of opulence which nobody can possess but themselves.
> Adam Smith, *The Wealth of Nations* (1776)

Best known for his influential book *The Wealth of Nations*, Adam Smith was one of the great eighteenth-century moral philosophers whose ideas led to modern-day theories.

He is also regarded as the world's first political economist. Born in Kirkcaldy, Fife, he was sent to Oxford at the age of 17. On his return home, he joined 'the brilliant circle in Edinburgh which included David Hume, John Home, Hugh Blair, Lord Hailes and Principal Robertson'. In 1751, aged 28, he became professor of logic at Glasgow University. In 1752, he took the chair of moral philosophy, and his *Theory of Moral Sentiments* was published in 1759. A shy, clumsy and absent-minded man, he lived a quiet bachelor's life with his mother. Loved by his students, he had the gift of oratory and a considerable reputation as a lecturer. He was a good friend of David Hume, and discussed his ideas with the great thinkers of his day, including Samuel Johnson and Benjamin Franklin. In 1760, he travelled to France, where he met Voltaire and began writing *An Inquiry into the Nature and Causes of the Wealth of Nations*, a book which transformed the economic theories of the day by analysing the results of economic freedom, and recognising the division of labour, rather than land or money, as the main ingredient of economic growth. Smith moved to London in 1776 and the book was published that year. In 1778, he returned to Edinburgh as commissioner of Customs. He died on 17 July 1790, after an illness. His grave is over on the far left against the rear wall of the Old Tolbooth.

BOOK LOVERS' EDINBURGH

SEE ALSO: David Hume, John Home, Samuel Johnson.

FURTHER READING: I.S. Ross, *The Life of Adam Smith* (Clarendon, 1995).

Grave of Robert Fergusson (1750–74)
Poet who was a major influence on Robert Burns

> Mr Fergusson died in the cells.
> Entry in the superintendent's log, Edinburgh's Bedlam, 16 October 1774

'O thou, my elder brother in Misfortune/By far my elder brother in the Muse,' wrote Robert Burns in epitaph on Robert Fergusson. Fergusson's poetry had a deep influence on Burns; his 'The Farmer's Ingle' clearly inspired 'The Cotter's Saturday Night'. Robert Fergusson was born in Edinburgh on 5 September 1750 in the Cap and Feather Close, near Niddry's Wynd (now Niddry Street). The Close was demolished with the construction of North Bridge, which provided easier access to the seaport of Leith and the land on which the New Town now stands. Robert was a second son born into a lower-middle-class family. His father, a clerk, came from Aberdeen farming stock. Educated privately at the Royal High School in Edinburgh for four years, Robert was awarded a bursary from the Donald Fergusson fund, enabling him to attend the Dundee High School and then St Andrews University. He enjoyed university life. He was a good singer – with a voice encouraged by a glass or several – and was popular amongst his fellow students. The University was less enamoured with the young man and on at least one occasion he stood on the doorstep of expulsion. The 'rabbit grace' best illustrates his relationship with the staff and students. At that time it was the practice in the University

CANONGATE

Detail from David Annand's 2004 sculpture of Fergusson outside the Kirk gates

for lecturers and students to eat dinner together. Each day, the students had to take it in turn to say grace over the food. Robert recited a quatrain that he had quilled:

> For rabbits young and for rabbits old
> For rabbits hot and rabbits cold
> For rabbits tender and for rabbits tough
> Our thanks we render for we've had enough.

The staff frowned, the students cheered, and it was reported that there were fewer rabbits purchased after that event. In May 1768, following the death of his father, Robert abandoned his studies without graduating and returned to Edinburgh to support his mother and family. In September 1778, he was working as a clerk copyist in the Commissary Records Office, quilling page after page of copperplate script at a penny a page. When the Tron Kirk bell chimed eight o'clock, the town stopped work. Robert enjoyed life; he danced, he sang, he drank, he became a member of the Cape Club. Each member of this club was dubbed with a 'knighthood'. Robert became Sir Precenter. His first poems were published in *Ruddiman's Weekly Magazine* in 1771 and were written in imitation of the English style. 'Daft Days' was his first Scots poem, published in 1772, and a slim volume of his works appeared in 1773, inspiring Burns to emulate his artistic vigour.
Tragically, however, Fergusson suffered from manic depression and, following a fall which exacerbated this condition, he was committed to the public asylum. He died shortly afterwards in Darien House, which, originally built in 1698 as the offices and stores of the Darien Company, had degenerated in the following century into a pauper lunatic asylum. The Bedlam Asylum stood behind the building which is now the Bedlam Theatre in Forrest Road. Fergusson's body was interred in a pauper's grave two days after his death. A young doctor, Andrew

Duncan, had attended him in the last few weeks of his life. Appalled by the conditions and treatment of the inmates in Bedlam, Andrew Duncan went on to pioneer methods for improving the treatment of the insane.

Robert Fergusson wrote 33 poems in Scots and 50 poems in English, and will chiefly be remembered for 'Auld Reikie' (1773), which traces a day in the life of the city. Other well-known poems include 'Elegy on the Death of Scots Music', 'Hallow Fair', 'To the Tron Kirk Bell', 'Leith Races' and 'The Rising of the Session'.

Burns was saddened to discover that Fergusson had been buried in an unmarked grave and, in February 1787, he sought permission to erect a headstone. After it was in place, Burns took five years to settle his account with the Edinburgh architect who designed the stone, commenting in a letter that 'He was two years in erecting it, after I commissioned him for it; and I have been two years paying him, after he sent me his account; so he and I are quits ... He had the hardiesse to ask me interest on the sum; but considering that the money was due by one Poet, for putting a tomb-stone over another, he may, with grateful surprise, thank Heaven that ever he saw a farthing of it.'

Erected and commissioned by the Friends of Robert Fergusson, a bronze figure sculpted by David Annand commemorates the poet outside the gates of the kirkyard. The statue was the brainchild of George Philp and Bob Watt (1932–2008), and was unveiled on 17 October 2004. Stewart Conn, the Edinburgh Makar, composed and delivered a poem to mark the occasion.

Robert Fergusson (1750–74)
On the unveiling of his statue in the Canongate, Sunday, 17 Oct 2004, by Stewart Conn

> The image uppermost in my mind
> was of him crouching in his cell in squalor,

> his head adorned with a crown of straw
> he had neatly plaited with his own hand.
> Now we see this trig figure
> caught in mid-stride among the thrang,
> a reminder that guid gear can gang
> intil sma' buik – not just in literature.
> Though too late to revivify a spirit broken
> in his lifetime it rekindles recognition
> of his artistry, humanity and vision
> and the plain braid Scots he spoke in.
> Besides cocking a snook at the literati
> of his day, his presence will regenerate
> the native vigour of the Canongate
> (no need to muster the black banditti).
> Long may those sturdy 'wee rosiers'
> spring from his grave; his affinity
> with common folk, his ribaldry and pity,
> move us to laughter and to tears.
> So let us – in fancied ritual – celebrate
> his genius by washing down our oysters
> with reaming noggins … raised in roisterous
> praise of Auld Reikie's peerless laureate.

SEE ALSO: Robert Burns, Scottish National Portrait Gallery, St Giles.

FURTHER INFORMATION: Fergusson's grave is situated close to the western wall of the church, bordered by a low chain fence. The statue and the grave are the primary memorials for Robert Fergusson, but there are a number of other tributes in the city, as follows: a plaque in St Giles'; a plaque in the new Royal High School; the male and female wards in the Royal Edinburgh Hospital, which are named after him; a lock of his hair in Edinburgh University Library; and his portrait hangs in the Scottish National Portrait Gallery. Fergusson destroyed his papers just before he died. There are inscribed copies of his 1773 *Poems* and some scraps among the Cape Records, MSS 2041–4, in the National Library of Scotland.

CANONGATE

The headstone placed by Robert Burns on Fergusson's unmarked grave

FURTHER READING: A. Law, *Robert Fergusson and the Edinburgh of his Time* (Edinburgh City Libraries, 1974); D. Irving, *The Life of Robert Fergusson* (1799); T. Sommers, *The Life of Robert Fergusson, the Scottish Poet* (1803).

Grave of Mary Brunton (1778–1818)
Novelist

> I am looking over *Self-Control* again, & my opinion is confirmed of its being an excellently-meant, elegantly-written Work, without anything of Nature or Probability in it.
> Jane Austen, 1813

Born on the island of Burray in Orkney, Mary Brunton (née Balfour) is best remembered for her novel *Self-Control*, published anonymously in 1812. Anonymity was often not a choice but a necessity for women writers in the early nineteenth century, who could not be seen to step over the boundaries of the home and their household duties. Not only were they denied the credit for their art, but, as in Brunton's preface in *Self-Control*, they were often made to feel apologetic for it: '[it] was begun at first merely for my own amusement, and to reconcile my conscience to the time which it has employed, by making it in some degree useful'. She married the Revd Alexander Brunton in 1798 and lived in Bolton, near Haddington, East Lothian, before moving to Edinburgh in 1803 when her husband took on the chaplaincy at Greyfriars. Their first home was at 3 St John Street, opposite the Masonic lodge. Her other works included *Discipline* (1814) and *Emmeline* (1819).

FURTHER INFORMATION: The tablet marking Mary Brunton's grave is fixed to the western wall, near the top-left corner of the kirkyard.

Grave of Dugald Stewart (1753–1828)
Philosopher and biographer

> Wealth, honours, and all that is extraneous of the man, have no more influence with him than they will have at the Last Day.
> Robert Burns

Dugald Stewart held the chair of moral philosophy at Edinburgh University for 25 years and became a celebrated philosopher and masterful teacher, whose persuasive arguments influenced many of his students, including Walter Scott and philosopher James Mill. Stewart was a disciple of Thomas Reid's 'common sense' philosophy and taught the first course on economics given in Britain. He is best remembered for his *Elements of the Philosophy of the Human Mind* (three volumes, 1792, 1814, 1827). A circular Corinthian monument was erected to his memory on Calton Hill in 1831. His nondescript tomb is situated in the north-west corner of the kirkyard, first on the left as you enter the area dominated by the tall monument erected to the memory of the soldiers who died in Edinburgh Castle.

SEE ALSO: Calton Hill, Walter Scott, Robert Burns, Edinburgh Castle.

Grave of James Ballantyne (1772–1833)
Childhood friend, printer, publisher and secret business partner of Sir Walter Scott

> In prospect of absolute ruin, I wonder if they would let me leave the Court of Session. I would like, methinks, to go abroad, 'And lay my bones far from the Tweed.'
> Sir Walter Scott, Journal (1826)

James Ballantyne's friendship with Scott began during their boyhood at Kelso Grammar School in the Scottish Borders, where they shared a bench together. Ballantyne went on to study law, but in 1797 he set up as a printer and launched the *Tory Kelso Mail*, and in 1802 printed the first two volumes of Scott's *The Minstrelsy of the Scottish Border*. Scott encouraged him to move to Edinburgh and, with money loaned from Scott, he moved to a small shop at Abbeyhill, near Holyroodhouse, where the third volume of *The Minstrelsy* was printed. He later moved to larger premises in the Canongate and in 1805 Scott bought a quarter share in Ballantyne's printing business, setting up James and his younger brother John in a publishing business four years later in Hanover Street. Scott's involvement in these ventures, which eventually led to his financial downfall, were kept intensely secret.
John Buchan, in his biography of Scott, describes James Ballantyne as 'enthusiastic, excitable, a muddler in finance, incapable of presenting at any time an accurate statement of his assets and liabilities'. Lockhart sums up his father-in-law's madcap partnership in his *Life*:

> It is an old saying, that wherever there is a secret there must be something wrong; and dearly did he pay the penalty for the mystery in which he had chosen to involve this transaction ... Hence, by degrees, was woven a web of entanglement from which neither Ballantyne nor his adviser had any means of escape.

Although the printing business was successful, the publishing side was a disaster. Its complex credit structure, coupled with its tangled involvement with Archibald Constable, who was ruined in 1826, inevitably led to Ballantyne's downfall the same year, with debts amounting to around £130,000. Scott subsequently wrote his way out of most of the debt, a task which took him six years. Buchan recalls that in 1829, 'James Ballantyne was no longer the jolly companion he had been, for he had lost his wife, retired to the country, and taken to Whiggism and piety.' He died four years later and is buried beside his brother John (see below).

SEE ALSO: John Ballantyne, Sir Walter Scott, J.G. Lockhart, R.M. Ballantyne, John Buchan, Archibald Constable.

FURTHER INFORMATION: In 1870, the Ballantynes moved to Clare House in Newington, following the expansion of Waverley Station. In 1878, a London branch was opened and in 1916 the Edinburgh printing works finally closed. James Ballantyne's nephew was the novelist R.M. Ballantyne.

Grave of John Ballantyne (1774–1821)
Childhood friend, printer, publisher and secret business partner of Sir Walter Scott

> I believe Scott would as soon have ordered his dog to be hanged, as harboured, in his darkest hour of perplexity, the least thought of discarding 'jocund Johnny'.
> J.G. Lockhart, *The Life of Sir Walter Scott* (1837–8)

CANONGATE

John Ballantyne, the younger brother of James, Walter Scott's school friend, was born in Kelso and was described by Lockhart as 'a quick, active, intrepid little fellow ... so very lively and amusing ... liked his bottle and his bowl, as well as, like Johnny Armstrong, "a hawk, a hound, and a fair woman"'. His father sent him to London where he worked in a banking house and he later trained as a tailor. Success, however, eluded him in life. In 1805, his goods were sold off to cover his debts, and his brother James offered him a post as clerk in his printing business. Both brothers became inextricably linked with Scott when he secretly bought a share of their printing business and later created a publishing house to be run by John, a move which would end in insolvency for Scott and the Ballantynes. Lockhart recalls a touching scene beside John Ballantyne's grave in his *Life*:

> As we stood together a few days afterwards, while they were smoothing the turf over John's remains in the Canongate churchyard, the heavens, which had been dark and slaty, cleared up suddenly, and the midsummer sun shone forth in his strength. Scott, ever awake to the 'skiey influences', cast his eye along the overhanging line of the Calton Hill, with its gleaming walls and towers, and then turning to the grave again, 'I feel,' he whispered in my ear, 'I feel as if there would be less sunshine for me from this day forth.'

He died as he had lived: ignorant of the situation of his affairs, and deep in debt.

SEE ALSO: James Ballantyne, Sir Walter Scott, J.G. Lockhart.

FURTHER INFORMATION: The Ballantynes are buried in unmarked graves. Take the path leading round the right-hand side of the church going downhill. On your right is the tomb of William Fettes, where a plaque at the bottom left marks the spot.

BOOK LOVERS' EDINBURGH

Grave of Clarinda (Agnes McLehose 1759–1841) Inspiration for Robert Burns's 'Ae Fond Kiss'

> I'll ne'er blame my partial fancy,
> Naething could resist my Nancy:
> But to see her was to love her;
> Love but her, and love for ever.
> Robert Burns, from 'Ae Fond Kiss'

Robert Burns first met Mrs Agnes (Nancy) McLehose after she engineered an invitation for him to a tea party given by Miss Erskine Nimmo at her brother's flat in Alison Square (now demolished), off Nicolson Street, on 4 December 1787. They seem to have been well and truly smitten with each other, and that night she hurriedly sent him a letter inviting him to tea at her house in Potterrow. He never kept the appointment as he dislocated his knee shortly afterwards when his coach reputedly overturned on his way home following an evening of revelry. And so the circumstances fell into place for the start of an impassioned correspondence between the two from December until mid-March, during which time around 80 letters were written between them, and a relationship blossomed which would eventually inspire Burns to write one of his greatest love songs.

It is doubtful whether today's postal system could have coped with their copious correspondence – sometimes six letters each a day – but since 1773 the Edinburgh penny post had been in operation, offering deliveries of letters and small parcels every hour throughout the day. Burns, who was then lodging at 2 St James Square (now demolished), used the penny post, but Nancy, careful of her reputation, often used her maid, Jennie Clow, to convey her letters.

On 8 December, Burns wrote to Nancy, stating:

> I cannot bear the idea of leaving Edinburgh without seeing you – I know not how to account for it – I am strangely taken with some people; nor am I often mistaken. You are a stranger to me; but I am an odd being: some yet unnamed feelings; things not principles, but better than whims, carry me farther than boasted reason ever did a philosopher.

Nancy replied:

> These 'nameless feelings' I perfectly comprehend, tho' the pen of Locke could not define them ... If I was your sister, I would call on you; but tis a censorious world this; and in this sense 'you and I are not of this world'. Adieu. Keep up your heart, you will soon get well, and we shall meet. Farewell. God bless you.

Nancy has been described by an acquaintance as 'short in stature, her form graceful, her hands and feet small and delicate. Her features were regular and pleasing, her eyes lustrous, her complexion fair, her cheeks ruddy, and a well-formed mouth displayed teeth beautifully white.' Another said she was 'of a somewhat voluptuous style of beauty, of lively and easy manners, of a poetical cast of mind, with some wit, and not too high a degree of refinement or delicacy'. She was also married to, but estranged from, James McLehose, a Glasgow lawyer whom she had married when she was 18 and whom she had borne four children (two dying in infancy) by the time she was 23. McLehose ended up in a debtors' prison and afterwards sailed to a new life in Jamaica, leaving Nancy struggling to make ends meet as a single parent in a flat at General's Entry (now demolished) off Potterrow on Edinburgh's Southside.

Although separated, Nancy was still in the eyes of the law a married woman and therefore had to be careful in her letters to Burns that she was not in any way compromised. Soon, therefore, they adopted for discretion's sake the Arcadian noms de plume Sylvander and Clarinda. Burns's injury made it difficult for him to have any opportunity to consummate the relationship and some of his letters – through frustration – got a little overheated, one stating 'had I been so blest as to have met with you in time, it might have led me – God of love only knows where'. To which Nancy replied, 'When I meet you, I must chide you for writing in your romantic style. Do you remember that she whom you address is a married woman?'

They did meet after Burns recovered, but there is no evidence that their relationship ever became sexual. Burns eventually left Edinburgh in February 1788, later marrying his former lover Jean Armour. They did, however, meet once more before Nancy's departure to join her husband in Jamaica in a failed attempt to rebuild her marriage. Her diary entry at the time reveals she was still in love with Burns 'till the shadow fell ... This day I can never forget. Parted with Robert Burns in the year 1791 never more to meet in this world. Oh may we meet in heaven.' Before her departure, Burns sent her a card with a lyric scrawled on it from Sanquhar Post Office in Dumfriesshire, which began 'Ae fond kiss, and then we sever, Ae fareweel, and then – for ever ... '

Nancy outlived Burns by 45 years, dying aged 82 in 1841 at her flat beneath Calton Hill. Her grave is situated against the eastern wall of Canongate Kirkyard. The site of the house where she corresponded with Burns is marked by a plaque at the corner of Potterrow and Marshall Street.

In November 1788, Nancy's maid, Jennie Clow, gave birth to Burns's illegitimate son, conceived while acting as courier for Sylvander and Clarinda.

CANONGATE

SEE ALSO: Robert Burns.

FURTHER INFORMATION: It was the Clarinda Burns Club that proposed that a plaque should be erected on the site of Clarinda's house at General's Entry in Potterrow on the wall of Bristo School in 1937. Edinburgh Corporation Education Committee thought 'the idea was totally unacceptable. It is beneath the dignity of our city to sanction such a tablet in view of Clarinda's character.' Questions were raised in the House of Commons. However, the Clarinda Burns Club stood firm, and a plaque was finally erected on 22 January 1937.

Clarinda's gravestone. Note the a absence of her real name and birth and death dates

149 CANONGATE
Acheson House
Formerley 'The Cock and Trumpet'
Public house, brothel, and den of thieves
Haunt of James McLevy (1796-1875)
Edinburgh's first detective
and crime writer

There are certain duties we perform of which we are scarcely aware, and which consist in a species of strolling supervision among houses, which, though not devoted to resetting, are often yet receptacles of stolen goods, through a mean of the residence there of women of the lowest stratum of vice and profligacy ... It was a feature of the portly landlady that she never knew (not she) that such things were in the house. 'Some of thae rattling deevils o' hizzies had done it. The glaikit limmers, will they no be content wi' their ain game, but maun turn common thieves?' Then her surprise was just as like the real astonishment as veritable wonder itself. 'And got ye that in my *house, Mr M'Levy? Whaur in a' the earth did it come frae? And wha brought it to The Cock and Trumpet? I wish I kent the gillet.'*
James McLevy, from 'The Cock and Trumpet',
McLevy: The Edinburgh Detective

Regarded as Edinburgh's first detective, James McLevy was involved in over 2,000 cases during his career, and such were his powers of deduction, he was consulted by parliament for his advice. 'He was of medium height, square-faced, and clean-shaven,' wrote the *Edinburgh Evening News* in 1922, 'and always wore a tall silk hat, from beneath the broad brim of which a pair of quick black eyes scrutinised the crowd ... '
James McLevy was born in Ballymacnab, county Armagh, Ireland, in 1796, to John McLevy, a weaver and farmer,

CANONGATE

Entrance to Acheson House with the Acheson family crest of the Cock and Trumpet carved above the door

and Catherine Dourie. When he was thirteen he became a weaver's apprentice, and in 1815 he arrived in Edinburgh where he was employed as builder's labourer. Fifteen years later, in 1830, he joined the city police force as a nightwatchman, aged 34, where his talents did not go unnoticed. In 1833 he was promoted and became Edinburgh's first criminal officer detective – CO1 – Criminal Officer number 1. Many of his adventures he recorded with his pen in later life, and his writing style is embedded in the Victorian Edinburgh of its time, but he had, for his day, a unique understanding and often a deep compassion for criminals. He was pre-Conan Doyle, but more streetwise than Sherlock Holmes. No doubt Conan Doyle had read him, and perhaps even been inspired by him, but had McLevy lived through the glory days of the fictional periodical, from around 1880 to the late 1920s, as Holmes did, who knows what his future might have been.

'I have often heard it said,' wrote McLevy, 'that the past part of my life must have been a harassing and painful one; called on, as my reputation grew, in so many cases, – obliged to get up at midnight, to pursue thieves and recover property in so wide a range as a city with 200,000 inhabitants, and often with no clue to seize, but obliged in so many instances, to trust to chance. All this is true enough, and yet it fails in being a real description, insomuch as it leaves out the incidents that maintain and cheer the spirit, – for I need scarcely say, that if any profession now-a-days can be enlivened by adventure, it is that of a detective officer.' James McLevy died, a local criminology legend, on 6 December 1873, aged 76, and is buried in Canongate Kirkyard.

SEE ALSO: Conan Doyle, Ian Rankin, Val McDermid, Quintin Jardine, Canongate Kirkyard.

FURTHER INFORMATION: Acheson House was built in 1633 for Sir Archibald Acheson, who was King Charles I's

Secretary of State for Scotland. Throughout history it has had many owners and tenants; some reputable, and some not so. In the eighteenth century the house was divided up into various dwellings, and by the early nineteenth century it housed a brothel and the Cock and Trumpet pub, the name inspired by the carvings in the Acheson family crest above the doorway. In recent years it has undergone major refurbishment and parts of it have been incorporated into the Museum of Edinburgh next door.

FURTHER READING: J. McLevy, *McLevy: The Edinburgh Detective* (Mercat, 2001); J. McLevy, *Curiosities of Crime in Edinburgh during the last thirty years* (Gale, 2010). David Ashton wrote the McLevy radio series for the BBC, and several Inspector McLevy mystery novels based on the series, including *Shadow of the Serpent* and *Fall from Grace* (Two Roads, 2016).

McLevy: The Edinburgh Detective was first published by Mercat Press in 2001. The stories were originally published in 1861 in *Curiosities of Crime in Edinburgh* and *The Sliding Scale of Life*

HOLYROOD

FOOT OF THE ROYAL MILE
The Palace of Holyroodhouse and Holyrood Abbey

The apartments are lofty, but unfurnished; and as for the pictures of the Scottish kings, from Fergus I to King William, they are paltry daubings, mostly by the same hand, painted either from the imagination, or porters hired to sit for the purpose.
Tobias Smollett, *The Expedition of Humphry Clinker* (1771)

The Palace of Holyroodhouse

HOLYROOD

The twelfth-century Abbey of the Holy Rood is a roofless ruin today, but the Palace still stands in its high-born glory after 500 years of turbulent history. Construction was started by James IV (1473–1513) and finished off by his son James V (1513–42) after his father fell at Flodden Field in 1513.

William Dunbar (*c*.1460–*c*.1520) was one of many poets in history who depended on Court patronage for their survival, and during the reign of James IV he was frequently outspoken and candid, often criticising the powers that be with the clout of his piercing verse. Little is known of his life, but he is said to have been born in East Lothian, attended St Andrews University and then entered the priesthood. He later became secretary to some of James IV's embassies to foreign courts. In 1500, he was given a Royal pension and in 1503 he wrote the political allegory *The Thrissill and the Rois*, the thistle being James IV, and the rose his wife, Margaret Tudor. Other poems included *Tua Mariit Wemen and the Wedo* and *The Dance of the Sevin Deidly Synnis*. His name disappears from all records after the Battle of Flodden, indicating he probably died in battle.

Poet and playwright David Lyndsay (*c*.1490–1555) also sought patronage from the court of James IV. His hilarious and irreverent political satire *The Thrie Estaites* was first performed in Cupar, Fife, in June 1552 and is the earliest Scottish play to have survived.

The Palace is best known for being the home of Mary, Queen of Scots (1542–87), who was twice married in the Abbey and who witnessed the murder of her secretary, David Rizzio, by her jealous husband, Lord Darnley, in her antechamber where, reputedly, the bloodstains can still be seen. Mary was the daughter of James V, King of Scots, by his second wife, Mary of Guise, and she arrived at Holyrood from France in 1561, a Catholic queen in a Protestant country. All her literary output was in French, which was widely spoken by the Scottish nobility. Her library held more than 300 books, which included the largest collection of French and Italian poetry in Scotland. She wrote sacred poems and love sonnets, but little of her work was published during her lifetime. This was rectified in 1873 when the *Poems of Mary, Queen of Scots* were edited and published by Julian Sharman. Mary was beheaded in 1587 when she was implicated in a plot against her cousin, Elizabeth I. An extract from a sonnet written during her incarceration at Fotheringay reveals her despair:

> Que suis-je hélas? Et de quoi sert ma vie?
> Je ne suis fors qu'un corps privé de coeur,
> Une ombre vaine, un objet de malheur
> Qui n'a plus rien que de mourir en vie.
> (Alas what am I? What use has my life?
> I am but a body whose heart's torn away,
> A vain shadow, an object of misery
> Who has nothing left but death-in-life.)

The other turbulent event that took place at Holyrood Palace was during the 1745 Jacobite uprising, when the Palace served briefly as the headquarters of Bonnie Prince Charlie, recreated by Sir Walter Scott in *Waverley* (1814):

> They reached the Palace of Holyrood, and were announced respectively as they entered the apartments ...
> It is not, therefore, to be wondered that Edward, who had spent the greater part of his life in the solemn seclusion of Waverley-Honour, should have been dazzled at the liveliness and elegance of the scene now exhibited in the long-deserted halls of the Scottish Palace. The accompaniments, indeed, fell short of splendour, being such as the confusion and hurry of the time admitted; still, however, the general effect was striking.

HOLYROOD

The roofless ruin of the Abbey of the Holy Rood

Sir Arthur Conan Doyle's father, Charles Doyle (1832–93), a talented artist and designer, was a clerk of works at the Office of Works in the Palace in the mid-nineteenth century, and is credited with designing its fountain. His son, Arthur, recounts Rizzio's murder in his story 'The Silver Mirror'. In the spring of 1933, John Buchan was made Lord High Commissioner to the General Assembly of the Church of Scotland and his headquarters were at the Palace, which he recalled in his autobiography *Memory Hold-the-Door* (1940) as a place 'where he entertains the Church and the World according to his means and his inclination'.

David I founded the Abbey of Holy Rood in 1128 on the spot where a stag which was about to gore him vanished into thin air, leaving him holding the holy rood (cross). The Abbey was run by the Augustinian Order and has seen a succession of Scottish monarchs married, crowned and buried there. Much of it was destroyed during the Reformation, and it was pillaged by the Earl of Hertford on his march through Scotland in 1544. In 1688, it was again plundered, by a mob celebrating the accession of William of Orange, when royal coffins were smashed and the head of Darnley was stolen. A new roof was erected in 1758, but was such a botched job it collapsed ten years later, and was never replaced, resulting in the ruin we see today.

The Holyrood Abbey Sanctuary was a safe haven for over 700 years for debtors trying to avoid imprisonment. Whether aristocrat or commoner, all were given refuge. In literary history, it is famous for giving shelter to the poverty-stricken Thomas De Quincey (1785–1859), who was imprisoned for debt on numerous occasions and was forced to take refuge there for a time, and in Joan Lingard's children's book *The Sign of the Black Dagger*, the Comte D'Artois arrives from France seeking shelter at the sanctuary.

The sanctuary was established in the twelfth century under a charter granted by King David I. On entering the sanctuary, a debtor had to submit an application to the Bailie of Holyrood for the 'benefit and privilege' of sanctuary. If the Bailie ruled in the debtor's favour, he was issued with 'letters of protection' and allowed to reside within the sanctuary grounds out of reach of the law. Holyrood Park was within its boundary and most of its accommodation was provided by lodging houses and inns at the foot of the Canongate, some of which are still standing in Abbey Strand, at the bottom of the Canongate, between the roundabout and the gates of the Palace. On

Sundays, the Abbey lairds (debtors) were free to step outside the sanctuary's boundary as legal proceedings could not be implemented on Sunday under Scots law. Part of its boundary is marked today by a row of three S-shaped brass studs sunk into the top of Abbey Strand where the cobbles meet the tarmac. Although imprisonment for debt was abolished in 1880, Holyrood's ancient right of sanctuary has never been revoked.

SEE ALSO: Thomas De Quincey, Sir Arthur Conan Doyle, Sir Walter Scott, John Buchan, Robert Louis Stevenson, Tobias Smollett, Holyrood Park.

FURTHER READING: J. Lingard, *The Sign of the Black Dagger* (Puffin, 2005); S. Mapstone, *William Dunbar, 'The Nobill Poyet'* (Tuckwell Press, 2001); R. Bell (ed.), *Bittersweet Within My Heart: The Love Poems of Mary, Queen of Scots* (Chronicle Books, 1993); R. Sabatini, *The Historical Nights' Entertainment* Vol. 1 (House of Stratus, 2001); Mr Chrystal Croftangry relates tales of the sanctuary in Sir Walter Scott's *Chronicles of the Canongate* (Penguin, 2003).

Thomas De Quincey, serial debtor and frequent guest of the Abbey Sanctuary. Photogravure after an 1885 drawing by James Archer

HOLYROOD PARK

There are not many cities in the world that can boast a 650-acre geological spectacle within walking distance of the city centre, encompassing ancient volcanoes, fossilised beaches, crags and lochs. Sometimes known as the Queen's Park (or the King's Park, depending on the gender of the ruling monarch), wordsmiths have often utilised and been stimulated by its primeval beauty.

Salisbury Crags

At St Anthony's Well, Robert Wringham 'was subject to sinful doubtings' and had a heavenly vision while contemplating murdering his brother in James Hogg's *The Private Memoirs and Confessions of a Justified Sinner* (1824). The discovery in 1836 of 17 miniature coffins of wood, each containing a wooden image of a human figure dressed for burial, in a recess of the rock on the north-east side of Arthur's Seat inspired Ian Rankin to weave miniature coffins into the plot of *The Falls* (2001). Rankin also used the top of Salisbury Crags as the setting for the suicide of Jim Margolies in the prologue of *Dead Souls* (1999):

> 'Salisbury Crag' has become rhyming slang in the city. It means skag, heroin. 'Morningside Speed' is cocaine. A

snort of coke just now would do him the world of good, but wouldn't be enough. Arthur's Seat could be made of the stuff: in the scheme of things, it wouldn't matter a damn.

In the 1830s, Thomas De Quincey relished the immunity his strolls in the park gave him from his creditors, falling, as it did, within the boundary of the Holyrood Abbey Sanctuary for debtors. If he'd still been around a few decades later, he would have spotted a young Robert Louis Stevenson, who, when not skating on Duddingston Loch, was filching kestrels' eggs from the high rocks of Arthur's Seat, which he described as 'a hill for magnitude, a mountain by reason of its bold design'. The Crags are said to have inspired young Edinburgh medical student Arthur Conan Doyle to create the towering plateau in *The Lost World* (1912). Sir Walter Scott used the mustering of the Jacobite army in the Park to great effect in *Waverley* (1814) and gives us a striking description of Salisbury Crags in *The Heart of Midlothian* (1818), depicting them as 'a close-built, high-piled city, stretching itself out beneath in a form, which, to a romantic imagination, may be supposed to represent that of a dragon'. Beneath the Crags runs the Radical Road, built in 1820 at Scott's suggestion by a group of unemployed weavers who were believed to hold radical political views following the end of the Napoleonic wars. J.G. Lockhart, Scott's biographer and son-in-law, proposed on Scott's death in 1832 the erection of 'a huge Homeric Cairn on Arthur's Seat – a land and sea mark'. It was the Scott Monument on Princes Street which finally became Scott's memorial, though had it been erected on the top of Arthur's Seat, it would have stood out like a beacon for miles.

SEE ALSO: Sir Walter Scott, Thomas De Quincey, Robert Louis Stevenson, Ian Rankin, Sir Arthur Conan Doyle, James Hogg, J.G. Lockhart.

CALTON

WATERLOO PLACE
Old Calton Burial Ground

Tomb of David Hume (1711–76)
Philosopher, historian and political thinker

In all ages of the world, priests have been enemies of liberty.
David Hume, *Essays Moral, Political and Literary* (1741–2)

Empiricist and sceptic, David Hume's powerful arguments exposed serious defects in accepted accounts of rationality, causation and morality, concluding that the domain of reason in human affairs was more narrow than had been supposed, and tradition and custom were the principal sources of accepted morality. He is best remembered for *A Treatise of Human Nature* (1739), *Political Discourses* (1752) and his *History of England* (5 volumes, 1754–62). Fearful that the rumour that he had entered into a conspiracy with the Devil was taken seriously, his friends, in order to prevent any violation of his grave, mounted guard over his tomb for eight nights after his funeral with pistols and lanterns. No physical or metaphysical intrusion was recorded.

SEE ALSO: Riddle's Court.

FURTHER INFORMATION: As you climb the steps from street level, David Hume's imposing tomb can be seen in the top-right corner.

Grave of Peter Williamson (1730–99)
Also known as 'Indian Peter'
Possible inspiration for David Balfour in Stevenson's *Kidnapped*

Robert Louis Stevenson based many of his characters on real people. W.E. Henley inspired Long John Silver, and a John Silver is buried in Old Calton Burial Ground. A John Pew, immortalised as 'Blind Pew' in *Treasure Island*, is buried in South Leith Churchyard. The name and description of Alan Breck appears in the custom records of Leith. Stevenson would, without a doubt, have read Peter Williamson's colourful accounts of his kidnapping and adventures in the Americas. It cannot be proved, but it is certainly probable, that Peter Williamson was a stimulus in the creation of David Balfour and *Kidnapped* (1886). Williamson was born at Hinley Farm, near the village of

Aboyne in Aberdeenshire. When he was a boy, visiting his aunt in Aberdeen, he was kidnapped from the quayside, shipped off to America and sold into slavery. After seven years of servitude, he married and began life as a farmer, but in 1754 his farm was attacked by Indians during the French and Indian War (1754–63) and he was forced to travel with them as a slave. He later escaped and joined the British Army to fight the French and their Indian allies. Captured by the French after his regiment surrendered, he was eventually freed after a POW exchange and made his way back to Scotland. He settled in Edinburgh where he established a coffee room in Parliament House in Old Parliament Close. In 1770, he organised the city's first penny post and in 1773 he produced the first Edinburgh street directory.

SEE ALSO: Robert Louis Stevenson, W.E. Henley, The Hawes Inn.

FURTHER INFORMATION: Peter Williamson was interred in an unmarked grave 15 paces north-east of the political martyrs' monument. The Williamson family memorial (an 8-ft-square pillar) marks the spot.

FURTHER READING: D. Skelton, *Indian Peter* (Mainstream, 2004); Peter Williamson, *The Travels of Peter Williamson* (R. Fleming, 1768); Peter Williamson, *French and Indian Cruelty* (Bryce and Paterson, 1758); Peter Williamson, *Life and Curious Adventures* (John Orphoot, 1812).

Grave of William Blackwood (1776–1834)
Bookseller and publisher of *Blackwood's Magazine*

It is ironic that William Blackwood is buried just a few yards from his great publishing rival, Archibald Constable. Blackwood was a Tory and Constable was a Whig, but political differences aside, both men contributed enormously to Edinburgh's literary heritage. Born in Edinburgh, Blackwood was apprenticed at 14 to the

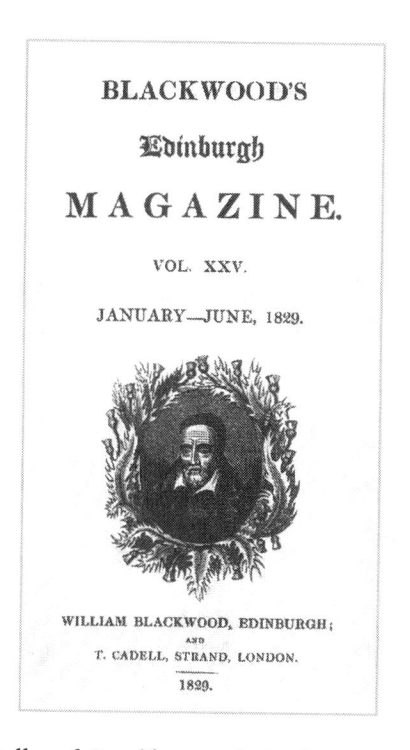

bookseller Bell and Bradfute at their shop in Parliament Square. After a period in London and Glasgow, he established himself as a bookseller and publisher in 1804, when he set up his own business at 64 South Bridge. In 1816, he took the extremely radical step of relocating his business to the New Town at 17 Princes Street; this was an unprecedented move, as traditionally the bookselling and publishing trade was located in the Old Town. Contrary to popular opinion, Blackwood wasn't ruined – his business prospered – and his new premises were described by J.G. Lockhart in *Peter's Letters to his Kinsfolk* as 'the only great lounging bookshop in the New Town of Edinburgh'. He became the Scottish agent of Byron's publisher, John Murray, and spotted the talent of John Galt and Susan Ferrier. In 1817, as a rival to Constable's *Edinburgh Review*, he founded *Blackwood's Magazine*, which evolved into a highly influential magazine that launched many writers' careers during its 180 years until its closure in 1980. William Blackwood died on 16 September 1834 and was succeeded by his two sons, Alexander and Robert.

SEE ALSO: *Blackwood's Magazine*, John Wilson, J.G. Lockhart, James Hogg, Archibald Constable, *Edinburgh Review*, John Galt, Susan Ferrier, National Library of Scotland.

FURTHER INFORMATION: When entering the graveyard from Waterloo Place, walk straight up the path and follow it round to the right. Keep walking until you can go no further. The black gates of Blackwood's tomb, which backs on to Waterloo Place, are directly in front of you. The Blackwood archives can be consulted at the National Library of Scotland, George IV Bridge.

FURTHER READING: F.D. Tredrey, *The House of Blackwood, 1804-1954* (W. Blackwood & Sons, 1954); M. Oliphant, *Annals of a Publishing House* (W. Blackwood & Sons, 1897).

Grave of Archibald Constable (1774-1827)
Regarded as the first modern publisher

Archibald Constable was born in Carnbee, Fife, where his father was land steward to the Earl of Kellie. In 1788, aged 14, he was apprenticed to Peter Hill, an Edinburgh bookseller, and in 1795 he went into business for himself as a dealer in rare and curious books on the Royal Mile. His business soon flourished, and he bought *The Scots Magazine* in 1801 and launched the *Edinburgh Review* in 1802, which became notorious for its savage literary articles. Apart from his natural flair for publishing and his regard for editorial independence, one of the reasons for his success was that he actually paid writers fees which matched their talents, something unheard of in early-nineteenth-century publishing. Lord Henry Cockburn (1779-1854) described Constable in *Memorials of his Times* (1856) as a man who 'confounded not merely his rivals in trade, but his very authors, by his unheard-of prices. Ten, even twenty, guineas for a sheet of review, £2,000 or £3,000 for a single poem ... [he] drew authors from dens where they would otherwise have starved.' In 1805, jointly with Longman & Co., Constable published Walter Scott's *Lay of the Last Minstrel*, followed by *Marmion* in 1808. In 1812, he purchased the rights to the *Encyclopaedia Britannica*. He suffered insolvency in 1826 due to the collapse of his London agents, but surfaced again in 1827 when he published *Constable's Miscellany*, an early form of mass-market literature, reproducing works on art, literature and science in cheap editions. He died on 21 July 1827 and can rightly be called the first modern publisher.

SEE ALSO: *Edinburgh Review*, Francis Jeffrey, Thomas Carlyle, Walter Scott, *Blackwood's Magazine*, William Blackwood, Lord Henry Cockburn, National Library of Scotland.

FURTHER INFORMATION: When entering the graveyard from Waterloo Place, walk straight up the path and follow it round to the right. Keep walking until you can go no further. Constable's grave is on your right in the corner, possibly obscured by ivy. Some of Constable's correspondence and business papers are held by the National Library of Scotland, George IV Bridge.

Archibald Constable

CALTON HILL
Monument to Dugald Stewart (1753–1828)
Philosopher and biographer

An exalted judge of the human heart.
Robert Burns

The rhetoric and elegant prose of Dugald Stewart has excited and inspired many, including the young Walter Scott, who remembered his 'striking and impressive eloquence'. Another student wrote, 'To me his lectures were like the opening of the heavens. I felt I had a soul.'
Born and educated in Edinburgh, Dugald Stewart was the son of the professor of mathematics at Edinburgh University, a post that father and son held jointly from 1775. He was professor of moral philosophy from 1785 to 1810 and became one of the most distinguished philosophers in Britain. He was greatly influenced by Thomas Reid's 'common sense' philosophy and his lectures on political economy were attended by all four founding members of the *Edinburgh Review*. He was in France during the French Revolution, where he met Benjamin Franklin and Thomas Jefferson, and while on holiday in Ayrshire he met Robert Burns. He returned with a copy of Burns's Kilmarnock edition of poems, which he showed to Henry Mackenzie, who subsequently wrote his famous influential review in *The Lounger*. This review contributed significantly to Burns's success. It was Stewart who first compared Edinburgh to Athens, christening his native city 'the Athens of the North' for posterity.
He was a prolific writer and is best known for *Elements of the Philosophy of the Human Mind* (three volumes, 1792, 1814, 1827). His other work includes *Outlines of Moral Philosophy* (1793), *Philosophical Essays* (1810) and *Biographical Memoirs* (1810), which chronicles the lives of Adam Smith, William Robertson and Thomas Reid.

CALTON

The monument to him on Calton Hill, built in 1831, was designed by William Playfair, and is modelled on one erected by Lysicrates in Athens in the fourth century.

Stewart lived for many years in Horse Wynd, Canongate (now the site of the Scottish Parliament) and from 1806 to 1812 at Whitefoord House in the Canongate, afterwards moving to 7 Moray Place, where he died in 1828. He is buried near the south-west corner of Canongate Kirkyard.

SEE ALSO: Canongate Kirkyard, *Edinburgh Review*, Henry Mackenzie, Robert Burns, Adam Smith, William Playfair.

William Playfair's Athenian tribute to Dugald Stewart on Calton Hill

REGENT ROAD
The Burns Monument

Ah, Robbie, ye asked them for bread and they hae gi'en ye a stane.
Agnes Burnes, mother of Robert Burns.

Situated on the south side of Calton Hill, this monument crowns a rock ten feet higher than the level of the street and was erected in 1830, after a design by Thomas Hamilton. It is a circular Corinthian cyclo-style of twelve columns, raised on a quadrangular base, surmounted by a cupola in imitation of the monument of Lysicrates at Athens (as is the monument to Dugald Stewart), and contains a bust of Burns by W. Brodie and, reputedly, a number of relics connected to the poet. A marble statue of Burns – sculptor John Flaxman's last work – which stood formerly in the monument is now in the National Portrait Gallery.

SEE ALSO: Anchor Close, St James Square, Buccleuch Street, Burns Monument, Canongate Kilwinning Lodge, White Hart Inn, St Giles, William Smellie, William Creech, The Writers' Museum, Sciennes Hill House, Robert Fergusson, Clarinda, Jean Lorimer, Henry Mackenzie, Thomas Blacklock.

New Calton Burial Ground
Site of the Stevenson family tomb

10 May 1887
Sir, The favour of your Company to attend the Funeral of my father, from his house here, to the place of Interment in the

CALTON

New Calton Burial Ground, on Friday the 13th curt at 1/2 past 2 o'clock, will much oblige, Sir your obedient servant
Robert Louis Stevenson

The walled tomb of the Stevensons is the last resting place of this dynasty of engineers and their families, notably RLS's parents, Thomas (1818–87) and Margaret (1828–97), and his grandparents, Robert (1772–1850) and Jean (1799–1846). Other family members interred here include Jean's father, Thomas Smith (1752–1815), Robert's son, Alan (1807–1865), and Alan's son, Bob Stevenson (1847–1900).

Thomas Stevenson died in the early hours of Sunday, 9 May 1887, at 17 Heriot Row. His funeral 'would have pleased him', wrote Louis. 'It was the largest private funeral in man's memory here.' Louis, sadly, was too ill to attend. His mother's diary entry for 13 May, the day of the funeral, reads, 'My darling was "gathered to his fathers" today in the new Calton burying ground. Lou had cold and could not be present. Bob was chief mourner.'

SEE ALSO: Howard Place, Inverleith Terrace, Heriot Row, Pilrig House, Colinton Manse, Swanston Cottage, Baxter's Place, Glencorse Kirk, Rutherford's Howff, Old Calton Burial Ground, St Giles, Hawes Inn, Rullion Green, W.E. Henley, Alison Cunningham, Henderson's School, Deacon Brodie, The Writers' Museum, *Kidnapped* Statue, Museum of Scotland, George Mackenzie, Martyrs' Monument, Edinburgh Castle, Old College, Parliament Hall, Holyrood Park, Royal College of Surgeons' Museum, R.M. Ballantyne, RLS Memorial.

FURTHER INFORMATION: The entrance to the New Calton Burial Ground is situated beside the monument to Robert Burns on Regent Road. On entering, walk straight ahead down the path in front of you, following it round to the right. The Stevenson tomb is against the eastern wall, about halfway along on your left.

THE SOUTHSIDE

INFIRMARY STREET
Site of the old Royal Infirmary
Where Arthur Conan Doyle was taught
the science of deduction

> The students were pouring down the sloping street which led to the infirmary – each with his little sheaf of note-books in his hand. There were pale, frightened lads, fresh from the high schools, and callous old chronics, whose generation had passed on and left them. They swept in an unbroken, tumultuous stream from the university gate to the hospital. The figures and gait of the men were young, but there was little youth in most of their faces. Some looked as if they ate too little – a few as if they drank too much. Tall and short, tweed-coated and black, round-shouldered, bespectacled, and slim, they crowded with clatter of feet and rattle of sticks through the hospital gate.

Conan Doyle describing his fellow students attending extramural classes at the Royal Infirmary in 'His First Operation' from *Round the Red Lamp* (1894)

In 1726 a Faculty of Medicine was founded at Edinburgh University, but before it could become a complete medical school the building of a hospital in which medicine and surgery could be practised had to be built. In 1729, through money raised by subscription, Edinburgh's first Royal Infirmary was opened in Robertson's Close, just

THE SOUTHSIDE

Engraving, by Paul Sandby, of the Royal Infirmary, founded in 1738

off Infirmary Street. Known as the 'Little House', it was only a six-bed hospital amid a city with a population of around 30,000, but it was a beginning. In 1738 a new and larger Royal Infirmary was founded, again by public subscription, on the south side of Infirmary Street (on your right walking downhill), a site now occupied by buildings which were once part of a Victorian school.

The new hospital, which was completed in 1741, had 228 beds and was on four floors, with an east wing for men and a west wing for women, and perched on the top floor was a 200-seat amphitheatre and operating theatre complete with glass windows in the roof for maximum light. This was progress, but to say it resembled hospital care as we know it today would be stretching it. Two of its most serious defects were a lack of understanding about hygiene and the dire inefficiency of the nursing system. Nurses were untrained and ignorant of what their proper duties were. They were underpaid, ill fed and poorly housed. They were servants rather than nurses, but in the mid-nineteenth-century one English woman changed everything. Her name was Florence Nightingale, the founder of modern nursing. Trained Nightingale nurses started to arrive at the Infirmary in the early 1870s, and hospital care began to resemble what we know today. But it still had a long way to go.

BOOK LOVERS' EDINBURGH

The old and new Surgical Hospitals, which were once part of the Royal Infirmary (now owned by the University of Edinburgh) at the foot of Infirmary St

Conan Doyle entered the medical faculty of Edinburgh University at Old College a few years later in 1876, and began his extramural training at the Royal Infirmary, just a short distance away on the other side of South Bridge. Outside the walls of the faculty, in local hospitals and teaching establishments, under the auspices of experienced medical men, the extramural method of teaching was introduced at Edinburgh in 1855, allowing students to take at least half their classes extracurricularly. These classes were extremely popular, often outnumbering those within the faculty walls.

'There were no attempts at friendship, or even acquaintance, between professors and students at Edinburgh,' wrote Conan Doyle. 'It was a strictly business arrangement by which you paid, for example, four guineas for anatomy lectures and received the winter's course in exchange, never seeing your professor save behind his desk and never under any circumstances exchanging a word with him.'

His professors may have been businesslike and formal, but they were a group of remarkable men who made a lasting impression on him, and he accumulated many of their names, temperaments and idiosyncrasies in his memory for future use.

There was Professor Sir Robert Christison who taught Materia Medica (Pharmacology), an expert in toxicology, who once swallowed a poisonous calabar bean to register its consequences. Fortunately he survived, but Conan Doyle recalls the incident in *A Study in Scarlet* when Watson describes Holmes as 'a little too scientific for my tastes – it approaches to cold-bloodedness. I could imagine his giving a friend a little pinch of the latest vegetable alkaloid, not out of malevolence, you understand, but simply out of a spirit of inquiry in order to have an accurate idea of the effects. To do him justice, I think he would take it himself with the same readiness. He appears to have a passion for definite and exact knowledge.'

Conan Doyle would have attended Sir Henry Littlejohn's lectures on medical jurisprudence. Littlejohn became Edinburgh and Scotland's first Medical Officer of Health in 1862. As police surgeon to the city he came into contact with many criminal cases and acted as expert medical witness for the Crown. He would also have had contact with Joseph Lister, founder of antiseptic medicine.

'There was also,' recalled Conan Doyle, 'the squat figure of Professor Rutherford with his Assyrian beard, his prodigious voice, his enormous chest and his singular manner. He fascinated and awed us. I have endeavoured to reproduce some of his peculiarities in the fictitious character of Professor Challenger. He would sometimes start his lecture before he reached the classroom, so that we would hear a booming voice saying: "There are valves in the veins", or some other information, when the desk was still empty.'

BOOK LOVERS' EDINBURGH

The first Dr Watson Conan Doyle ever met was Dr Patrick Heron Watson, forensic expert and inspiration for Holmes's Watson. Joseph Bell, who became his model for Sherlock Holmes, lectured in clinical surgery at the Extramural School of Medicine and, in October 1878, Conan Doyle, now a second-year medical student with poor marks, paid his fee of four guineas and enrolled on Bell's course. That same year Conan Doyle was appointed as Bell's outpatient clerk, an experience he described in his autobiography *Memories and Adventures* in 1924:

> On my return [from an Arctic whaling voyage] I went back to medicine in Edinburgh again. There I met the man who suggested Sherlock Holmes to me – here is a portrait of him as he was in those days … I was clerk in Mr Bell's Ward. A clerk's duties are to note down all the patients to be seen, and muster them together. Often I would have seventy or eighty … I would show them in to Mr Bell, who would have the students gathered round him. His intuitive powers were simply marvellous. A case would come forward. 'Cobbler, I see.' [Bell would say.] Then he would turn to the students and point out to them that the inside of the knee of the man's trousers was worn. That was where the man rested the lapstone – a peculiarity only found in cobblers. All this impressed me very much. He was continually before me – his sharp piercing grey eyes, eagle nose, and striking features. There he would sit in his chair with fingers together – he was very dexterous with his hands – and just look at the man or woman before him. He was most kind and painstaking with students – a real good friend – and when I took my degree and went to Africa the remarkable individuality and discriminating tact of my old master made a deep and lasting impression on me, though I had not the faintest idea that it would one day lead me to forsake medicine for story writing.

THE SOUTHSIDE

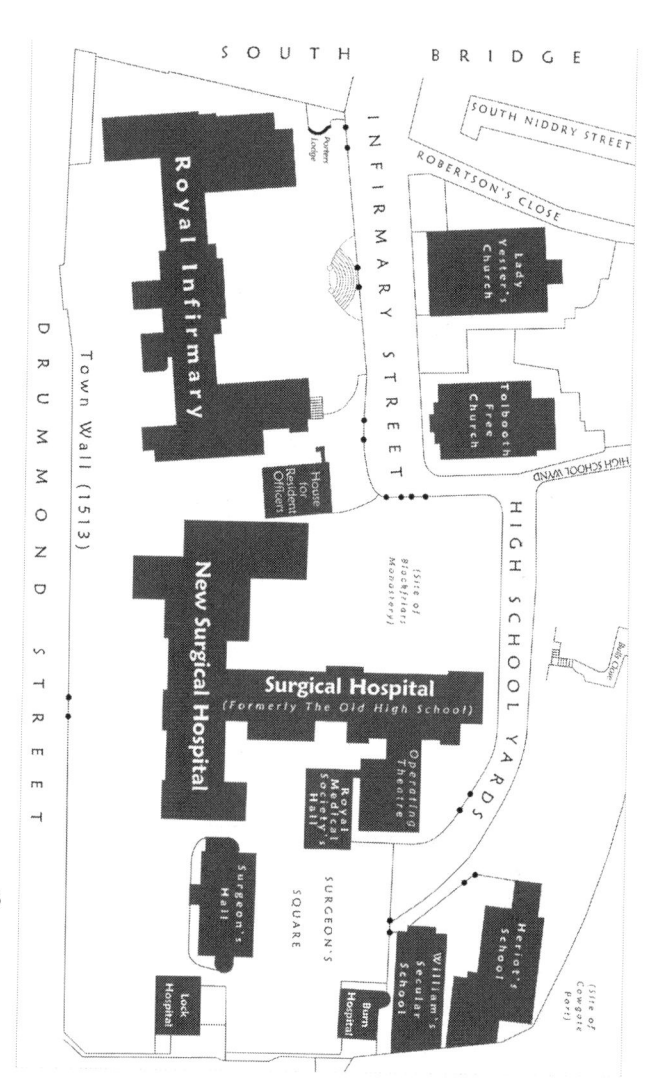

The Infirmary area shortly after the completion of the New Surgical Hospital in 1853 (Map Crispin Sage)

When Bell made Conan Doyle his outpatient clerk, it gave him the opportunity to study Bell's methods at close quarters. The position of clerk, although a privileged one, was a common post to be given to a student. It was a sharp learning curve, which taught a student to think fast, write fast, and communicate swiftly with patients. Often there would be 70 or 80 patients to assemble and

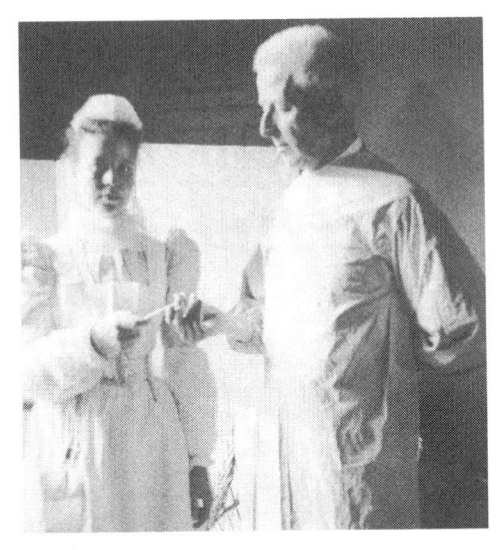

Left: Joseph Bell in surgical gown Right: Joseph Lister, founder of antiseptic medicine and aseptic surgery

write notes on before Bell began his outpatient clinic, and woe betide Doyle if he didn't have them ready on time. He would then usher them in, one by one, to a large room in which Bell sat surrounded by students, where, 'with a face like a Red Indian, [he would] diagnose the people as they came in, before they had even opened their mouths. He would tell them their symptoms. He would give them details of their lives, and he would hardly ever make a mistake.'

This was an age before X-rays and scans. What Bell was trying to do was to emphasise to his students the use of the powers of perception: taste, touch, smell and what they could hear through their stethoscopes. To do this he had various tricks up his sleeve. One of them was a classic, which to this day may possibly be used as an example to medical students.

Bell would hold a phial of bilious looking liquid aloft for all his students to see. 'This, gentlemen, contains a most potent drug. It is extremely bitter to taste. Now I wish to see how many of you have developed the powers of observation that God granted you. But sir, ye will say, it can be analysed chemically. Aye, aye, but I want you to taste it – by smell and taste. What! You shrink back? As I don't ask anything of my students which I wouldn't do alone wi' myself, I will taste it before passing it around.' Bell would then dip a finger into the obnoxious liquid and place it in his mouth, followed by an expression of disgust. 'Now you do likewise,' and the students proceed to pass the phial amongst themselves. When the vile concoction eventually returned to Bell he would sigh in despair, saying 'Gentlemen, I am deeply grieved to find that not one of you has developed his power of perception, the faculty of observation which I speak so much of, for if you had truly observed me, you would have seen that, while I placed my index finger in the awful brew, it was my middle finger – aye – which somehow found its way into my mouth.'

SEE ALSO: Conan Doyle, Surgical Hospital, New Surgical Hospital, Surgeon's Hall Museum, Old College, St Andrew Square, Mauricewood, Dean Cemetery, Robert Louis Stevenson.

FURTHER INFORMATION: In 1879 a new Royal Infirmary was opened on Lauriston Place, and the old Royal Infirmary buildings on the south side of Infirmary Street were demolished in 1884.

FURTHER READING: A. Turner, *The Story of a Great Hospital, The Royal Infirmary of Edinburgh 1729–1929* (Oliver & Boyd, 1937).

BOOK LOVERS' EDINBURGH

High School Yards
Former High School of Edinburgh
and alma mater of Sir Walter Scott

I was never a dunce, nor thought to be so, but an incorrigibly idle imp, who was always longing to do something else than what was enjoined him.
J.G. Lockhart, *The Life of Sir Walter Scott* (1837–8)

Facing you at the foot of Infirmary Street is the former building of the old High School in High School Yards. In October 1779, at the age of eight, young Wattie entered the second class, taught by Mr Luke Fraser, 'a good Latin scholar'. Younger than most of his classmates, Wattie's Latin was rusty, and he made little headway, until three years later when he entered the class of the headmaster, Dr Adam. Through Adam's inspirational teaching, Wattie began to learn the value of knowledge, and what before had been a burdensome task evolved into a lifelong love affair with Latin poetry and prose.
In J.G. Lockhart's *The Life of Sir Walter Scott* (seven volumes, 1837–8) he fondly recalled his schooldays:

> Among my companions, my good nature and a flow of ready imagination rendered me very popular. Boys are uncommonly just in their feelings, and at least equally generous. My lameness, and the efforts which I made to supply that disadvantage, by making up in address what I wanted in activity, engaged the latter principle in my favour; and in the winter play-hours, when hard exercise was impossible, my tales used to assemble an admiring audience round Lucky Brown's fireside, and happy was he that could sit next to the inexhaustible narrator. I was also, though often negligent of my own task, always ready to assist my friends; and hence I had

THE SOUTHSIDE

a little party of staunch partisans and adherents, stout of hand and heart though somewhat dull of head – the very tools for raising a hero to eminence. So on the whole, I made a brighter figure in the yards than in the class.

Scott's father also employed a private tutor for him during these years, but in the spring of 1783 he left the High School to spend the summer with his Aunt Janet in Kelso, prior to entering university in the autumn.

SEE ALSO: Birthplace of W.S., childhood home of W.S., townhouse of W.S., Lasswade Cottage, Parliament Hall, Greyfriars Kirkyard, St John's Churchyard, The Heart of Midlothian, Holyrood Park, The Writers' Museum, Old College, Sciennes Hill House, Scott Monument, Assembly Rooms, J.G. Lockhart, Portobello Sands, Canongate Kirkyard.

FURTHER INFORMATION: The High School of Edinburgh, known today as the old High School, was built in 1777 by Alexander Laing at a cost of £4,000. In 1829, a new Royal High School was opened on the side of Calton Hill to be closer to the expanding New Town and the old school closed.

An 18th century engraving of the old High School

High School Yards
The Surgical Hospital
Where Joseph Bell studied under
'The Napoleon of Surgery',
Dr James Syme (1799-1870)

'The Napoleon of Surgery': Dr James Syme

After the closure of the old High School in 1829, the building reopened as a surgical hospital in 1832, and became part of the Royal Infirmary. It was here that Joseph Bell taught his students, including Conan Doyle, the art of surgery. But who introduced Bell to the skills of deductive reasoning? Who were the men who honed his analytical mind? There were several medical legends on the faculty during Bell's student years, all of whom would have affected his development, including Joseph Lister, surgeon and antiseptic pioneer; James Young Simpson, Professor of

Midwifery and anaesthetic pioneer; and surgeons James Miller and James Spence, but the one who rose head and shoulders above them all, in Bell's eyes, was his mentor, Dr James Syme, affectionately known as 'The Napoleon of Surgery'.

Syme was the son of an Edinburgh lawyer, who taught clinical surgery at the Infirmary for thirty-six years, from 1833 to 1869, and who had a formidable reputation as a teacher and a surgeon. He was not a showy or elegant surgeon. He had no flourish or dash, but his knowledge and skill saved many lives. One of Syme's assistants commented that 'he never wasted a word, a drop of ink, or a drop of blood'. Joseph Bell was closer to Syme than most as Syme had chosen Bell as his dresser. Bell wrote:

> Unless it was raining, the students attending Syme's wards might, if they chose, run down a steep flight of stairs, past one or two old houses, across a square of rough gravel surrounding a plot of measly grass, generally decorated by old broken iron bedsteads or decaying mattresses, to a low two-storied building in severely classical style ... In the angle, dark and confined, of the lower floor of the Surgical Hospital admitting to the general surgical waiting rooms ... The large operating theatre, a really finely-proportioned and well-arranged building, with some small wards, house surgeon's rooms – extended beyond the main lines of the old High School, and formed part of a quaint old square, now nearly demolished, called Surgeon's Square ... I saw Dr. Syme daily for the greater part of his last fifteen years. His hospital life was on this wise – two clinical lectures a week, operations two days more (perhaps three), a ward visit when he wished to see any special cases ... before his select class he examined each new and interesting case that could walk in ... Mr. Syme then and there made his diagnosis, which to us young ones seemed magical

and intuitional ...

Then if it was a lecture day, a tremendous rush of feet would be heard of the students racing to get the nearest seats in the large operating theatre ... Chairs in the arena were kept for colleagues or distinguished strangers; first row for dressers on duty; operating table in centre; Mr. Syme on a chair in left-centre. House surgeons a little behind, but nearer the door; instrument clerk with his well-stocked table under the big window. The four dressers on duty march in (if possible in step), carrying a rude wicker basket, in which, covered by a rough red blanket, the patient peers up at the great amphitheatre crammed with faces. A brief description ... and then the little, neat, tyro sees at once a master of his craft at work – no show, little elegance, but absolute certainty, ease and determination; rarely a word to an assistant – they should know their business.

In 1859, Joseph Bell graduated. Ten years later, in April 1869, James Syme suffered an apoplectic seizure and was forced to retire from the chair of clinical surgery. He died on 26 June 1870, aged 70, and was interred in the family vault at St John's Episcopal Church, at the West End of Princes Street.

THE SOUTHSIDE

Left: Joseph Bell when he was a young medical student
Right: The old Surgical Hospital. Formerly the High School of Edinburgh

SEE ALSO: Conan Doyle, Surgeons' Hall Museum, Old College, Royal Infirmary, St. Andrew Square, Mauricewood, Dean Cemetery, Robert Louis Stevenson.

FURTHER INFORMATION: The buildings in High School Yards are now part of Edinburgh University, but the public are free to wander through the grounds. The old Surgical Hospital with its pillared entrance faces you at the bottom of Infirmary Street. The operating theatre referred to by Bell was behind the main building and was part of the wing which projects into the square at the rear, now fronted by a modern extension. A plaque can be seen to the right of the entrance (behind the pillars) dedicated to Syme and Lister. Surgeons' Square can be seen by walking through the tunnelled passageway to the right of the entrance. Here you will find the 'steep flight of stairs' and the 'plot of measly grass' (now a neat lawn) described by Joseph Bell. The stairs divide the old seventeenth-century Surgeons' Hall (on your left) and what became known as the New Surgical Hospital built in 1853, and which is now part of the university (on your right). The land that is now High School Yards was once the site of the monastery of the Black Friars, the Dominicans, which was destroyed by an accidental fire in 1528.

FURTHER READING: R. Paterson, *Memorials Of The Life Of James Syme, Professor Of Clinical Surgery In The University Of Edinburgh, Etc.* (1874) (Kessinger Publishing, 2008); E. M. Liebow, *Dr. Joe Bell* (Bowling Green University Popular Press, 1982).

53–62 SOUTH BRIDGE
Blackwell's
Site of James Thin's Bookshop
Formerly the largest bookselling
establishment in the city

Alf Jamieson, who used to run our antiquarian and second-hand books department, could be quite sharp with customers. One day, two eminent Free Church Professors were questioning him on the price of a book they were interested in, and hinting that they hoped for a slight reduction. Alf impatiently barked, 'What do you think this is, a bloody bazaar?' turned on his heel and left them to it.
From *James Thin, 150 Years of Bookselling 1848–1998*

The founder, James Thin, from the painting by Henry W. Kerr, 1904

THE SOUTHSIDE

In 1836 James Thin (1823–1915) was apprenticed to the bookseller James McIntosh at 5 North College Street. His starting wage was two shillings and sixpence a week, out of which he had to provide himself with pen and pencil. His working hours were from 9 a.m. to 9 p.m. and meals were eaten in the shop. After twelve years of training, he set himself up in business in 1848, when he bought the stock of a failed bookseller and leased a shop at 14 Infirmary Street. His first day's sales totalled five shillings and sevenpence. Concentrating mainly on academic books and working closely with the University, his business prospered and expanded. He was also a keen hymnologist and had a personal collection of 2,500 hymn books. Three generations later, his family were still controlling the business. In 1891, aged 67, James Thin was interviewed by *The Publisher's Circular*, who drew from him a delightful insight into Edinburgh's literati and their tastes:

> Mr Thin has met most of the famous men who have visited Edinburgh, or been associated with its history during the past half-century. He remembers Macaulay well, and speaks with enthusiasm of the historian's oratorical power. He also knew Christopher North, 'the lion-headed'. 'A man of great power,' said Mr Thin, 'who never did himself justice, and who seems to be entirely forgotten by the younger generation.' De Quincey used to visit Mr Thin's shop in search of scarce books. The author of *The Confessions of an Opium Eater* was described by Mr Thin as a meagre, nervous, shrivelled little man, who went skulking about after nightfall as if he could not stand the garish light of day … But of all the great men whom he has known, Mr Thin speaks with the greatest cordiality of Carlyle – indeed, he talks of the sage of Chelsea with a deep and open reverence … Mr Thin remembers the sudden rise of 'Pickwick' and the slower ascent of Thackeray. In those days, it

BOOK LOVERS' EDINBURGH

was all Dickens. Now the better class of readers are forsaking him for his once-neglected rival – a circumstance that strikes Mr Thin rather favourably ... Lord Tennyson is, of course, immensely popular; and since their death Arnold and Newman have both been much in demand, especially the former. It does not appear that academic Edinburgh cares much for Mr Ruskin.

Left: James Thin in 1998
Right: Blackwell's opposite the imposing visage of Old College

The customer might always be right, but they are not necessarily always understood. A Thin's customer once appeared to make the following request: 'I want a book on fashion.'
'Yes. You'll find the fashion books at the back of the front shop and up the steps to the left.'
'Not fashion; fushin!'
'Oh, sorry. The nuclear fission books are upstairs in the technical department.'
To this, the exasperated customer retorted, 'Fushin! With a rod and line!'

FURTHER INFORMATION: The Blackwell's bookshop chain took over James Thin on South Bridge in 2002.

THE SOUTHSIDE

SOUTH BRIDGE
The University of Edinburgh
Old College

Men bred in the universities of Scotland cannot be expected to be often decorated with the splendours of ornamental erudition, but they obtain a mediocrity of knowledge, between learning and ignorance, not inadequate to the purposes of common life ...
Samuel Johnson, A Journey to the Western Islands of Scotland (1775)

The literal translation from Latin of alma mater is 'bounteous mother', and Old College – and the Tounis College, which stood on the same site before it – can certainly lay claim to a staggering roll call of literary offspring. The thirteen-year-old Walter Scott attended Old College intermittently from 1783 to 1786, where he studied for a general Arts degree, and recalled the moral philosophy class of Mr Dugald Stewart, 'whose striking and impressive eloquence riveted the attention even of the most volatile students'. He left Old College in 1786 and became apprenticed to his father's legal firm. Divinity student Thomas Carlyle enrolled in 1809 and left ten years later without taking his degree, bemoaning the fact that 'within its learned walls, I have not one single friend, not even an acquaintance that I value; which, after 15 years' residence, says but little for my moral qualities.' Robert Louis Stevenson attended Old College from the late 1860s until 1875, first studying engineering, before transferring to law. A bohemian at heart, the world of academia didn't hold much attraction for RLS, who frequently rushed out in the middle of lectures for 'pencils'; in reality, this was an excuse for sinking a pint at Rutherford's, across the road in Drummond Street. Stevenson was also a member of The Speculative Society, the University's literary and debating society, founded in 1764, and whose members have included Sir Walter Scott, Francis Jeffrey and Hugh MacDiarmid. Arthur Conan Doyle began studying medicine at Edinburgh in 1876, and would regularly walk between Old College and the Surgical Hospital where the University held its anatomy classes at the foot of Infirmary Street (formerly the old High School). As a student, he was taught by Dr Joseph Bell (his inspiration for Sherlock Holmes) and the father of antiseptic surgery, Joseph Lister. Although Doyle was born and studied in Edinburgh, he never had any great love for the city or its university, commenting, 'Edinburgh University may call herself, with grim jocoseness, the "alma mater" of her students, but if she is to be mother at all, she is one of a very stoic and Spartan cast, who conceals her maternal affection with remarkable success. The only signs of interest she ever deigns to evince towards her alumni are upon those not infrequent occasions when guineas are to be demanded from them.'

Conan Doyle in graduation robes, 1881

In 1878, J.M. Barrie entered Old College, where he struggled with mathematics but was inspired by the lectures of the great scholar Professor Masson. Barrie never experienced any great financial hardships at university, but did recall 'three undergraduates who lodged together in a dreary house at the top of a dreary street; two of them used to study until two in the morning, while the third slept. When they shut up their books, they woke number three, who rose, dressed and studied until breakfast time.' S.R. Crockett, another exponent of the Kailyard School, existed for three years on nine shillings a week while attending university, living on meals of porridge and penny rolls washed down with milk.

Other literary alumni include Henry Mackenzie, David Hume, Oliver Goldsmith, Charles Darwin, John Brown, Norman MacCaig, Robert Garioch and Peter Mark Roget. Former Lord Chancellors of the University include J.M. Barrie and John Buchan; in 1866, Thomas Carlyle became Lord Rector.

The original College of the University of Edinburgh was founded in 1583 by the Town Council of Edinburgh and for many years it was known as the Tounis College of Edinburgh. It was built in the grounds of the Collegiate Church of St Mary's in the Fields, known locally as Kirk o' Field, and it was here that Mary, Queen of Scots' second husband, Lord Darnley, was murdered in 1567. The new building, now known as Old College, was started in 1789 and took 40 years to complete. The original plan of the building was by Robert Adam, who died in 1792, before it was completed. Work was then interrupted by the Napoleonic Wars, but in 1816 William Playfair was appointed to complete the building, which he finally accomplished in the late 1820s. Much of Adam's design survived in the building, including the huge vaulted entrance on South Bridge. Playfair was responsible for the vast quadrangle, the surrounding terrace and the 190-ft-long Playfair Library hall. At the rear of the building is the Talbot Rice Gallery.

SEE ALSO: Sir Walter Scott, Robert Louis Stevenson, J.M. Barrie, Conan Doyle, Joseph Bell, Thomas Carlyle, S.R. Crockett, Henry Mackenzie, David Hume, Norman MacCaig, Robert Garioch, John Buchan, Rutherford's Howff, Samuel Johnson.

FURTHER INFORMATION: Old College is not open to the public, but visitors may stroll around the quadrangle.

FURTHER READING: R. Footman, B. Young, *Edinburgh University: An Illustrated Memoir* (Edinburgh University, 1983).

THE SOUTHSIDE

Rowland Anderson's Old College Dome, erected in 1887, on top of which stands John Hutchinson's 'Golden Boy', added in 1888. The statue was modelled on Edinburgh athlete Anthony Hall.

8 DRUMMOND STREET
Hispaniola
Formerly Rutherford's Howff
Favourite drinking den
of Robert Louis Stevenson (1850–94)

Last night as I lay under my blanket in the cockpit ... There was nothing visible but the southern stars, and the steersman there out by the binnacle lamp ... the night was as warm as milk; and all of a sudden, I had a vision of – Drummond Street. It came to me like a flash of lightning; I simply returned thither, and into the past. And when I remembered all that I hoped and feared as I pickled about Rutherford's in the rain and the east wind: how I feared I should make a mere shipwreck, and yet timidly hoped not; how I feared I should never have a friend, far less a wife, and yet passionately hoped I might; how I hoped (if I did not take to drink) I should possibly write one little book, etc. etc. And then, now – what a change! I feel somehow as if I should like the incident set upon a brass plate at the corner of that dreary thoroughfare, for all students to read, poor devils, when their hearts are down.

RLS writing to his friend Charles Baxter aboard the yacht *Casco* in the South Pacific on 6 September 1888

Until its closure and subsequent conversion into an extension of a nearby Italian restaurant in the winter of 2007, Rutherford's still retained the sparse decor and friendly atmosphere of the traditional Scottish howff (tavern). It first opened its doors in 1834 and became a popular watering hole for the students of Edinburgh University just around the corner in South Bridge. Electric lights had been installed and the price of a pint had increased dramatically, but one got the feeling that Rutherford's hadn't changed very much since the late 1860s when the young velvet-jacketed engineering student Robert Louis Stevenson sauntered through its doors to down his first pint of the day after tedious hours of note taking on the stress factors of lighthouses.

Stevenson was no model student, regularly playing truant, dozing and doodling in class. Despite coming from a family of engineers, he eventually gave up engineering to study law, passing his Bar exams in 1875. He never, however, actually practised law. No stranger to the howffs of the Old Town and its squalid underbelly, drink, revelry and the haunches of a whore were a delight to him. 'I was the companion,' he said, 'of seamen, chimney-sweeps and thieves; my circle was being continually changed by the action of the police magistrate.'

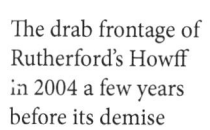

The drab frontage of Rutherford's Howff in 2004 a few years before its demise

Of all his haunts, Rutherford's seemed to hold a special place in his heart, which he never forgot. Among the many other thirsty undergraduates and wordsmiths to have regularly entered Rutherford's portals were Arthur Conan Doyle and the poet Hugh MacDiarmid. J.M. Barrie, who was ten years younger than Stevenson, also studied at Edinburgh University. The two admired each other greatly and corresponded in later life, but never met, much to

BOOK LOVERS' EDINBURGH

Barrie's sincere regret. Long after Stevenson's death, Barrie wrote about a fictional encounter with him in the 1925 edition of Rosaline Masson's anthology of memoirs entitled *I Can Remember Robert Louis Stevenson*: 'he led me away from the Humanities to something that he assured me was more humane, a howff called Rutherford's where we sat and talked by the solid hour.'

SEE ALSO: Robert Louis Stevenson, Conan Doyle, Hugh MacDiarmid, J.M. Barrie.

FURTHER INFORMATION: Conan Doyle was another student regular at Rutherford's, setting his 1894 short story 'His First Operation' there. The wooden Victorian facade of Rutherford's is still intact and preserved on Drummond Street, but its interior has been completely gutted: a sad loss to literary Edinburgh and lovers of the good old Scottish drinking den. It is now an extension of the Italian restaurant Ciao Roma at 64 South Bridge round the corner from Drummond Street.

Left: Rutherford's reborn as The Hispaniola in 2007, and named after the pirate ship in *Treasure Island*
Right: San Francisco RLS fans toast their literary hero in old Rutherford's in 2004

THE SOUTHSIDE

Drummond Street
The New Surgical Hospital Where W.E. Henley, inspiration for Long John Silver, was hospitalised from 1873 to 1875

Out of the night that covers me,
Black as the pit from pole to pole,
I thank whatever gods may be
For my unconquerable soul.

In the fell clutch of circumstance
I have not winced nor cried aloud.
Under the bludgeonings of chance
My head is bloody, but unbowed.

Beyond this place of wrath and tears
Looms but the Horror of the shade,
And yet the menace of the years
Finds and shall find me unafraid.

It matters not how strait the gate,
How charged with punishments the scroll,
I am the master of my fate,
I am the captain of my soul.

W.E. Henley, 'Invictus'

The son of a Gloucester bookseller, William Ernest Henley (1849–1903) came to Edinburgh in 1873 to be treated by Professor Joseph Lister for tubercular arthritis, which, seven years previously, had resulted in the amputation of his left leg below the knee. Lister's skills saved his other leg and probably his life, but the treatment was so painful and prolonged, he was hospitalised in Edinburgh

W.E. Henley

for almost two years. Henley is chiefly remembered today as a poet, notably for his 'Invictus' (1875). 'It is grand literature,' wrote Conan Doyle, 'and it is grand pluck too; for it came from a man who, through no fault of his own, had been pruned, and pruned again, like an ill-grown shrub, by the surgeon's knife.' Henley's 'Hospital Sketches', first published in the *Cornhill Magazine* in 1875, grimly recall his distressing time at the Infirmary. He was also a critic and an editor, and first met Robert Louis Stevenson through their mutual friend and colleague Leslie Stephen, editor of the *Cornhill Magazine* and father of Virginia Woolf.

Stevenson described the meeting to Frances Sitwell in a letter dated 13 February 1875:

> Yesterday, Leslie Stephen, who was down here to lecture, called on me and took me up to see a poor fellow, a bit of a poet, who writes for him, and who has been eighteen months in our infirmary and may be, for all I know, eighteen months more ... Stephen and I sat on a couple of chairs and the poor fellow sat up in his bed, with his hair and beard all tangled, and talked as cheerfully as if he had been in a King's Palace, or the great King's Palace of the blue air. He has taught himself two languages since he has been lying there. I shall try to be of use to him.

Stevenson became a close friend of Henley, taking him out for carriage rides and even carrying an easy chair on his head all the way from Heriot Row to the Infirmary for Henley's use. They collaborated on a number of plays together between 1880 and 1885, none of which was successful. Henley held a series of editorships including *Pen* (1880) and *Magazine of Art* (1881–6), and in 1889 he returned to Edinburgh to edit the *Scots Observer*. A stinging critic and a fearless editor, Henley published the works of Hardy, Barrie, Kipling, H.G. Wells, Stevenson, Yeats and Henry James. He also published the struggling Joseph Conrad's *The Nigger of the Narcissus* in *The New Review*. 'Now that I have conquered Henley,' wrote Conrad, 'I ain't afraid of the divvle himself.'

His friendship with Stevenson was all but destroyed after their play-writing escapades, but when Henley accused Stevenson's wife of being a plagiarist over a story she'd had published, the slander was too much for Stevenson, who wrote to a friend saying, 'I fear that I have come to the end with Henley.' The incident terminated their friendship, and they never communicated again, but by then Stevenson had already immortalised him. 'It was the sight of your maimed strength and masterfulness,' he wrote in 1883, ' that begot John Silver in *Treasure Island*.' Jim Hawkins's last words on Silver could well be Stevenson's lament for Henley:

> Of Silver, we have heard no more. That formidable seafaring man with one leg has at last gone clean out of my life; but I dare say he met his old negress, and perhaps still lives in comfort with her and Captain Flint. It is to be hoped so, I suppose, for his chances of comfort in another world are very small.

Left: Long John Silver, by Frank Godwin, 1924
Right: The New Surgical Hospital

THE SOUTHSIDE

SEE ALSO: Robert Louis Stevenson, Conan Doyle, J.M. Barrie.

FURTHER INFORMATION: According to J.H. Millar, author of *A Literary History of Scotland*, W.E. Henley invented the phrase 'the Kailyard School', derived from the popular American novel *Mrs Wiggs of the Cabbage Patch*. The Kailyard (cabbage patch) School comprised a group of Scottish writers, namely J.M. Barrie, Ian Maclaren and S.R. Crockett, who created a false, cosy, sentimental and romantic image of Scottish life written in local patois, lasting from around 1888 to 1896. Henley was also an imperialist and a Tory, and much of his poetry was a platform for his jingoistic patriotism.

Henley used to address J.M. Barrie as 'friend' and, reputedly, Henley's only daughter, Margaret, mispronounced it as 'fwend' and 'fwendy-wendy'. This was Barrie's inspiration for the name of his Wendy in *Peter Pan*. Margaret died aged four in 1894. Henley is buried beside her in the churchyard of St John the Baptist, Cockayne Hatley, Bedfordshire.

FURTHER READING: J.M. Flora, *W.E. Henley* (Irvington, 1970); Bill Yule, *Matrons, Medics and Maladies: Edinburgh Royal Infirmary in the 1840s* (Tuckwell Press, 1999); A. Turner, *The Story of a Great Hospital, The Royal Infirmary of Edinburgh 1729-1929* (Oliver & Boyd, 1937).

5 SOUTH COLLEGE STREET
Site of William McGonagall's death
The world's best bad poet

> *And after spending his earnings foolishly he beats his wife –*
> *The man that promised to protect her during life –*
> *And so the man would if there was no drink in society,*
> *For seldom a man beats his wife in a state of sobriety.*
>
> *And if he does, perhaps he finds his wife fou',*
> *Then that causes, no doubt, a great hullaballo;*
> *When he finds his wife drunk he begins to frown,*
> *And in a fury of passion he knocks her down.*
>
> *And in that knock down she fractures her head,*
> *And perhaps the poor wife she is killed dead,*
> *Whereas, if there was no strong drink to be got,*
> *To be killed wouldn't have been the poor wife's lot.*
>
> William McGonagall, from 'The Demon Drink'

Described as the world's best bad poet, the popularity of William McGonagall (c.1825–1902) still flourishes and his poetry is still published all over the world, proof that poetry, no matter how execrable, can still find an audience. The son of an Irish cotton weaver, he was born in Edinburgh but grew up in Dundee, where his father had moved in search of work. One of five siblings, he worked from the age of 11 as a handloom weaver. He acted in amateur productions at Dundee's Royal Theatre and in 1878 published his first collection of poems, which included his famous 'Railway Bridge of the Silvery Tay'. He gave public readings to derisory applause, ducked missiles thrown at him and was crowned with the ridiculous honour of 'Sir

THE SOUTHSIDE

Topaz, Knight of the White Elephant of Burmah'. He sold his broadsheets in the street, and once walked all the way to Balmoral, where Queen Victoria denied him an audience. He also tried his luck in London and New York, but returned as he had arrived: penniless. During his lifetime, he published over 200 poems and his *Poetic Gems* was published in 1890.

He may have died in poverty at South College Street (above the Captains Bar), and is buried in a pauper's grave in Greyfriars Kirkyard, but the memory of the man, who disregarded everything that makes poetry worth reading, will live forever.

SEE ALSO: Greyfriars Kirkyard.

FURTHER INFORMATION: McGonagall's burial records give no clue as to where in Greyfriars Kirkyard he was laid to rest, but a plaque reading 'Buried near this spot' was erected in 1999. From the main entrance, follow the path round the right hand side of the kirk. Walk straight ahead and through the archway in the Flodden Wall. McGonagall's memorial plaque is in the top left corner, near the gate leading into George Heriot's School.

The Captains Bar. Den of traditional music and annual McGonagall night. A plaque to McGonagall can be seen to the right of the pub

6A NICOLSON STREET
Spoon Cafe (Formerly Nicolson's)
Where J.K. Rowling wrote some of the early chapters of *Harry Potter and the Philosopher's Stone*

We won't be selling any Harry Potter books ... It teaches people how to cast spells on people. Ordinary people can't cast spells, but you can by the power of Satan. It's not a laughing matter; it's quite serious. If you educate children to witchcraft, you don't know where it's going to end. It could even end with children dying.
Theodore Danson-Smith, Edinburgh bookseller,
The Scotsman, 10 June 2003

J.K. Rowling first appeared at the Edinburgh International Book Festival in 1997, an unknown writer promoting her first book about a boy wizard. Her audience totalled just 20 people. At the same festival in 2004, the event was closed off to everyone but herself and her fans. She was given her own purpose-built signing tent and her queue of devotees stretched into the street. Signed copies of first editions of the Harry Potter books now sell for colossal prices at auction and her books are sold in every corner of the planet.

Born and bred in the West Country, Rowling attended Exeter University, where she studied French. After various secretarial jobs, she went to Portugal when she was 26 to teach English as a foreign language, and it was while she was there that she began writing stories about Harry Potter. She met and married a Portuguese television journalist, and in 1993 their daughter Jessica was born. Four months later, however, their marriage collapsed, and Rowling decamped with her daughter to Edinburgh, where her younger sister lived. By this time, she was

THE SOUTHSIDE

> J. K. ROWLING Wrote some of the early chapters of HARRY POTTER in the rooms on the First Floor of this building

living on benefits and experiencing the plight of many single mothers: poverty, loneliness, poor housing and inadequate or expensive childcare. She lived in Leith, in a flat at South Lorne Place, for a few years (cashing her benefits from Leith Walk Post Office), before moving to Hazelbank Terrace in Shandon, off Slateford Road, in 1997.

She trained as a teacher at Moray House Teacher Training College in Holyrood Road, studying by day and writing at night, and it was while working as a French teacher that her first book, *Harry Potter and the Philosopher's Stone*, was accepted for publication. A few months later, the American rights were sold, and she was able to give up teaching and write full-time. She still lives in Edinburgh, but is rarely seen in cafes, although in her early days she was particularly fond of Nicolson's.

After her first book was published, she visited some pupils at Leith Academy, where she used to teach. 'They avoided the issue for half of the class,' she said, 'then someone said, "Miss! You're rich now, eh?"'

SEE ALSO: Edinburgh Book Lovers' Tour, Edinburgh International Book Festival.

18 NICOLSON STREET
Surgeons' Hall Museums
Royal College of Surgeons of Edinburgh
Location of the death mask of serial killer William Burke, who, together with accomplice William Hare, provided the inspiration for Robert Louis Stevenson's 'The Body Snatcher'

Stevenson's spine-chilling short story 'The Body Snatcher' was written in June 1881 at Kinnaird Cottage, Pitlochry, and was originally destined to be one of a series of horror stories, or 'crawlers' as he described them, in a book entitled *The Black Man and Other Tales*. From this collection of tales, 'Thrawn Janet' and 'The Merry Men' appeared in the *Cornhill Magazine*, but 'The Body Snatcher' was 'laid aside [by Stevenson] in a justifiable disgust, the tale being horrid'.

By 1884, however, he obviously thought the readers of *The Pall Mall* were ready to cope with it, as he submitted it for their Christmas edition, describing it to the editor as 'blood-curdling enough – and ugly enough – to chill the blood of a grenadier'. *The Pall Mall* responded by sending its publicity campaign for the story into overdrive, but when the campaign hit the streets, it was deemed so repulsive by the authorities that the police were ordered to suppress it.

Stevenson's inspiration for 'The Body Snatcher' was Edinburgh's most famous murdering duo, Burke and Hare, who, between 1827 and 1828, delivered at least 16 of their victims to the dissecting rooms of Dr Knox in Surgeons' Square for seven pounds and ten shillings a cadaver. Contrary to popular legend, no evidence has ever been uncovered confirming that Burke and Hare were grave-robbers. Rather, all their victims were murdered by suffocation – guaranteed undamaged and fresh on delivery.

William Burke and William Hare both left their native Ireland to work as labourers on the new Union Canal, but they did not become acquainted with each other until Burke and his partner, Helen McDougal, moved into Logs Lodging house in Tanners Close (now demolished) in the West Port, where Hare had settled with the widowed proprietress. One day, a male lodger died owing Hare four pounds in rent. To recoup his loss, Hare decided, with Burke's help, to sell the corpse to Dr Knox's Anatomy School at Surgeons' Square. At the funeral of the deceased

Death mask of William Burke

lodger, unbeknown to the mourners, the coffin was weighted with a sack of bark. After this incident, Burke and Hare got the taste for easy money, and their first murder victim was a sickly, bedridden miller who was boarding at their lodgings. After getting him drunk, they suffocated him and carted his corpse off to Dr Knox. From then on, their victims tended to be selected from the weak, the poor and the intoxicated lowlife of Edinburgh's squalid backstreets: people no one would miss. In the end, they got careless and lazy, and when their last victim was discovered under a bed at their lodgings, the game was up.

The trial began on Christmas Eve 1828. Hare turned King's evidence and was released in February 1829, as were both their partners, much to the public's anger, but Burke was found guilty and sentenced to hang. Between 30 and 40,000 people witnessed his execution at the Lawnmarket on Wednesday, 28 January 1829. Burke's corpse went the way of his victims and ended up on a slab in an anatomy class, where it was put on public display. His skeleton and an anatomy textbook covered with his skin are on display at the Surgeons' Hall Museum.

The authorities investigated Knox's role in the affair and decided that, though neither he nor his staff had been aware the cadavers were murdered, he had acted incautiously and should have made enquiries. This judgement, however, did not stop the public rioting outside Knox's house and burning his effigy. As a consequence of the Burke and Hare case, the Anatomy Act was passed in 1832 for regulating the supply of bodies to anatomy departments, sanctioning the bodies of the poor to be taken from hospitals and workhouses to be used in teaching. Today's Anatomy Act permits only bequests that have been written into the will or verbally agreed with relatives of the deceased before death.

THE SOUTHSIDE

Left: Surgeons' Sq., 1829
Right: Surgeons' Hall, Nicolson St., headquarters of the Royal College of Surgeons, designed by William Playfair

SEE ALSO: Old Glencorse Kirk.

FURTHER INFORMATION: William Burke's death mask and a few other related artefacts, including the anatomy text book covered with his skin, can be viewed at the museum. Surgeons' Square, where Dr Knox's Anatomy School was located, still exists and is behind the old High School at the foot of Infirmary Street, accessed through the vennel to the right of the building. Dr Knox's house and anatomy school were situated in the south-west corner of the square, to the right of the steps leading up to Drummond Street. The museum also highlights the College's connection with Joseph Bell, Conan Doyle's inspiration for Sherlock Holmes. The museums are open to the public, 7 days a week.

FURTHER READING: W. Roughead (ed.), *Burke and Hare* (W. Hodge, 1948); O.D. Edwards, *Burke and Hare* (Polygon, 1984); I. Rae, *Knox the Anatomist* (Oliver & Boyd, 1964).

38 WEST NICOLSON STREET
West Nicolson House (now The Pear Tree)
Former residence of Thomas Blacklock
Poet and friend of Robert Burns

A very elegant genius, of a modest backward temper, accompanied with that delicate pride which so naturally attends virtue in distress.
David Hume describing Dr Blacklock

Poet Dr Thomas Blacklock (1721–91) was born in Annan, the son of a bricklayer, and lost his sight after contracting smallpox as a child. He studied divinity at Edinburgh University and was ordained minister of Kirkcudbright in 1762, but blindness limited the duties he could perform and he retired on a small annuity in 1762. He survived by writing, tutoring and running a student lodging house. In the 1770s, Dr Blacklock and his wife lived in the upper floors of West Nicolson House (now The Pear Tree pub). He produced his first book of poems in 1746 and continued writing verse for the next 40 years, but he is probably best remembered for his association with Robert Burns.
Blacklock recognised the genius of Burns's poems, commenting that they had 'a pathos and a delicacy'. In September 1786, he wrote a letter to Burns encouraging

him to come to Edinburgh, where he might try for a second edition of his by then out-of-print Kilmarnock edition. Burns's life at this juncture was in turmoil. The Kilmarnock printer wanted money up front for a second edition, which Burns didn't have. Jean Armour was pregnant with twins and her parents were threatening legal action, and Burns was involved in a new relationship with Mary Campbell, a local nursery-maid. He was seriously planning to emigrate to the West Indies with Mary and had even booked a passage with a shipping agent. 'I had taken the last farewell of my friends,' he said in an autobiographical letter to Dr Moore, 'my chest was on the road to Greenock; I had composed my last song I should ever measure in Caledonia … when a letter from Dr Blacklock to a friend of mine overthrew all my schemes by rousing my poetic ambition. The Doctor belonged to a set of Critics for whose applause I had not even dared to hope. His idea that I would meet with every encouragement for a second edition fired me so much that away I posted to Edinburgh without a single acquaintance in town.'
Burns really had nothing to lose by going to Edinburgh. If all failed, his ship to the West Indies was departing from Leith anyway. He needn't have worried, as his debut in Edinburgh was a great success and not only resulted in a second edition but also brought him fame and celebrity. And had Dr Blacklock not written inviting Burns to Edinburgh, he may well have boarded the Roselle bound for Jamaica and never have been heard of again.

SEE ALSO: Robert Burns.

FURTHER INFORMATION: Dr Blacklock and his wife are buried in the graveyard of Buccleuch Church, on the west side of Chapel Street. Two indecipherable white stones on the west wall mark their graves.

18 BUCCLEUCH PLACE
Former residence of Francis Jeffrey (1773–1850) and birthplace of the *Edinburgh Review* (1802–1929)

This will never do!
Francis Jeffrey on Wordsworth's 'The Excursion' (1814) in the *Edinburgh Review*, November 1814

One of the greatest achievements of the publisher Archibald Constable was the launching of the *Edinburgh Review*, a magazine which, although not wholly literary, expressed its opinions on literature in an unreserved and often remorseless manner. Thomas Carlyle described it as 'a kind of Delphic oracle'. Byron was less romantic and penned his lengthy satirical poem, 'English Bards and Scotch Reviewers', as a retort to its acerbic reviews. The reading public, however, couldn't get enough of it, and its circulation rose rapidly, reaching a peak of 14,000 monthly copies in 1818.
It was founded by the Reverend Sydney Smith and advocates Henry Brougham, Francis Horner and Francis Jeffrey at Jeffrey's third-floor flat at 18 Buccleuch Place in the spring of 1802. The idea for a Whig review was Smith's, who at that time was a private tutor. Jeffrey, who was initially sceptical of the idea, became its first editor. Henry Brougham wrote:

> There was himself [Smith] ready to write any number of articles, and to edit the whole; there was Jeffrey, *facile princeps* in all kinds of literature; there was myself, full of mathematics and everything relating to the colonies; there was Horner for political economy, and Murray for political subjects. Besides, might we not, from our great and never-to-be doubted success, fairly hope to receive help

from such leviathans as Playfair, Dugald Stewart, Thos. Brown, Thomson and others? All this was irresistible.

The first issue contained no fewer than 29 articles and 252 pages. Early contributors included William Hazlitt, Thomas Carlyle, John Allen, George Ellis and Henry Hallam. Walter Scott was also a frequent contributor until Jeffrey published a savage 35-page review of *Marmion* in April 1808:

> To write a modern romance of chivalry, seems to be such a phantasy as to build a modern abbey or an English pagoda. For once, however, it may be excused as a pretty caprice of genius, but second production of the same sort is entitled to less indulgence, and imposes a sort of duty to drive the author from so idle a task, by a fair exposition of the faults which are, in a manner, inseparable from its execution.

Francis Jeffrey

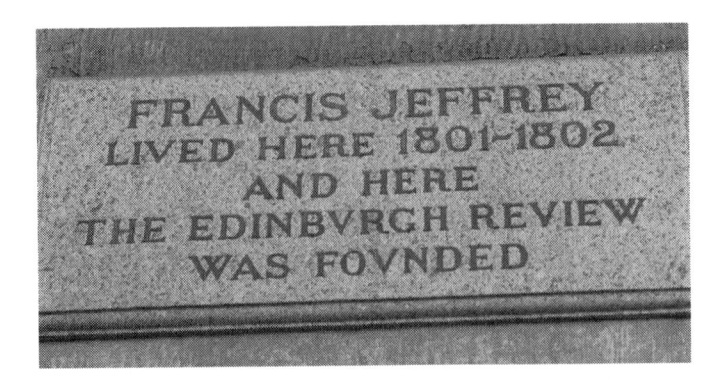

> FRANCIS JEFFREY
> LIVED HERE 1801-1802
> AND HERE
> THE EDINBVRGH REVIEW
> WAS FOVNDED

Jeffrey effectively shot himself in the foot with this review, as Scott, along with his 'pretty caprice of genius', transferred his allegiance shortly afterwards to the new London-based magazine, the *Quarterly Review*.

Jeffrey was enthusiastic about Keats and Byron, but was never passionate about the Lake school of poetry and often responded with scathing reviews. The Irish poet Thomas Moore became so incensed at Jeffrey's articles that he challenged him to a duel in 1806, which was fortunately halted by the police.

In 1829, Jeffrey gave up his editorship and was elected dean of the Faculty of Advocates. He continued to write articles and, in 1830, he obtained a seat in the House of Commons after becoming lord advocate of Scotland. The *Edinburgh Review* continued publication for another 100 years, publishing most of the major writers and critics of the nineteenth and early twentieth centuries, until its demise in 1929.

SEE ALSO: Dean Cemetery, Archibald Constable, *Blackwood's Magazine*, Thomas Carlyle, Sir Walter Scott.

FURTHER INFORMATION: Francis Jeffrey was born at 7 Charles Street. He also lived at 62 Queen Street, 92 George Street, 24 Moray Place and Craigcrook Castle off Craigcrook Road, the former home of Archibald Constable. Jeffrey is buried in Dean Cemetery.

THE SOUTHSIDE

18 Buccleuch Pl. Residence of Francis Jeffrey, and birthplace of the *Edinburgh Review*

BOOK LOVERS' EDINBURGH

CHARLES STREET
Site of The Paperback, the first paperback bookshop in Britain, and the infamous burning of *Lady Chatterley's Lover*

Sexual intercourse began
In nineteen sixty-three
(which was rather late for me) -
Between the end of the "Chatterley" ban
And the Beatles' first LP.
Philip Larkin, from 'Annus Mirabilis' (1967)

The 1960 burning of *Lady Chatterley's Lover* outside The Paperback. Jim Haynes second from the left in front of the rhino head. Photo Alan Daiches

Jim Haynes hailed from Louisiana, and in the fifties he was conscripted into the US Air Force, and posted to Kirknewton, near Edinburgh, where his primary duties were listening in on the Russian Air Defence System. 'Almost immediately,' wrote Jim, 'I went to see the base commander and said, "I've been up to the University and they said I can go to classes. May I have permission to have permanent night duty and to live in a small room off the base at my own expense?" He said, "My boy, of course, we will try to help anyone who wants to further himself."

THE SOUTHSIDE

I didn't want to further myself; I just wanted to escape the military. But he gave me permission.'

Weary of the military, Jim was soon granted early release and pursued his idea of starting a bookshop next to the university. With his demob money he went in search of premises, and, walking along Charles Street next to the university, he spotted an old junk shop at No. 22A, which he acquired and converted into 'a real bookshop' in 1959.

> I started by writing letters to publishers, saying that I was going to start a paperback bookshop, it was going to be mainly for the students and staff of the University of Edinburgh, and that if they wanted to trust me with their books I would sell them and pay them. Of course, this was early days, when the paperback revolution hadn't really come to Britain, and there I was, quite unknown and demanding credit ... but the books just started rolling in. And so The Paperback opened ... It was an immediate success: the only bookshop in Britain to stock every serious paperback in print, not just British paperbacks but a wide range of American and European ones ... Mine was the first bookshop to arrange paperbacks by subject, rather than publisher ... I also sold a lot of books that were supposedly not to be sold for one reason or another – so-called obscene publications ... So when Penguin published *Lady Chatterley's Lover*, I naturally placed a very large order. Then suddenly the word went out that there was going to be a court case and that we were not to sell *Lady Chatterley*. Despite that, I found more and more people coming into the bookshop demanding it and of course I sold it.
>
> One day a curious woman came in and asked if I had *Lady Chatterley* in stock. I said, 'Yes' and she said, 'Can you save me a copy? I'll be right back', and left. I thought there was something funny going on so I rang up Alan Daiches, a photographer friend, and the local press.

BOOK LOVERS' EDINBURGH

They all came by in time to witness the return of the woman. She arrived holding a pair of coal tongs; she put the money down and wouldn't touch the book, but picked it up with tongs and carried it out in front of the bookshop. There she poured some kind of liquid, probably kerosene, on top of the book and proceeded to rant and rave and put a match to it, 'this iniquitous document'. The scene was documented by Alan, who had his camera there, and made all the papers in England and Scotland – even some international press. It added substantially to the shop's notoriety – everyone talking about this crazy woman burning *Lady Chatterley's Lover* outside The Paperback. I even got a letter of support from Allen Lane, the founder of Penguin, who later visited the shop on several occasions.

The rhino head was discovered by me when walking down Princes Street one sunny morning with a friend. Workmen were carrying it out of The New Club. When they said they were going to destroy it, I asked if I could have it. They were pleased to give it to me. My friend and I took it to Charles Street in a taxi and by chance there was a spike available to hang it immediately onto the wall.

The Paperback evolved, becoming not just a bookshop, but a salon, a coffee house, a gallery, and a meeting place, all squashed within its quaking shelves of books. There were also concerts and readings by writers, notably the great Russian poet, Yevgeny Yevtushenko, and French writers Nathalie Sarraute, Marguerite Duras, and Alain Robbe-Grillet. Jim also

THE SOUTHSIDE

co-founded The Traverse Theatre on the Lawnmarket in 1963 and became a catalyst for the Edinburgh Fringe Festival. The Paperback closed in 1967.

SEE ALSO: The International Writers' Conference.

FURTHER INFORMATION: A bronze sculpture of a rhino head marking the site of The Paperback in Charles Street was unveiled by Jim in 2012, and can be seen protruding from the wall of Edinburgh University's Informatics building. The identity of the mysterious book-burning lady remains unknown, although she was rumoured to have been a missionary in Africa. But she was also a symbol of the moral conflict of the time, which would determine the path of human rights. And when *Lady Chatterley's* publisher, Penguin Books, was eventually acquitted by the jury at the Old Bailey on 2 November 1960 of charges under the Obscene Publications Act, it became a signpost for human rights and the floodgates slowly began to open with the decriminalisation of homosexuality, abortion reform, the abolition of capital punishment and theatre censorship, and radical changes in the divorce laws. To this day many people still dismiss *Lady Chatterley's Lover* as a sex romp, but then it was really about the freedom of the written word and a reflection of the constrained social mores of its time. Penguin Books dedicated the second edition of *Lady Chatterley's Lover* to the Old Bailey jury.

FURTHER READING: C. Rolph, *The Trial of Lady Chatterley: Regina v. Penguin Books Limited* (Penguin, 1990); J. Haynes, *Thanks for Coming* (Faber & Faber, 1984); *Thanks for Coming! Encore!* (Polwarth, 2014).

Left: The bronze rhino head, Charles St.
Right: Jim Haynes, Paris, 2016

TEVIOT PLACE
McEwan Hall
Venue for the 1962
International Writers' Conference
The world's first international
literary festival

> *People jumping up to confess they were homosexuals; a Registered Heroin Addict leading the young Scottish opposition to the literary tyranny of the Communist Hugh MacDiarmid ... An English woman novelist describing her communications with her dead daughter, a Dutch homosexual, former male nurse, now a Catholic convert, seeking someone to baptise him; a bearded Sikh with hair down to his waist declaring on the platform that homosexuals were incapable of love, just as (he said) hermaphrodites were incapable of orgasm (Stephen Spender, in the chair, murmured that he should have thought they could have two). And all this before an audience of over two thousand people per day, mostly, I suppose, Scottish Presbyterians. The most striking fact was the number of lunatics both on the platform and in the public. One young woman novelist was released temporarily from a mental hospital in order to attend the Conference, and she was one of the milder cases. I confess I enjoyed it enormously.*
> Mary McCarthy writing to Hannah Arendt, describing the International Writers' Conference in 1962.

From Monday 20 to Friday 24 August 1962 an audience of over 2,000 people packed the McEwan Hall daily to hear writers discussing the topic of the day, which included censorship, the future of the novel, and Scottish writing. They discussed censorship when censorship was still

McEwan Hall

in place. They talked about sex when it was barely even written about, let alone talked about. They argued with each other, they insulted each other, they confronted each other; and in doing so entertained the 2,300-strong daily audience and made literary history.

Writers came from far and wide, and included Norman Mailer, Henry Miller, Lawrence Durrell, Mary McCarthy, William Burroughs, Rebecca West, Erich Fried, Rosamond Lehmann, Stephen Spender and Khushwant Singh, as well as Scotland's own Muriel Spark, Hugh MacDiarmid, Edwin Morgan, Alexander Trocchi and many others.

The media, as it tends to do with unknown quantities, treated the idea with scepticism. *The Scotsman* newspaper,

BOOK LOVERS' EDINBURGH

Khushwant Singh and Lawrence Durrell

however, proved the exception: 'Everything went wrong. Crowds were still milling outside the hall long after the advertised starting time. Microphones sulked. The speech of welcome, on tape, didn't materialise. Promised stars failed to turn up. And yet, despite all this – or even because of it – the first international writers' conference to be held at the Edinburgh Festival got off to a splendid start.'

The title 'International Writers' Conference' is today a fairly mundane one: not exactly catchy or sexy. A better, slightly less formal, label might have described it as an International Literary Festival, but as there had never been an international literary festival before 1962, it is possibly only hindsight that makes the conjecture appear wise.

'It was never repeated,' wrote writer Joan Lingard. 'Not in that form at least, but in 1967, inspired by the memory of it, a number of us who were members of Scottish International PEN and the Society of Authors, began to run small scale book Conferences of our own during the Edinburgh International Festival ... until, in 1983, the first Edinburgh International Book Festival was launched ... On the night before the opening we had a party to celebrate and I remember feeling the same buzz of excitement that I had sitting in the McEwan Hall sixteen years before.'

THE SOUTHSIDE

SEE ALSO: The Paperback bookshop, Edinburgh International Book Festival.

FURTHER INFORMATION: The 1962 International Writers' Conference was the brainchild of Jim Haynes, who ran the Paperback Bookshop across the street, publisher John Calder, and Sonia Orwell, widow of George Orwell.

FURTHER READING: A. Bartie and E. Bell (eds), *The International Writers' Conference Revisited: Edinburgh 1962* (Cargo Publishing, 2012).

Clockwise, from top left:
William Burroughs, Alexander Trocchi (centre), Mary McCarthy, Norman Mailer, Henry Miller

5 GEORGE SQUARE
Former location of George Watson's Ladies College
School of novelist and journalist Rebecca West (1892–1983)

Rebecca West could handle a pen as brilliantly as ever I could and much more savagely.
George Bernard Shaw

Once a household name, Rebecca West's popularity has waned in recent years, probably due mainly to the difficulty in categorising her work. She wrote in every literary genre, including biography, essays, novels, history and investigative journalism. Her association with H.G. Wells, which forever labelled her as a famous novelist's mistress, didn't help either.
She was born Cicily Isabel Fairfield in London's Paddington in 1892 and was the youngest of three sisters. Her father, Charles Fairfield, was a journalist who deserted his family in 1901 and sailed to Africa, where he died penniless five years later. Her mother, Isabella Mackenzie, was a former governess, who, following the collapse of her marriage, returned with her family to her native city of Edinburgh in 1902. Their first home was at 2 Hope Park Square, and they later moved to Buccleuch Place.
West was enrolled at George Watson's Ladies College on 13 January 1903 and won the school's junior essay prize in 1907. Notebooks were discovered in 1996 at the Rebecca West archive in Tulsa University which were the draft of a novel entitled *The Sentinel*. The start of the manuscript was dated 1909 and written when West was still a schoolgirl. Watson's later became John Thompson's Ladies College in her 1922 novel, *The Judge*. On leaving school, she briefly pursued an unsuccessful acting career.

She began her writing career as a columnist on the suffragist weekly *The Freewoman* in 1911, and it was here she first used the pen name Rebecca West, taken from the strong-willed heroine of Henrik Ibsen's drama *Rosmersholm*. She contributed to various newspapers and socialist magazines, and her first book, *Henry James*, was published in 1916.

She first met H.G. Wells after writing an unfavourable review of his novel *Marriage* in 1912. 'Mr Wells is the Old Maid among novelists,' she wrote. 'Even the sex obsession that lay clotted on *Ann Veronica* like cold white sauce was merely old maid's mania, the reaction towards the flesh of a mind too long absorbed in airships and colloids.' Shortly afterwards, aged nineteen, she began an affair with her 'old maid' which lasted ten years. Their son and her only child, Anthony West, was born in 1914.

She was a staunch supporter of the suffragist movement, participating in marches, protests and riots, but she was never imprisoned. Her essay *A Reed of Steel* (1933), about Emmeline Pankhurst, is arguably one of her best works.

Her first novel, *The Return of the Soldier* (1918), about a shell-shocked soldier, was followed by *The Judge* (1922), *The Strange Necessity* (1928) and *Harriet Hume* (1929). Her autobiographical novel, *The Fountain Overflows*, was published in 1956.

Rebecca West

23 GEORGE SQUARE
Home of Arthur Conan Doyle from 1876 to 1880

This is the residence most associated with Conan Doyle in Edinburgh and, compared to his other homes in the city, George Square was by far the most select and affluent. The boyhood home of Sir Walter Scott (1771–1832) was at No. 25, and Thomas Carlyle (1795–1881) wooed Jane Welsh at No. 22.

The Doyles moved into No. 23 in the summer of 1876 from their cramped flat at 2 Argyle Park Terrace, just a few minutes' walk away on the southern edge of The Meadows. The street-level rooms at No. 23 George Square were occupied by the Doyles and their lodger, Bryan Waller, who paid the £85 annual rent. Waller was a consultant pathologist who had recently inherited his family estate and cash flow did not appear to be one of his immediate problems.

From No. 23, Conan Doyle would have walked across the Square to the university medical faculty and the Royal Infirmary on South Bridge. In 1881 the family moved to nearby Lonsdale Terrace, and in the summer of 1882, Bryan Waller, accompanied by the Doyles, retired to his estate in Yorkshire.

In the early 1960s much of George Square was demolished to make way for a new university campus; this was considered by many to be a disgraceful act of architectural vandalism. Fortunately, No. 23 on the western side of the Square survived, along with a few houses in the north east corner, but the Square remains one of Edinburgh's most controversial redevelopments. 23 George Square is marked by a small plaque and is currently home to Edinburgh University's Catholic Chaplaincy.

SEE ALSO: Conan Doyle, Joseph Bell.

THE SOUTHSIDE

23 George Square

25 GEORGE SQUARE
Childhood Home of Sir Walter Scott

Born for nae better than a gangrel scrape-gut ...
The teenage Walter Scott described by his father

George Square was designed by the architect James Brown and pre-dates the New Town by 20 years. It wasn't named after royalty or a worthy man of letters, but James's brother George. It was a fashionable place to live, but more importantly it was a healthy place to live, especially if you'd just arrived in 1772, like the Scotts had, from a tenement ghetto in the Old Town, where six of their children had died in infancy.

Young Wattie, however, did not spend his early childhood at George Square. In 1773, when he was about 18 months old, he contracted poliomyelitis and lost the use of his right leg, which left him with a limp for the rest of his life. Doctors could do nothing for him, and on the advice of his grandfather, Dr Rutherford, he was sent to live with his paternal grandfather at Sandyknowe Farm in the Scottish Borders where, it was hoped, fresh air and exercise would improve his health.

Thus began Wattie's lifelong love affair with the Border country. Amongst his earliest memories were being wrapped in the newly flayed skin of a sheep to attempt a cure, being carried by the ewe-milkers to the crags above the house, and winter evenings round the fireside listening to his grandmother's tales. Border life didn't mend his leg, but his general health improved, and when he was four years old, the family decided to try another remedy.

In the summer of 1775, he left the Borders with his Aunt Janet for the waters of Bath. The visit didn't cure his lameness, but he did pick up an English accent and learn the rudiments of reading at a local dame-school. They returned to

25 George Square

Sandyknowe the following summer, and two years later, between the ages of seven and eight, he returned to George Square. 'I felt the change,' he wrote, 'from being a single indulged brat, to becoming a member of a large family, very severely.'

His mother, Anne, was a small, plain woman, who was sagacious and friendly, and lived to the ripe old age of 87. She had a head full of ballads and stories which she passed on to Wattie, and was the first person to introduce him to the world of poetry. Her husband, Walter, was a solicitor and a staunch Calvinist. Almost teetotal, he possessed no hobbies, but had an intense interest in theology, doling out long sermons from the family Bible on the Sabbath. Anne and Walter's marriage was a happy one, apart from the day he threw out of the window a cup in which his wife had thoughtlessly given tea to the traitor Murray of Broughton, who betrayed his fellow Jacobites after Culloden. History does not record if any passers-by or any of the Scotts' illustrious neighbours were injured. These neighbours included the Lord Advocate Lord Melville, writer Henry Mackenzie and the 'hanging judge'

Lord Braxfield, the inspiration for the eponymous hero of Robert Louis Stevenson's *Weir of Hermiston.*

Scott's siblings consisted of four brothers and one sister. Robert, the eldest, joined the Navy and later the East India Company, and died of malaria aged 41. John became a soldier and died aged 47. Thomas (his favourite brother), a couple of years younger than Wattie, died a regimental paymaster in Canada, aged 50. Daniel, the youngest, ended up being employed on a plantation in Jamaica, where he was accused of cowardice during a slave uprising, indelibly staining the family name. Wattie shunned him on his return and did not attend his funeral or wear mourning for him. His only sister, Anne, a year younger than him, was a highly strung and sickly girl who was terribly accident-prone. Her perilous escapades included crushing her hand in an iron door, almost drowning in a pond and seriously burning her head after her cap caught fire. She died in her late 20s.

In 1779, when he was eight, Wattie attended the High School in Infirmary Street, and in 1783, aged thirteen, he entered Edinburgh University. His studies were frequently interrupted by ill health and in 1784–5 he was forced to convalesce once again in the Borders at his Aunt Janet's house in Kelso. By this time, he was a voracious reader, reading 10 times the average quota for a boy his age. He had mastered French and by the time he was 15 he was proficient enough in Italian to read Dante and Ariosto in the original.

In 1786, he signed up for a five-year apprenticeship in his father's legal firm, where the laborious task of copying legal documents (he once wrote 10,000 words without rest or food) was invaluable training for his future career as a novelist, and in 1792 he qualified as an advocate.

As a teenager, his lameness didn't seem to be any great impediment. Long walks and horse-riding did not daunt him. He could lift a blacksmith's anvil by the horn, and

THE SOUTHSIDE

James Hogg described him as the strongest man of his acquaintance. He became involved in the city's social life and was accustomed to the hard drinking and revelry of gentlemen's clubs, often not returning home until the early hours, prompting his father to complain once that he was 'born for nae better than a gangrel scrape-gut'. One of these clubs was the famous Speculative Society, a hub of literary and legal talent.

As an advocate, he walked the floor of Parliament Hall waiting to be hired. He defended destitute prisoners for no fee, and on his Border circuits his clients included sheep stealers, poachers and drunkards. It was his exploration of the Borders which drew him deeper into its ancient traditions and inspired him to collect its ballads and tales before they vanished forever. A Tory who valued tradition and the monarchy, Scott was prompted by the country's fear of rising republicanism and the threat of a French invasion to join the newly formed Royal Edinburgh Volunteer Light Dragoons in 1797. In July of the same year, he met French émigrée Charlotte Carpenter while holidaying in the Lake District, and after a whirlwind romance they were married on Christmas Eve in St Mary's Church, Carlisle. Shortly afterwards, the couple moved into rented accommodation on the second floor of 108 George Street, then to 10 Castle Street and finally to 39 North Castle Street, his townhouse for the next 28 years.

SEE ALSO: Birthplace of W.S., townhouse of W.S., Lasswade Cottage, Heart of Midlothian, Greyfriars Kirkyard, Scott Monument, Holyrood Park, St John's Churchyard, The Writers' Museum, High School, Old College, Sciennes Hill House, Assembly Rooms, Parliament Hall, J.G. Lockhart, Portobello Sands, Canongate Kirkyard.

FURTHER READING: S. Kelly, *Scott Land: The Man Who Invented a Nation* (Polygon, 2010).

MAYFIELD

MARCHHALL CRESCENT
Abden House, home of John Buchan (1875–1940)

A fool tries to look different: a clever man looks the same and is different.
John Buchan, from *The Thirty-Nine Steps* (1915)

John Buchan, father of the modern espionage novel and best remembered as the author of *The Thirty-Nine Steps*, was a frequent visitor to Edinburgh. In 1907, he became a partner in the Edinburgh publishing house of Thomas Nelson & Sons, through his old Oxford friend Tommy Nelson. Although mainly based at their London office, he was, together with his wife Susan, very familiar with the city. Nelson's Parkside works were situated opposite the Commonwealth Pool, between Holyrood Park Road and Parkside Terrace, on the site now occupied by an insurance company. Buchan became editor of Nelson's new magazine, the *Scottish Review*, and his intentions were 'to make it the centre of a Scottish school of letters such as Edinburgh had [in the *Edinburgh Review* and *Blackwood's Magazine*] a hundred years ago'. The magazine's readership, however, had other intentions, and it folded after two years. He next edited the famous Nelson Sixpenny Classics.
During their first visit to Edinburgh, the newly-wed Buchans stayed at Abden House, a Gothic villa which is now in the grounds of Edinburgh University's Pollock

MAYFIELD

Halls of Residence off Dalkeith Road. 'It was enormous,' recalled Buchan's wife Susan, 'even judged by the standards of yesterday, but we existed happily in a corner of it with two excellent Scots servants. The garden had sweeping green lawns and a view of Arthur's Seat which redeemed the gloom of the heavy carved woodwork and the sombre curtains which almost stood up by themselves.' Buchan resigned from Nelson's in 1929.

SEE ALSO: Thomas Nelson, Holyrood Palace, Old College.

FURTHER INFORMATION: *The Thirty-Nine Steps* was first published as a serial in *Blackwood's Magazine* in the summer of 1915 under a pseudonym. In October of the same year it was published as a book with John Buchan's name on the spine, selling 33,000 copies in the first three months. Buchan's life and legacy can be explored at The John Buchan Story Museum, The Chambers Institution, High Street, Peebles, in the Scottish Borders. Abden House today is a conference and events venue.

FURTHER READING: J.A. Smith, *John Buchan* (Hart-Davis, 1965); A. Lownie, *John Buchan, The Presbyterian Cavalier* (Pimlico, 2002).

Frontispiece of a Nelson's Sixpenny Classic

SCIENNES

SCIENNES HOUSE PLACE
Sciennes Hill House
Site of the only meeting of Walter Scott and Robert Burns

Scott met Burns only once in his life: when he was a lad of 15 in 1786–7, at Sciennes Hill House, the residence of philosopher and historian Adam Ferguson. He graphically recalled this meeting in Lockhart's *Life of Sir Walter Scott*:

> I saw him one day at the late venerable Professor Ferguson's, where there were several gentlemen of literary reputation, among whom I remember the celebrated Mr Dugald Stewart. Of course we youngsters sate silent, looked and listened. The only thing which I remember which was remarkable in Burns's manner, was the effect produced upon him by a print of Bunbury's, representing a soldier lying dead in the snow, his dog sitting in misery on the one side, on the other his widow, with a child in her arms ... He actually shed tears. He asked whose the lines [written beneath] were, and it chanced that nobody but myself remembered that they occur in a half-forgotten poem of Langhorne's called by the uncompromising title of 'The Justice of the Piece'. I whispered my information to a friend present, who mentioned it to Burns, who rewarded me with a look and a word, which, though of mere civility, I then received, and still recollect, with very great pleasure. His person was strong and robust: his manners rustic,

not clownish; a sort of dignified plainness and simplicity … the eye alone, I think, indicated the poetical character and temperament. It was large and of a dark cast, and glowed (I say literally *glowed*) when he spoke with feeling or interest. I never saw such an eye in a human head, though I have seen most distinguished men of my time. His conversation expressed perfect self-confidence, without the slightest presumption. Among the men who were the most learned of their time and country, he expressed himself with perfect firmness, but without the least intrusive forwardness; and when he differed in opinion he did not hesitate to express it firmly, yet at the same time with modesty. I do not remember any part of his conversation distinctly enough to be quoted, nor did I ever see him again, except in the street, where he did not recognise me, as I could not expect he should.

SEE ALSO: Sir Walter Scott, Robert Burns, Old College.

FURTHER INFORMATION: A plaque on the restored remains of the mid-eighteenth-century Sciennes Hill House (aka Sciennes Hall) commemorates the only meeting of Scott and Burns. Partly demolished in 1868, it is the back of the original house that faces the street today, and the modified front faces the rear. Originally, it was the home of Robert Biggar, who lost his fortune after investing in the Darien Scheme. An old Jewish burial ground lies opposite. Sciennes is a corruption of Sienna, and the name is derived from St Catherine of Sienna, to whom was dedicated a convent erected here about 1514.

MARCHMONT

ARDEN STREET
Former home of Ian Rankin (1960–) and the fictitious Inspector Rebus

Described by the crime fiction writer James Ellroy as the 'king of tartan noir', Ian Rankin was born in 1960 in the village of Cardenden in Fife. He now lives and works in Edinburgh, where most of his novels are set, graphically contrasting the picturesque 'Athens of the North' with its concrete housing schemes and criminal underclass.
Rankin writes in his introduction to *Rebus: The Early Years* (1999):

> I was living in a room in a ground-floor flat in [No. 24] Arden Street, so my hero, John Rebus, had to live across the road. When the book was published, I found to my astonishment that everyone was saying I'd written a whodunit, a crime novel. I think I'm still the only crime writer I know who hadn't a clue about the genre before setting out ...

'Before setting out', Rankin had a variety of jobs: chicken factory worker, alcohol researcher, swineherd, grape-picker, punk musician, tax collector, assistant at the National Folktale Centre in London and journalist with the monthly magazine *Hi-Fi Review*. Rankin attended Edinburgh University, where he won several literary prizes. One of his short stories evolved into a novel called *The Flood*, but in the mid-'80s he started writing a book which updated

MARCHMONT

Ian Rankin

Dr Jekyll and Mr Hyde to present-day Edinburgh. *Knots and Crosses* was published in 1987 and appropriately introduced Detective Sergeant John Rebus with 'water seeping into his shoes' standing before the grave of his father. Rebus was intended as a one-off, but the public's appetite for this sardonic, obstinate, world-weary cop has ensured his immortality with each successive bestseller. Rebus is now on a par with the legends of the detective genre, from Marlowe to Morse, but one of the great allures of Rebus is the way Rankin weaves real places and events into his stories: Arthur's Seat in *The Falls*, the new Scottish Parliament building in *Set in Darkness*, the Mull of Kintyre helicopter crash in *A Question of Blood*, and Rebus's and Rankin's local pub, the Oxford Bar.

In an interview on 17 November 2000, Ian Rankin explained the origins of Rebus's unusual name:

> I was a student of English Literature when I wrote the first Rebus book, *Knots and Crosses*, and I was studying deconstruction, semiotics, etc. A rebus is a picture puzzle, and it seemed to click ... so I made him Rebus, thinking it was only for one book (I never intended turning him into a series) so it didn't matter if I gave him a strange name. Recently, I bumped into a guy called Rebus in my local pub. He lives in Rankin Drive in Edinburgh. Truth is always stranger than fiction ...

THE GRANGE

GRANGE ROAD
Grange Cemetery
Grave of Thomas Nelson and Sons
Prolific Edinburgh publishers
and inventors of the rotary printing press

Thomas Nelson, senior

Thomas Nelson was born into a pious family on a small farm in Throsk, Stirlingshire, in 1780, and by the age of 16, he had become a teacher. After various jobs, he headed for London, where he became employed as a publisher's apprentice. When he was 18, he returned to Edinburgh and opened a second-hand bookshop in the Grassmarket. Within a few years, he began publishing affordable Christian works and classic literature for the 'common folk'.

His distribution and sales methods, which included selling books at fairs and auctions, low prices and sending out sales reps, were extremely innovative. The book trade was initially sceptical of this pious upstart, but his company soon began to flourish.

His two teenage sons, William and Thomas, joined the company in the 1830s and in 1839 took over its management. In 1844, a London office was opened and by 1853 Nelson had become the largest printing and publishing house in Scotland, specialising in religious works, school texts, and stories of travel and adventure for children.

Thomas Nelson Jr invented the rotary printing press in 1850 and revolutionised the industry. Using a continuous web sheet, the rotary press was faster than others and printed on both sides simultaneously. He exhibited his invention at the Great Exhibition of 1851 but, oddly, he never patented it, and it was copied throughout the world. In the 1840s, the company moved into premises at Hope Park on Edinburgh's Southside, where employees were well cared for – this included the provision of meals, often accompanied by a sermon from the clergy. The Hope Park premises were completely destroyed by fire in 1878 and new premises were built in Parkside on the edge of Holyrood Park. Nearby, Thomas Jr built himself a castellated Gothic mansion named St Leonards, now part of Edinburgh University's Pollock Halls on Dalkeith Road.

In the early 1900s, John Buchan became involved in the company's management through his friendship with Thomas Jr's son Tommy, to whom he dedicated *The Thirty-Nine Steps*. Buchan edited the Nelson Sixpenny Classics and in 1907 launched the short-lived magazine the *Scottish Review*. He also wrote a history of the First World War and the life of Montrose for Nelson.

Thomas Nelson, the company's founder, died in 1861. When informed that his death was approaching, he calmly replied, 'I thought so; my days are wholly in God's hands. He doeth all things well. His will be done!' He then lifted his Bible from his bedside table and said, 'Now I must finish my chapter.'

SEE ALSO: John Buchan.

BRUNTSFIELD

WARRENDER PARK CRESCENT
Former James Gillespie's High School for Girls
Inspiration for the Marcia Blaine School in
Muriel Spark's *The Prime of Miss Jean Brodie*

Give me a girl at an impressionable age and she is mine for life.
Muriel Spark, from *The Prime of Miss Jean Brodie*

Although Muriel Spark wrote over 20 novels, it was her sixth novel, *The Prime of Miss Jean Brodie*, published in 1961 and adapted for stage and screen, which is her best known and most discussed work. In fact, she could probably have written another 50 novels, but all roads would still lead back to this one, which, although easy to read and written in a relaxed style, is more complex in its theme and composition than it at first appears. And this is the reason why readers and critics keep returning to this novel, which can be read on many different levels and, like all great classics, refuses to fade into obscurity.

Muriel Spark was born in 1918 to Sarah and Bernard Camberg, an engineer, at 160 Bruntsfield Place. She was enrolled at James Gillespie's School in 1922, where she

Left: Muriel Spark in 1947
Right: The old James Gillespie's High School for Girls. Now Edinburgh University student accommodation

became known as the school's 'poet and dreamer'. Her work regularly appeared in the school magazine, and in 1932 she was crowned 'Queen of Poetry'. When she was 11, the young Muriel encountered Miss Kay, whose eccentric teaching and idealism formed the basis for the fictional character in her 1961 novel, *The Prime of Miss Jean Brodie*. Like many other pupils before her, Muriel was fascinated by Miss Kay and fell quickly under her spell, commenting that, 'Miss Kay predicted my future as a writer in the most emphatic terms. I felt I hardly had much choice in the matter.' But Miss Kay did not have love affairs with the art master and singing teacher, and was not dismissed for teaching treason and sedition to her students, as was Jean Brodie; the two, however, did share many similar characteristics, such as a love of music, Renaissance painters and exotic travel, and an admiration for Mussolini's Fascisti.

After leaving school, Spark attended Heriot Watt College in Chambers Street, and at 18 took a job in the office of Small's department store at 106 Princes Street. In 1937, aged 19, she married Sydney Spark in Salisbury, Southern Rhodesia, and their son Robin was born in Bulawayo a year later. Her husband became increasingly mentally unstable, and, following her return to Britain in 1944, the couple were divorced. She joined the political department of the Foreign Office secret intelligence service, MI6, during the Second World War. After the war, she remained in London, where she became general secretary of the Poetry Society and editor of the *Poetry Review* (1947–9). She started writing seriously after the war and in 1951 she won *The Observer*'s short story competition with 'Seraph and the Zambesi'. Her first collection of poems, *The Fanfario and Other Verse*, was published in 1952, and in 1954 she was converted to Roman Catholicism, an event which influenced her later writing. Her first novel, *The Comforters* (1957), was praised by Evelyn Waugh as 'brilliantly original and fascinating', and during the next four years she penned a further five novels: *Robinson* (1958), *Memento Mori* (1959), *The Bachelors* (1960), *The Ballad of Peckham Rye* (1960) and *The Prime of Miss Jean Brodie* (1961).

The Prime of Miss Jean Brodie was first published in *The New Yorker* magazine to great acclaim, prompting her move to New York in the early '60s, where she worked for the magazine with fellow contributors J.D. Salinger, John Updike and Vladimir Nabokov. During this period, she wrote two further novels, *The Girls of Slender Means* (1963) and the prize-winning *The Mandelbaum Gate* (1965). In the late '60s, she moved to Rome and in 1979 she settled in Tuscany. Her later works include *The Abbess of Crewe* (1974), *Loitering with Intent* (1981), *A Far Cry from Kensington* (1988) and *The Finishing School* (2004). Her autobiography, *Curriculum Vitae*, was published in 1992. Muriel Spark died in Tuscany in 2006, aged 88.

FURTHER INFORMATION: Christina Kay was born at 4 Grindlay Street, off Lothian Road, on 11 June 1878, the only child of Mary McDonald and Alexander Kay, a cabinet maker. She was enrolled at Gillespie's School at the age of five, and, except for two years at training college, there she remained until her retirement in 1943. She lived at Grindlay Street for most of

BRUNTSFIELD

her life, where she often entertained her pupils to tea. She never married, although she lost a lover in the Great War, and died on 25 May 1951 at Midhope, Hopetoun, South Queensferry, of chronic bronchitis and myocarditis, aged 72, unaware of the legend she would become. She is buried in Abercorn Churchyard, near South Queensferry.

Outwith her writing, Muriel Spark was well known for her public feud with her estranged son Robin Spark (1938-2016), whose belief that he was Jewish conflicted with his mother's claim that her family were Christians. 'You can be whatever you like … ' she wrote to him in 1981, 'but there is no use writing to me with all that pompous bureaucratic religiosity as if you were John Knox in drag.' Robin did not attend her funeral and was not mentioned in her will.

The building on Warrender Park Crescent, formerly James Gillespie's High School for Girls, is now Edinburgh University student accommodation. The Muriel Spark Archive is held by the National Library of Scotland, George IV Bridge.

FURTHER READING: A. Bold, *Muriel Spark* (Routledge, 1986); M. Stannard, *Muriel Spark: The Biography* (W&N, 2010); A. Taylor, *Appointment in Arezzo: A friendship with Muriel Spark* (Polygon, 2017).

James Gillespie's High School for Girls, Junior Class, 1930: Muriel Camberg, 3rd row, right; Miss Christina Kay, wearing hat

7 LEAMINGTON TERRACE
Former home of poet Norman MacCaig

> Hugh MacDiarmid: *After I am gone, my poetry will be remembered and read for hundreds of years, but after you have gone, your poetry will soon be forgotten.*
> Norman MacCaig: *Ah, but I am not planning to go!*

Norman MacCaig

Norman MacCaig (1910-96) was one of the great Scottish poets, who wrote not in Scots or Gaelic, but in English in a simple way, observing nature, people and especially his friends. From rhyme to free verse, MacCaig produced unique poetry which, despite MacDiarmid's tongue-in-cheek prediction, will not be 'forgotten'.

He was born on 14 November 1910 to Robert McCaig and Joan MacLeod. His father, who came from Haugh of Urr in Dumfriesshire, was a chemist who had a shop at 9 Dundas Street, and the family lived in a tenement flat at 11 Dundas Street. His mother, who had never been taught to read or write, was from Scalpay, off Harris. Norman was the youngest of four children; he was educated at the Royal High School and studied classics at Edinburgh University. He became a primary-school teacher and remained in teaching until 1967, when he was appointed as fellow in creative writing at Edinburgh University. In 1970, he joined the Department of English Studies at the University of Stirling and became a reader in poetry, retiring in 1978. His first volumes of poetry, *Far Cry* (1943) and *The Inward Eye* (1946), earmarked him as a devotee of the 'anti cerebral' New Apocalypse, a group of writers who, for a brief time in the 1940s, reacted against the 'classicism' of Auden with savage and disorderly verse. Other collections included *Riding Lights* (1955), *Rings on a Tree* (1968), *A Man in my Position* (1969) and *Collected Poems* (1985).

He first met the poets of the Scottish Renaissance (including Hugh MacDiarmid, Sydney Goodsir Smith and Sorley Maclean) in the Southern Bar in South Clerk Street in 1946. In a radio interview with Roderick Watson, he recalled his early meetings with them: 'For a while, they despised and rejected me, of course, because I write in English: "Lickspittle of the English ascendancy; stabber in the back of the Scottish movement; cultural quisling." But, of course, when they got to know me and found that I was tall, handsome, rich and could sing in tune, they decided I wasn't so bad after all and Douglas Young invented a phrase, he said, "It's a pity Norman doesn't write in Scots but he's got a Scots accent of the mind." Whatever that means.'

After the pubs had closed, the sessions of debate and flyting often continued at MacCaig's flat in Leamington Terrace, where he lived from 1943 to 1996. 'In his own house, he was a generous host,' recalled George Mackay Brown. 'In this, he had a good partner in Isabel, his wife. By 10 p.m., closing time in those days, the burn of lyricism and laughter was only beginning to gather head. Often a group of merry figures was to be seen at a bus stop, burdened with "cerry-oots".'

MacCaig never wrote long, continuous screeds of verse, and critics have sometimes claimed his poetry is lightweight and without political clout. Once, when asked how long it takes him to write a poem, he replied, 'Two fags. Sometimes, it's only one.' He died in the Astley Ainslie Hospital, Edinburgh, on 23 January 1996, aged 85.

SEE ALSO: Hugh MacDiarmid, Sydney Goodsir Smith.

MORNINGSIDE

CLINTON ROAD
East Morningside House
Former home of Susan Ferrier
'Scotland's Jane Austen'

One thing let me entreat you: if we engage in this undertaking, let it be kept a profound secret from every human being. If I was suspected of being accessory to such foul deeds, my brothers and sisters would murder me and my father bury me alive.
Susan Ferrier writing to her friend Charlotte Clavering, revealing her yearning to write a novel

Left: East Morningside House
Right: Susan Ferrier from an engraving after an 1836 portrait by R.Thorburn

Like many women writers throughout history who dared to defy convention and go beyond their expected duties of looking after the family and the home, Susan Ferrier, in order to avert scandal, wrote her first two novels anonymously. But unlike her contemporary Jane Austen, to whom she is often compared, Susan Ferrier has drifted into obscurity.

She was born in a flat in Lady Stair's Close, off the Lawnmarket, on 7 September 1782, the tenth child of Helen Coutts and James Ferrier, a successful lawyer who became principal clerk of session. When she was two years old, her family moved to 25 George Street and later acquired the first villa to be built in Morningside – East Morningside House – as a summer residence. In 1797, when Susan was 14 years old, her mother died. All of her siblings eventually married, while Susan remained unmarried, looking after her ageing father.

BOOK LOVERS' EDINBURGH

She wrote only three novels. The first two, *Marriage* (1818) and *The Inheritance* (1824), were published anonymously by Blackwood and were immensely popular. Her novels were intended to instruct, but were also filled with humour and astute observation. Published the same year as Jane Austen's *Northanger Abbey* and Mary Shelley's *Frankenstein*, her novel *Marriage*, she explained, would 'warn all young ladies against runaway matches'. In the moralising attitudes and manners of her day, she remarked, 'I expect it will be the first book every wise matron will put into the hand of her daughter, and even the reviewers will relax of their severity in favour of the morality of this little work.' Most of *Marriage* was written in the oak-panelled study at East Morningside House.

She was a good friend of Sir Walter Scott, who described her as 'simple, full of humour, and exceedingly ready at repartee, and all this without the least affectation of the blue-stocking'. Scott offered to negotiate with publishers Blackwood over her third novel, *Destiny*, which was published in 1831 and is dedicated to him. Scott was also a friend and colleague of Ferrier's father and was a regular visitor to East Morningside House.

Ill health, failing eyesight and conversion to the Free Church led to her abandoning writing in later life. She died aged 70 in her townhouse at 38 Albany Street in 1854 and is buried in the family grave in St Cuthbert's Churchyard in Lothian Road.

SEE ALSO: St Cuthbert's Churchyard, *Blackwood's Magazine*, John Wilson, Sir Walter Scott.

FURTHER INFORMATION: Legend has it that a white rose bush still grows in the garden from which Bonnie Prince Charlie and the Jacobite army plucked blooms for their bonnets as they passed along Cant's Loan (now Newbattle Terrace) en route to Holyrood Palace. An old willow tree which grows against the Clinton Road wall is said to have been grown from a cutting

MORNINGSIDE

taken from Napoleon's garden on St Helena. East Morningside House is not open to the public.

FURTHER READING: M. Cullinan, *Susan Ferrier* (Twayne, 1985); N. Paxton, *Subversive Feminism: A Reassessment of Susan Ferrier's* Marriage, *Women and Literature* (1976).

BOOK LOVERS' EDINBURGH

77 FALCON AVENUE
St Peter's Church
Church of Father John Gray (1866–1934), inspiration for Dorian Gray in Oscar Wilde's *The Picture of Dorian Gray*

It is false art and false to human nature. Mr Wilde has brains, art, and style; but if he can write for none but outlawed noblemen and perverted telegraph boys, the sooner he takes to tailoring (or some other decent trade) the better for his own reputation and morals.
Critic W.E. Henley's response to *The Picture of Dorian Gray*

The only novel of Oscar Wilde (1854–1900), *The Picture of Dorian Gray*, was condemned when it was first published in 1890 as an affront on polite society and contributed to his downfall, which ended in his imprisonment for homosexuality in 1895. It tells the story of young, handsome and hedonistic Dorian Gray who, after having his portrait painted, dreams of remaining young forever while his painted visage grows old and corrupt. Offering up a prayer, he volunteers his soul in exchange for perpetual youth.

Left: John Gray when he was 'made of ivory and gold'
Right: St Peter's Church

There is no single person who can be defined as the original inspiration for Dorian Gray – Wilde knew many fascinating and beautiful young men – but his friendship with John Gray, with whom he had an intimate relationship and from whom he received letters signed 'Dorian',

MORNINGSIDE

leads us to believe that if Wilde was not modelling Dorian on John Gray, he was certainly out to beguile him. Wilde at this time was besotted with Gray, who recalled 'having received from someone' a letter stating, 'The world is changed because you are made of ivory and gold. The curves of your lips rewrite history.'

A poet, critic and playwright, John Gray's origins were very different from the London literati he courted in 1890s Victorian London. He was born in London, the son of a wheelwright and carpenter. On leaving school, he became a metal turner at Woolwich Arsenal. Self-educated, he passed his civil service examinations and took up the position of clerk in the Foreign Office library.

He first met Wilde in the summer of 1889 at a supper party in a Soho restaurant and has been described by George Bernard Shaw as 'one of the more abject of Wilde's disciples'. In 1893, Gray's *Silverpoints*, a book of 29 poems, was published by the Bodley Head, with Wilde agreeing to underwrite the costs. This was a contract from which Wilde later withdrew. By this time, Gray's relationship with Wilde was sidelined by the ascendancy of Wilde's latest lover, Lord Alfred Douglas; the jilted Gray told friends he was seriously contemplating suicide.

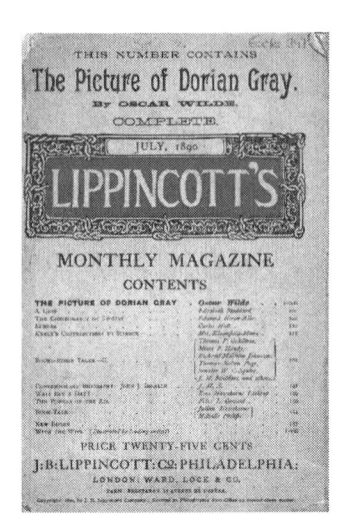

Left: The July, 1890 issue of *Lippincott's*, which first published *The Picture of Dorian Gray*
Right: The Revd John Gray c.1901

He was rescued from the depths of despair by an extremely wealthy Russian emigré Jew named André Raffalovich, who began publishing critical articles, poems and fiction and meeting many prominent men of letters in his 'at homes'. Raffalovich, now a Roman Catholic convert, fell in love with Gray. During these years, Gray and Raffalovich collaborated on several unsuccessful plays. Drawn towards Catholicism himself, Gray entered the Scots College in Rome in 1898 and was subsequently ordained as a priest. He served as curate initially at St Patrick's Church in the slum parish of Edinburgh's Cowgate.

Raffalovich was probably of the opinion that Gray deserved a lot better in life and made the archdioceses of St Andrews and Edinburgh an offer they couldn't refuse – a gift of the site and construction costs for a new church to be built in prospering middle-class Morningside, at a cost of around £5,500. There were no strings attached, except that he 'proposed' Gray as its new priest. No objections were raised.

What made Gray come to Scotland is a moot point. One obvious reason could have been that it was a very long way from London and the scandal of Wilde's trial and disgrace, although Gray's name was never mentioned in court. Who would think to connect a simple priest with the life of a dandy poet who once loved 'ponce and Sodomite' Oscar Wilde? And as Gray wrote himself in his 1931 elegy for Wilde: 'I warmed my hands and said aloud, I never knew the man.'

SEE ALSO: W.E. Henley.

FURTHER INFORMATION: Gray and Raffalovich are both buried at Mount Vernon Cemetery in Edinburgh. Gray is buried in the Priest's Circle, near the centre of the cemetery, where a circular arrangement of graves surrounds a large crucifix. The home of André Raffalovich, from 1907 until his death in 1934, was at 9 Whitehouse Terrace, Morningside.

MORNINGSIDE DRIVE
Morningside Cemetery
Grave of Alison Cunningham (1822–1913)
Devoted nurse of Robert Louis Stevenson

> *My second Mother, my first Wife,*
> *The angel of my infant life –*
> *From the sick child, now well and old,*
> *Take, nurse, the little book you hold!*

Robert Louis Stevenson,
'Dedication to Alison Cunningham from her boy',
A Child's Garden of Verses (1885)

She filled his head with bloodcurdling stories, pumped him full of puritan morals, sang him psalms, made him fear the Devil and was responsible in no short measure for fuelling his guilt-ridden, sin-soaked nightmares, but the ailing child who lay awake 'to weep for Jesus' probably owed his life to the double-edged sword that was Alison Cunningham. Known affectionately as 'Cummy', she was a formidable influence on the early life of RLS, who in adulthood wrote to her saying, 'You have made much that there is in me, just as surely as if you had conceived me.'
RLS's parents had worked their way through a succession of unsuitable nurses for their only child, one of whom had been dismissed for drinking in a public house with her charge. Alison Cunningham, who had probably never entered a pub in her life, let alone tasted alcohol, was hired as his nurse and surrogate mother in the spring of 1852, when he was 18 months old. She was a fisherman's daughter, from the village of Torryburn in Fife, and was brought up on a diet of porridge, Presbyterianism and the Covenanters. Cummy slept in the same room as Louis until he was almost ten years old, nursing him through

long nights of endless sickness: nights of hacking coughs, sweats and fevers. 'I remember with particular distinctness,' he recalled in *Memoirs of Himself* (1880), 'how she would lift me out of bed, and take me, rolled in blankets, to the window, whence I might look forth into the blue night starred with streetlamps, and see where the gas still burned behind the windows of other sick-rooms.'

When not stimulating his fears of hell or nursing him back to health, Cummy would take him for walks – often to the Royal Botanic Gardens or the cheery surrounds of Warriston Cemetery. *Cassell's Family Paper* was a regular purchase for them, enabling them to share the next thrilling instalment of their favourite adventure serial. She was friend, mentor and angel of mercy, and RLS never forgot the debt he owed her.

Cummy never married, but it was rumoured she once turned down a proposal of marriage because she was loath to part from her 'laddie'. She stayed with the Stevensons until 1871, when she left 'to keep her brother's house at Swanston'. In 1893, she lived at 23 Balcarres Street, ending her days with her cousin at 1 Comiston Place, where she died a Victorian icon in July 1913, aged 91.

SEE ALSO: Robert Louis Stevenson, St Giles.

FURTHER INFORMATION: The cemetery entrance on Morningside Drive is between Ethel Terrace and Dalhousie Terrace. On entering, take the first tree-lined path to the right. Cummy's white tombstone faces the left-hand edge of the path near the large war memorial.

'When Robert Louis Stevenson died,' wrote Julian Barnes in *Flaubert's Parrot*, 'his business-minded Scottish nanny quietly began selling hair which she claimed to have cut from the writer's head forty years earlier. The believers, the seekers, the pursuers bought enough of it to stuff a sofa.'

FURTHER READING: A. Cunningham, *Cummy's Diary* (1926).

CRAIGLOCKHART

219 COLINTON ROAD
Napier University Craiglockhart campus, formerly Craiglockhart War Hospital
Where soldier poets Siegfried Sassoon and Wilfred Owen were hospitalised during the First World War

Second Lieutenant
Siegfried Sassoon

CRAIGLOCKHART

> I am making this statement as an act of wilful defiance of military authority, because I believe the war is being deliberately prolonged by those who have the power to end it. I am a soldier, convinced that I am acting on behalf of soldiers. I believe that this war, upon which I entered as a war of defence and liberation, has now become a war of aggression and conquest. I believe that the purposes for which I and my fellow soldiers entered upon this war should have been so clearly stated as to have made it impossible to change them, and that, had this been done, the objects which actuated us would now be attainable by negotiation.
>
> I have seen and endured the suffering of the troops, and I can no longer be a party to prolong these sufferings for ends which I believe to be evil and unjust. I am not protesting against the conduct of the war, but against the political errors and insincerities for which the fighting men are being sacrificed. On behalf of those who are suffering now I make this protest against the deception which is being practised on them; also I believe that I may help to destroy the callous complacence with which the majority of those at home regard the continuance of agonies which they do not share, and which they have not sufficient imagination to realise.
>
> S. Sassoon, July 1917

Second Lieutenant Siegfried Sassoon (1886–1967) wrote his declaration of 'wilful defiance' whilst on convalescent leave after being wounded in France. He sent a copy of this statement to *The Times* and one to his colonel, fully prepared to accept that his action could result in a court martial. There was no question of cowardice. His war record was exemplary, even to the point of recklessness. His reputation for bravado on the battlefield earned him the nickname 'Mad Jack'. What probably saved him from a court martial was his friendship with fellow Welch Fusilier

BOOK LOVERS' EDINBURGH

Craiglockhart Hydropathic and staff during the First World War

CRAIGLOCKHART

Robert Graves (1895-1985), who got to know Sassoon while serving in France. Graves interceded and persuaded the military authorities to have Sassoon medically referred, and in July 1917 he was sent to Craiglockhart War Hospital, officially suffering from shell shock.

Formerly Craiglockhart Hydropathic which opened in 1880, this giant Italianate villa was requisitioned by the Army for use as a military hospital during the First World War. It was at Craiglockhart that Sassoon met poet Wilfred Owen (1893-1918), who was commissioned as a second lieutenant in the 5th Battalion, Manchester Regiment and was suffering from trench fever. Owen edited the hospital magazine *The Hydra* (a pun on Hydro) and nervously approached Sassoon to ask him to sign several copies of his 1917 collection of poems, *The Old Huntsman*. They soon struck up a friendship and Sassoon became a kind of mentor to Owen, regularly commenting on and criticising his poems. 'Anthem For Doomed Youth', written at Craiglockhart, especially interested Sassoon and his suggested amendments appear in his handwriting on the manuscript. While at Craiglockhart, Sassoon was 'treated' by the eminent Army psychologist W.H.R. Rivers (1864-1922), who had a reputation for curing shell-shocked soldiers compassionately. Sassoon's and Rivers's relationship at Craiglockhart was recounted in Pat Barker's acclaimed 1995 novel *Regeneration*, which was filmed in 1997 by Gillies MacKinnon, starring Jonathan Pryce as Rivers. 'Sassoon was the only one in Craiglockhart who didn't have shell shock,' says MacKinnon:

> He'd made this declaration against the war, even though he was an extremely brave and efficient soldier, so they sent him to a mental hospital to avoid having to court martial him. So Rivers has to take somebody who's entirely sane, and make him mad enough to go back and sacrifice himself for a cause he doesn't believe in.

Sassoon was eventually 'discharged to duty' on 26 November 1917 and returned to the front. He never forgot the support and faith Rivers gave him, and his influence on Sassoon can be discerned in the poems 'Revisitation', written after Rivers's death, and 'Repression of War Experience', written in July 1917.

Wilfred Owen arrived back in France on 31 August 1918 and was killed crossing the Sambre Canal on 4 November, a week before the armistice was signed. Only five of his poems were published during his lifetime.

> What passing-bells for these who die as cattle?
> Only the monstrous anger of the guns.
> Only the stuttering rifles' rapid rattle
> Can patter out their hasty orisons.
> No mockeries now for them; no prayers nor bells;
> Nor any voice of mourning save the choirs,
> The shrill, demented choirs of wailing shells;
> And bugles calling for them from sad shires.
>
> What candles may be held to speed them all?
> Not in the hands of boys, but in their eyes
> Shall shine the holy glimmers of goodbyes.
> The pallor of girls' brows shall be their pall;
> Their flowers the tenderness of patient minds,
> And each slow dusk a drawing-down of blinds.
>
> Wilfred Owen, 'Anthem for Doomed Youth'

CRAIGLOCKHART

FURTHER INFORMATION: During a fortnight of events in 1988 marking the 70th anniversary of the signing of the armistice on 11 November 1918, Napier University established the War Poets Collection, a commemorative collection within the library at the Craiglockhart campus, as a tribute to the poets of the Great War. Although the collection is centred on the lives and works of Wilfred Owen and Siegfried Sassoon, it also includes writings by other poets, such as Graves, Brooke and Blunden. The main purpose is to record the poets' work and to set it in its literary, historical and social context. The collection comprises in excess of 400 items and is on permanent display at Craiglockhart Campus Library.

FURTHER READING: J.M. Wilson, *Siegfried Sassoon: The Making of a War Poet* (Duckworth & Co., 2004); D. Hibberd, *Wilfred Owen* (Weidenfeld & Nicolson, 2002); P. Barker, *Regeneration* (Penguin, 1998). A disguised account of Craiglockhart appears in Sassoon's *Sherston's Progress* (Simon Publications, 2004).

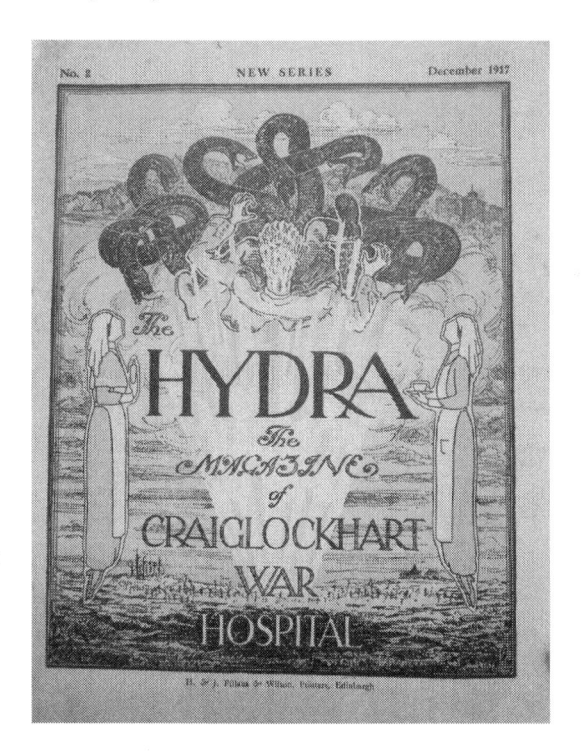

Left: Wilfred Owen
Right: December 1917 issue of *The Hydra*

GREENSIDE

PICARDY PLACE
Site of the birthplace of
Sir Arthur Conan Doyle (1859–1930)

The strain was something I could not endure any longer. Of course had I continued [to write Sherlock Holmes] *I could have coined money, for the stories were the most remunerative I have written; but as regards literature, they would have been mere trash.*
Conan Doyle, quoted in Stashower, *Teller of Tales* (1999)

Arthur Ignatius Conan Doyle, creator of the world's greatest fictional detective, was born on 22 May 1859, in a small flat at 11 Picardy Place (demolished in 1969). A bronze sculpture of Sherlock Holmes clutching his famous pipe, but minus his hypodermic syringe, now marks the site. Situated beside one of the city's busiest and noisiest road junctions, the gaslit streets, hansom cabs and grubby street urchins of Conan Doyle's era seem as remote as Mars.
Doyle is chiefly remembered today for his stories about the great sleuth, which, although they made him a fortune, also became a millstone round his neck. Few people today read his historical romances, the works he most wanted to be remembered for, and his obsession in later life with the occult greatly diminished his reputation and credibility.
Born of Irish-Catholic parentage, he was the second of ten children of Mary Foley and Charles Doyle, an assistant surveyor. Charles came from an artistic family and was himself a talented artist. All three of his brothers

Map of Picardy Place before the demolition of Conan Doyle's birthplace in 1969. The island of buildings where No 11 once stood was demolished to make way for a major traffic intersection (Map © Crispin Sage)

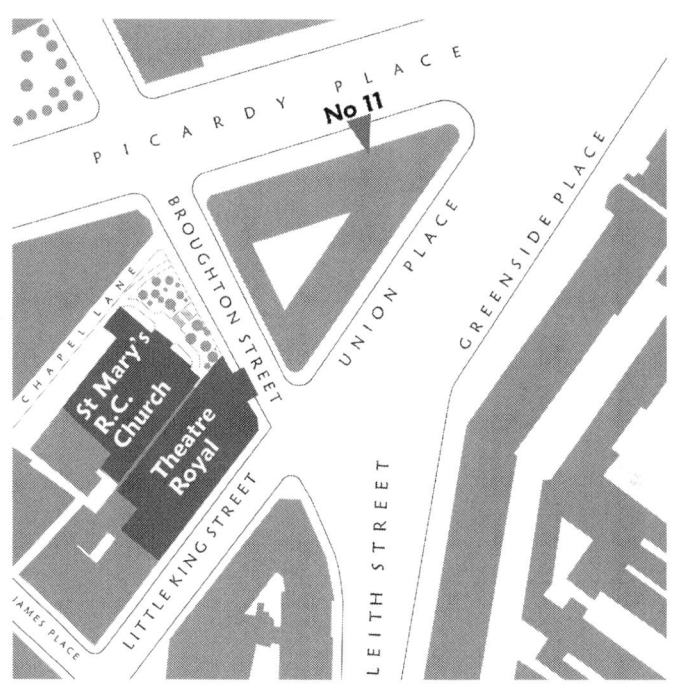

prospered in the art world; however, Charles, who was alcoholic and epileptic, did not. He was involved in designing a fountain at Holyrood Palace and a window at Glasgow Cathedral, and did occasional book illustration and sketching, but his career came to nothing. He was eventually institutionalised.

Conan Doyle described his mother in his autobiographical novel, *The Stark Munro Letters*, as having a 'sweet face' and being suggestive of 'a plump little hen'. She was known as 'the Ma'am', and was a voracious reader and storyteller. Conan Doyle recalled in his autobiography that 'as far back as I can remember anything at all, the vivid stories which she would tell me stand out so clearly that they obscure the real facts of life'.

The real 'facts of life' were that he had an alcoholic father to contend with, and life at home was a strain for all. In

Sherlock Holmes facing his creator's birthplace on Picardy Place

1868, when he was nine years old, his wealthy uncles sent him to a Jesuit boarding school in England – a move which may have lifted the stress of home life, but ended up destroying his Catholic faith. He went on to study medicine at Edinburgh, where the uncanny observational powers of his teacher, Dr Joseph Bell, made him the model for Sherlock Holmes. He received his Bachelor of Medicine and Master of Surgery qualifications in 1881, and after a short stint as a ship's medical officer, he set up as a GP in Southsea in 1882.

While still at university, he had his first short story published – 'The Mystery of Sasassa Valley' – in Edinburgh's *Chambers' Journal*, for which he was paid three guineas. Many other stories followed, usually resulting in a rejection slip. Doyle's income after his first year practising in Southsea was a mere £150. Patients were thin on the ground to begin with, and his consulting room was more a place in which to write stories than to consult.

The detective genre in 1886 had only been around for 40 years, and among the role models which were the inspiration for the Holmes character were Poe's Auguste Dupin and Emile Gaboriau's Monsieur Lecoq. On 8 March 1886, he began writing a story called 'A Tangled Skein', which introduced the characters Sherringford Holmes and Ormond Slacker. By April, the title had changed to 'A Study in Scarlet', and the characters had evolved into Sherlock Holmes and Dr Watson. After three rejections, it was accepted by Ward, Lock and Company. Doyle reluctantly sold the copyright for £25 and it was published as the main story in the November 1887 issue of *Beeton's Christmas Annual*. Shortly afterwards, it appeared in book form, with pen and ink drawings by Doyle's father. 'The Sign of Four' followed in 1890, but it wasn't until *The Strand* magazine published 'A Scandal in Bohemia', and subsequent monthly short stories, that the public developed an insatiable appetite for Sherlock Holmes. And so the legend was born, adding 100,000 copies to *The Strand*'s monthly circulation.

While churning out Holmes stories, Doyle was also busy working on his real love – historical fiction: *Micah Clarke* (1889), *The White Company* (1891), *Brigadier Gerard* (1896), *Rodney Stone* (1896) and *Sir Nigel* (1906). Later came *The Lost World* (1912) and the Professor Challenger stories. Although all these books were extremely competent literary efforts, they never eclipsed the popularity of Sherlock Holmes, much to the dismay of Doyle, who wanted so much to be remembered as a writer of 'quality' fiction.

Eighteen months after the appearance in *The Strand* of his first piece, Doyle was so fed up with his creation that he pitched Holmes over the Reichenbach Falls in 'The Final Problem'. This caused a tremendous public outcry. Doyle may have buried Holmes, but he also buried his bank account along with him. Eight years later, in 1902, he revived them both with *The Hound of the Baskervilles*. Shortly afterwards, the American magazine *Collier's Weekly* offered him a staggering $45,000 for 13 stories. Holmes was back, and he was here to stay.

Doyle stated in his 1924 autobiography, *Memories and Adventures*, that he was giving up his 'congenial and lucrative' writings for the psychic crusade, 'which will occupy, either by voice or pen, the remainder of my life'. In the Journal of the Society for Psychical Research, he claimed he had been contacted by Charles Dickens and asked if he would complete his unfinished novel, *The Mystery of Edwin Drood*. 'I shall be honoured, Mr Dickens,' Doyle replied to his spirit. As far as we know, Doyle never did carry out this project.

After his first wife's death from tuberculosis in 1906, he married Jean Leckie. Doyle died in 1930 and the couple are buried beneath an oak tree in All Saint's churchyard, Minstead, Hampshire.

GREENSIDE

SEE ALSO: Joseph Bell, Palace of Holyroodhouse, Holyrood Park, Rutherford's Howff, *Blackwood's Magazine*, Old College.

FURTHER INFORMATION: A Sherlock Holmes statue was erected on Picardy Place in 1991 marking Conan Doyle's birthplace. Conan Doyle stayed at various addresses in the city as a young medical student, including 2 Argyle Park Terrace and 32 George Square. Picardy Place is so called because it is the site of the village of Picardy formed by French refugees from the province of that name who came to Edinburgh after the revocation of the Edict of Nantes in 1685.

FURTHER READING: A.C. Doyle, *Memories and Adventures* (Oxford, 1989); J.D. Carr, *Life of Sir Arthur Conan Doyle* (Carroll & Graf, 2003); M. Booth, *The Doctor and the Detective* (Thomas Dunne Books, 2000); D. Stashower, *Teller of Tales* (Penguin, 2001); R.L. Green and J.M. Gibson, *A Bibliography of A. Conan Doyle* (Clarendon, 1983); J. Cooper, *The Case of the Cottingley Fairies* (Pocket Books, 1998).

Arthur with his father, Charles Doyle

1 BAXTER'S PLACE
Former home of Robert Stevenson (1772–1850) and birthplace of Thomas Stevenson (1818–87), grandfather and father of Robert Louis Stevenson

There is scarce a deep sea light from the Isle of May north about to Lerwick, but one of my blood designed it, and I have often thought that to find a family to compare with ours in the promise of immortal memory we must go back to the Egyptian Pharaohs.
Robert Louis Stevenson

1-3 Baxter's Place

GREENSIDE

Robert Stevenson, RLS's paternal grandfather, was the archetypal Victorian: a pious, right-wing, patriotic, power-house of a man, whose skill as an engineer ranks him alongside Brunel. He was involved in the design and construction of 23 Scottish lighthouses, notably the Bell Rock off Arbroath, and was also a consulting engineer for roads, railways, canals, bridges and harbours. He was born in Glasgow to Alan Stevenson, a merchant, and Jean Lillie, a builder's daughter. When he was only two, his father tragically died in the Caribbean, leaving his mother penniless. Thirteen years later, she married Thomas Smith, a ship owner, underwriter and engineer to the fledgling Board of Northern Lighthouses. Robert studied engineering in Glasgow and Edinburgh, eventually becoming his stepfather's partner. When he was 27, he married his 20-year-old stepsister, Jean Smith, 'a pious, tender soul' who bore him three sons – Alan, David and Thomas. 'The marriage of a man of 27 and a girl of 20 who have lived for 12 years as brother and sister is difficult to conceive', wrote RLS.

1 Baxter's Place (now numbered 1–3) was built in 1804 for Thomas Smith, and Robert inherited it on Smith's death, along with the business and his post as engineer to the Board of Northern Lighthouses. Robert died six months before his famous grandson was born, but RLS left us a nostalgic description of Baxter's Place:

> No. 1 Baxter's Place, my grandfather's house, must have been a paradise for boys. It was of great size, with an infinity of cellars below, and of garrets, apple-lofts, etc., above; and it had a long garden, which ran down to the foot of the Calton hill … There was a coming and going of odd, out-of-the-way characters, skippers, light-keepers, masons, and foremen of all sorts, whom my grandfather, in his patriarchal fashion, liked to have about the house, and who were a never-failing delight to the boys.

'The boys' were all destined to become engineers, and the family became known as 'The Lighthouse Stevensons'. Thomas, RLS's father, was a skilled and creative engineer, who invented the first wave dynamometer. Thomas and his brothers were educated at the old High School on Infirmary Street, and later at its new premises on Regent Road. RLS gave the following account of this in his *Memories and Portraits* (1887):

> He never seems to have worked for any class that he attended, and he drifted through school 'a mere consistent idler' ... he bravely encouraged me to neglect my lessons, and never so much as asked me my place in school. What a boy should learn in school, he used to say, is 'to sit upon his bum.' So were his days bound each to each by this natural suspicion and contempt for formal education.

Despite his loathing for school, Thomas forged himself a successful career in engineering. He never achieved the feats of his father, though, and is remembered more by history for siring his famous son, who wrote of him: 'When the lights come out at sundown along the shores of Scotland, I am proud to think they burn more brightly for the genius of my father!'

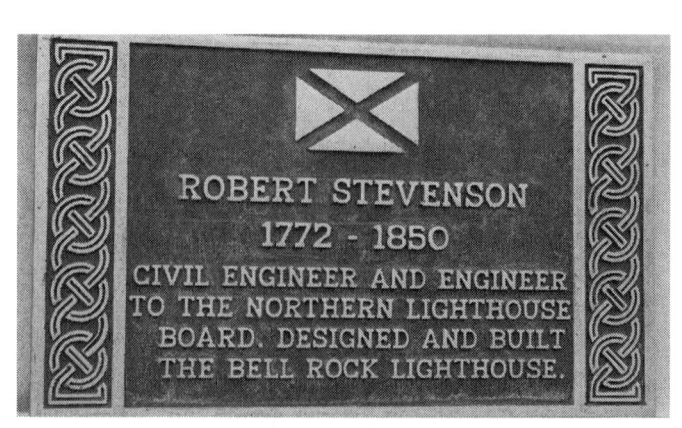

Left: Plaque at the entrance of 1-3 Baxter's Place
Right: Site of the former stationer's shop on the corner of Antigua and Union Street

GREENSIDE

SEE ALSO: Howard Place, Inverleith Terrace, Heriot Row, Pilrig House, Colinton Manse, Swanston Cottage, Glencorse Kirk, Rutherford's Howff, New Calton Cemetery, Old Calton Burial Ground, St Giles, Hawes Inn, Rullion Green, W.E. Henley, Alison Cunningham, Henderson's School, Deacon Brodie, The Writers' Museum, Kidnapped Statue, RLS Club, Museum of Scotland, George Mackenzie, Martyrs' Monument, Edinburgh Castle, Old College, Parliament Hall, Holyrood Park, Royal College of Surgeons' Museum, R.M. Ballantyne, RLS Memorial.

FURTHER INFORMATION: Baxter's Place was sold by the Stevenson family in 1856. The Stevensons' office was at the headquarters of the Commissioners of Northern Lights at 84 George Street. It was here that the map of Treasure Island was redrawn (the original having been lost) for inclusion in the first edition of 1883. The Stevenson family engineering papers are held in the National Library of Scotland, George IV Bridge.

Directly across the street from Baxter's Place, on the corner of Antigua Street and Union Street, there used to be a stationer's shop which RLS was fond of visiting as a child in which 'all the year round, there stood displayed a theatre' and where he would buy plays and sets for his own toy Skelt theatre. In his essay 'A Penny Plain and Twopence Coloured' (1887), Stevenson describes the excitement of his visits there.

FURTHER READING: C. Mair, *A Star for Seamen: The Stevenson Family of Engineers* (J. Murray, 1978); B. Bathurst, *The Lighthouse Stevensons* (Perennial, 2005).

2 GAYFIELD SQUARE
Gayfield Square Police Station
Home of the Historic Cases Unit
H.Q. of Detective Chief Inspector Karen Pirie, Val McDermid's fictional detective who solves the unsolvable

Nine o' clock and Karen was in the poky office at the back of the Gayfield Square station that housed the Historic Cases Unit. They were squeezed into the furthest corner, as if the high command wanted them out of sight and out of mind.
Val McDermid, from *Out of Bounds* (2016)

Val McDermid's novels have been translated into 30 languages and sold over ten million copies worldwide. Today she is one of the biggest names writing in the crime genre. Born in 1955, she grew up in a working class background in Kirkcaldy, on the east coast of Scotland. She attended Kirkcaldy High School and, at 17, became the first pupil from a Scottish state school to read English at St Hilda's College, Oxford, and one of the youngest undergraduates to have studied there. She always had a passion to write novels, but rather than risk starving in a garret, she joined the treadmill of journalism. She spent two years training in Devon, where she made her first attempt at writing a novel, and won the Trainee Journalist of the Year award. For the next 14 years she worked on national newspapers in Glasgow and Manchester. In 1984, after dabbling with writing drama, and being influenced by the new wave of American women crime writers, she began writing *Report for Murder*, featuring cynical lesbian journalist, Lindsay Gordon, which was published by The Women's Press in 1987. After having written nine books in five years she decided to quit her day job in April, 1991, and became a full-time writer.

GREENSIDE

Detail of Gayfield Square Police Station. A strong contender for the least photogenic police station in Scotland

BOOK LOVERS' EDINBURGH

Val McDermid

Most of her novels can be categorised into one of four series featuring the following characters: journalist, Lindsay Gordon; private investigator, Kate Brannigan; psychologist, Tony Hill, and Detective Chief Inspector Carol Jordan; and DCI Karen Pirie. She has also written a number of stand-alone novels, as well as collections of short stories and works of non-fiction. Edinburgh plays a role in many of her novels. In *Killing the Shadows*, geographic profiler Fiona Cameron stays at Channings Hotel in South Learmonth Gardens and walks around Comely Bank in the dark. In *A Darker Domain*, the second Karen Pirie novel, one of the characters, living in Marchmont because of its proximity to the Sick Children's Hospital where she has a very ill son, walks across the Meadows to a coffee shop on George IV Bridge. In *The Skeleton Road*, the third Karen Pirie novel, the story begins with the discovery of a human skeleton in a relatively inaccessible roof turret of a former Edinburgh private school. And in the fourth novel of the Karen Pirie series, *Out of Bounds*, much of the action takes place in Edinburgh, where Karen is now based in Gayfield Square Police Station, and has moved into a flat on Western Harbour Breakwater with stunning views over the Firth of Forth to her native Fife. Among the places she visits in this novel are the General Register

Office at the east end of Princes Street, the Thai restaurant on Craig's Close off Cockburn Street, Ryrie's pub at Haymarket, the Sheriff Court and the Restalrig Railway Path, where she has several surprising encounters.

In 2014 McDermid published *Northanger Abbey,* a reworking of Jane Austen's novel in the contemporary setting of the Edinburgh International Festival and the Scottish Borders. The book was part of HarperCollins' Austen Project, a series in which authors, including Joanna Trollope (*Sense and Sensibility*) and Alexander McCall Smith (*Emma*), tackled the retelling of Austen's six novels. Predictably, some critics condemned the idea of treading on hallowed ground, and in the words of Dorothy Parker, 'you can't teach an old dogma new tricks'. McDermid's *Northanger Abbey* is Jane Austen's comedy of manners with smartphones, Facebook, and bloodsucking vampires. But still, it's a young girl's voyage of discovery Austen would have loved – once, that is, she had been chaperoned through its haze of buzzwords and technology. 'Austen is such a shrewd reader of character,' wrote McDermid, 'the building blocks were all in place. All I had to do was find a contemporary equivalent for their concerns. John Thorpe is obsessed with impressing Catherine with his carriage; it was only a short leap of the imagination to think, "Ah. Top Gear." Then I was home and dry … What makes Jane Austen as relevant today as when she was scribbling quietly in a corner of the drawing room is that she understood what makes people tick. More than that, she found a way to tell us in continually developing ways. Austen truly is the gift that keeps on giving.'

In 2010 Val McDermid was awarded one of crime fiction's highest honours: the Crime Writers' Association Cartier Diamond Dagger for outstanding achievement.

SEE ALSO: Edinburgh International Book Festival, Conan Doyle, Ian Rankin, Quintin Jardine, James McLevy.

PILRIG

PILRIG STREET
Pilrig House
Birthplace of Lewis Balfour, grandfather of Robert Louis Stevenson

I was thus in the poorest of spirits, though still pretty resolved, when I came in view of Pilrig, a pleasant gabled house set by the walkside among some brave young woods. David Balfour arrives at Pilrig House in Stevenson's *Catriona* (1893)

RLS's maternal grandfather, Lewis Balfour, was born at Pilrig House in 1777, the third son of the second laird of Pilrig. The Balfours were a prosperous landowning family who had fingers in lots of pies, including the ill-fated Darien Company, which attempted colonising and trading in Central America in 1700. When the company collapsed, it left the Balfours almost ruined. In 1719, the government decided to compensate those who had lost their capital, and with their new-found wealth, James Balfour purchased the estate of Pilrig. James fathered 17 children and the eldest, also named James, was Lewis's father. James Balfour (1705–95) was an advocate, to whom his great-grandson gave immortality when he wove him into the plot of *Catriona*. He was also sheriff-substitute of Midlothian and famously held the chair of moral philosophy at Edinburgh University, denying the post to David Hume, whose religious scepticism ensured he was never in the running.

PILRIG

Pilrig House

'Some part of me played there in the eighteenth century,' wrote RLS in *Memories and Portraits* (1887), 'and ran races under the green avenue at Pilrig; some part of me trudged up Leith Walk, which was still a country place ... All this I had forgotten; only my grandfather remembered and once reminded me.' Lewis Balfour entered the ministry and married Henrietta Scott Smith. The couple moved to Colinton Manse in 1823, where RLS's mother, Margaret, was born in 1828.

SEE ALSO: David Hume, Howard Place, Inverleith Terrace, Heriot Row, Pilrig House, Colinton Manse, Swanston Cottage, Baxter's Place, Glencorse Kirk, Rutherford's Howff, New Calton Cemetery, Old Calton Burial Ground, St Giles, Hawes Inn, Rullion Green, W.E. Henley, Alison Cunningham, Henderson's School, Deacon Brodie, *Kidnapped* Statue, RLS Club, Museum of Scotland, George Mackenzie, Martyrs' Monument, Edinburgh Castle, Old College, The Writers' Museum, Parliament Hall, Holyrood Park, Royal College of Surgeons' Museum, R.M. Ballantyne, RLS Memorial.

FURTHER INFORMATION: Pilrig House was built in 1638 by Gilbert Kirkwood, a wealthy goldsmith who died of the plague. It was built on a ridge over the site of an old peel tower, hence the name Pilrig – the peel on the ridge. The best view of the house is from Pilrig Park, off Pilrig Street, but it can also be approached from the rear via Pilrig House Close. The Balfours worshipped at South Leith Parish Church, 6 Henderson Street, where the family is interred in the churchyard.

WEST END

PRINCES STREET
St John's Churchyard

St John's Church was erected in 1818 and designed by W. Burn, who copied many of the details from St George's Chapel at Windsor. One of the ministers at St John's was Revd Dean Ramsay, author of Reminiscences of Scottish Life and Character.

Grave of Anne Rutherford (1732–1819)
Sir Walter Scott's mother

Described by J.G. Lockhart as 'short of stature ... and by no means comely', Anne Rutherford was said to be plain-featured like her father, John Rutherford, professor of medicine at Edinburgh University. Her mother's family, the Swintons, were descendants of the Earls of Douglas. In April 1758, Anne married Walter Scott, a young solicitor, with whom she had twelve children, six of whom died in infancy. Her favourite child was 'wee Wattie', born in 1771, to whom she passed on her love of ballads, folk traditions and poetry. 'She was a strict economist,' Scott wrote to Lady Louisa Stuart, 'which she said enabled her to be liberal; out of her little income of about £300 a year she bestowed at least a third in well-chosen charities, and with the rest lived like a gentlewoman, and even with hospitality more general than seemed to suit her age; yet I could never prevail upon her to accept of any assistance.' She died aged 87 at 75 George Street.

WEST END

SEE ALSO: Birthplace of W.S., childhood home of W.S., townhouse of W.S., Lasswade Cottage, Parliament Hall, Greyfriars Kirkyard, The Heart of Midlothian, Scott Monument, Holyrood Park, The Writers' Museum, High School, Old College, Sciennes Hill House, Assembly Rooms, J.G. Lockhart, Portobello Sands, Canongate Kirkyard.

FURTHER INFORMATION: Anne Rutherford's grave is marked by a small white stone in the Dormitory Garden at the eastern end of the church.

St John's Church

5 LOTHIAN ROAD
St Cuthbert's Churchyard

The origins of St Cuthbert's are obscure, but in 1127 King David I granted a charter conferring all land below the Castle to St Cuthbert's. The land around the church has been a burial ground for over 1,000 years, but interments ceased at the end of the nineteenth century. In 1738, incidents of grave-robbing were becoming commonplace and the perimeter walls were raised to 8 ft. By 1803, it had become such a scourge that a crenellated watchtower was built to house guards throughout the night; this can still be seen today in the south-west corner of the churchyard.

The crenellated watchtower in St Cuthbert's graveyard

Grave of Susan Ferrier (1782–1854)
'Scotland's Jane Austen'

Much admired by Walter Scott, Ferrier's novels were as instructive as they were amusing. Although she is often compared to Jane Austen, the penetrating satire in her novels is probably more akin to Tobias Smollett. Her first novel, *Marriage*, published in 1818, tells of the marriage of Juliana to an impoverished Scottish officer. A novel of provincial social manners, it warns against impetuous and foolhardy marriage. Her other two novels are *The Inheritance* (1824) and *Destiny* (1831).

SEE ALSO: Former home of Susan Ferrier.

FURTHER INFORMATION: Susan Ferrier's tombstone is roughly in the centre of the wall opposite the Princes Street side of the church.

Grave of Thomas De Quincey (1785–1859)
Prolific opium-addicted essayist who influenced Edgar Allan Poe, Baudelaire and the French Symbolists

I have often been asked – how it was, and through what series of steps, that I became an opium-eater. Was it gradually, tentatively, mistrustingly, as one goes down a shelving beach into a deepening sea, and with a knowledge from the first of the dangers lying on that path; half-courting those dangers, in fact, whilst seeming to defy them?
Thomas De Quincey, from *Confessions of an English Opium-Eater* (1822)

Thomas De Quincey's life has become synonymous with two words – opium and debt – and outside his bestselling *Confessions of an English Opium-Eater*, which made his name, little of his work is ever discussed, perhaps because most of it was journalism, written to put bread on the table for his eight children. He was born into a wealthy family of Manchester textile merchants, the fifth of eight children. His father, who was of Norman descent, died when De Quincey was seven. An extremely bright but unhappy scholar, De Quincey ran away from school when he was 17 and ended up living on the streets of London. In 1804, he studied at Oxford – where he first used opium, as a relief from neuralgia – but left without taking his degree. In 1807, he met Samuel Taylor Coleridge (who also started taking opium for pain relief) in Bath, which led to his becoming acquainted with the Lakeland poets Wordsworth and Southey, and to his forming a close friendship with John Wilson (Christopher North). In 1809, he rented Dove Cottage in Grasmere, where he lived for ten years after it had been vacated by Wordsworth. He experimented with opium while living in the Lake District, but it was a series of illnesses in his late 20s which induced him to take copious doses of the painkiller laudanum, prepared from opium, which turned him into a habitual user.

In 1816, De Quincey married Margaret Simpson, with whom he had had an illegitimate child. By now, he was committed to trying seriously to earn money from his writings, as his family inheritance had dried up. He edited the local *Westmoreland Gazette* and in 1821 moved to London, where he wrote for *Blackwood's Magazine* and the *London Magazine*, publishing *Confessions of an English Opium-Eater* the following year to great acclaim. His Blackwood's connection, and spiralling debts, prompted the family, which had now swelled to eight children, to move to Edinburgh in 1826. He became encumbered by more and more debt, for which he was eventually imprisoned in 1831, and was convicted twice more in 1833 and three times in 1834, forcing him to take refuge in Edinburgh's Holyrood Abbey Sanctuary. One of his sons died aged two in 1832 and his wife died in 1837. As if this wasn't enough suffering for De Quincey, another of his sons died shortly afterwards fighting, ironically, in the Chinese Opium Wars.

In 1843, he retired with his family to a cottage in Polmont Bank, Lasswade, a village on the River Esk, south-east of Edinburgh, where he finished *The Logic of Political Economy* (1844) and wrote *Suspiria de Profundis* (1845), a sequel to *Confessions*. In 1850, he returned to Edinburgh, where he died on 8 December 1859, just as his collected works were about to be published; this knowledge must have brought him great satisfaction after such a tortuous and stressful life.

SEE ALSO: John Wilson, *Blackwood's Magazine*, the Palace of Holyroodhouse, Holyrood Abbey, James Thin.

WEST END

FURTHER INFORMATION: Entering from Lothian Road, walk straight down the path and turn right up the short steps just before the church. Follow the path round. De Quincey's grave is situated against the centre of the wall facing King's Stables Road. During his 30-odd years in the city, De Quincey resided at various addresses, including 1 Forres Street, 29 Ann Street (home of John Wilson), 9 Great King Street, 113 Princes Street, 71 Clerk Street, 42 Lothian Street (now demolished) and Mavis Bush Cottage, Lasswade.

FURTHER READING: G. Lindop, *Opium Eater: A Life of Thomas De Quincey* (Weidenfeld & Nicolson, 1993); E. Sackville West, *A Flame in Sunlight: The Life and Work of Thomas De Quincey* (Bodley Head Ltd, 1974); H.A. Eaton, *Thomas De Quincey* (1936).

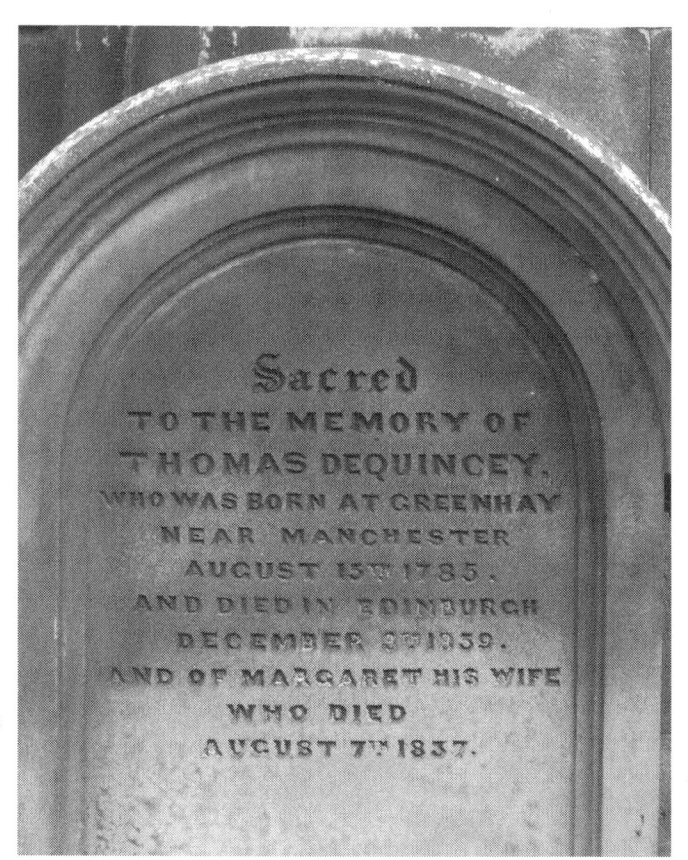

Final resting place of Thomas De Quincey

23 RUTLAND STREET
Former home of Dr John Brown (1810–82) Physician and essayist known as the 'Scottish Charles Lamb'

> They ken your name, they ken your tyke,
> They ken the honey from your byke;
> But mebbe after a' your fyke,
> (The truth to tell)
> It's just your honest Rab they like,
> An' no yoursel'.
> Robert Louis Stevenson,
> from 'To Doctor John Brown', *Underwoods* (1887)

Dr John Brown didn't leave the world much to remember his literary talents by, but what little he did leave ranks him amongst the world's foremost essayists. Most of his writings are contained in the three-volume *Horae Subsecivae* (*Leisure Hours*, 1858–82), which includes 'Our Dogs' (1862), 'Marjorie Fleming' (1863), 'Minchmore' (1864) and his masterpiece set in the streets of Edinburgh, 'Rab and his Friends' (1859), one of the best insights into the human nature of dogs ever written. Set in the days before anaesthetic (chloroform was first used in Edinburgh by obstetrician James Young Simpson in 1847), the following scene describes an operation at the city's Minto House Hospital which then stood on Chambers Street. A local carter's wife named Ailie has 'a kind o' trouble in her breest' and is operated on by surgeons in an amphitheatre filled with excited medical students. Also present in the theatre is her husband James and their dog Rab:

> The operating theatre is crowded; much talk and fun, and all the cordiality and stir of youth. The surgeon with his staff of assistants is there. In comes Ailie: one look at

her quiets and abates the eager students. That beautiful old woman is too much for them; they sit down, and are dumb, and gaze at her. These rough boys feel the power of her presence. She walks in quickly, but without haste; dressed in her mutch, her neckerchief, her white dimity short-gown, her black bombazine petticoat, showing her white worsted stockings and her carpet shoes. Behind her was James with Rab. James sat down in the distance, and took that huge and noble head between his knees. Rab looked perplexed and dangerous; forever cocking his ear and dropping it as fast.

Ailie stepped up on a seat, and laid herself on the table, as her friend the surgeon told her; arranged herself, gave a rapid look at James, shut her eyes, rested herself on me, and took my hand. The operation was at once begun; it was necessarily slow; and chloroform – one of God's best gifts to his suffering children – was then unknown. The surgeon did his work. The pale face showed its pain, but was still and silent. Rab's soul was working within him; he saw that something strange was going on, – blood flowing from his mistress, and she suffering; his ragged ear was up, and importunate; he growled and gave now and then a sharp impatient yelp; he would have liked to have done something to that man. But James had him firm, and gave him a GLOWER from time to time, and an intimation of a possible kick; all the better for James, it kept his eye and his mind off Ailie.

It is over: she is dressed, steps gently and decently down from the table, looks for James; then, turning to the surgeon and the students, she courtesies, and in a low, clear voice begs their pardon if she has behaved ill. The students – all of us – wept like children; the surgeon happed her up carefully, and, resting on James and me, Ailie went to her room, Rab following. We put her to bed.

BOOK LOVERS' EDINBURGH

The son of a minister, John Brown was born in Biggar and moved to Edinburgh in 1822, aged 12, where he was educated at the old High School and the University of Edinburgh. He qualified as an MD and lived for 60 years in Edinburgh, counting among his friends Francis Jeffrey, Ruskin, Thackeray and Mark Twain.

He became acquainted with Samuel Clemens (Mark Twain) in the summer of 1873 when the Clemenses visited Edinburgh and resided at Veitch's Hotel, 125 George Street. Mrs Clemens took ill on her arrival, and Samuel, who knew of Dr John Brown, obtained his address and consulted him. Under Dr Brown's care, she made a swift recovery and for almost a month the couple were his close companions, accompanying him on his rounds almost daily. The Clemenses would bring along books to read while they waited, and Dr Brown would comment, 'Entertain yourselves while I go in and reduce the population.' Samuel Clemens described Dr Brown as having 'a sweet and winning face, as beautiful a face as I have ever known. Reposeful, gentle, benignant; the face of a saint at peace with all the world and placidly beaming upon it the sunshine of love that filled his heart'. Dr Brown died on 11 May 1882, aged 71.

SEE ALSO: Scott Monument, Royal High School, Old College, Francis Jeffrey, Mark Twain.

Left: Dr Brown
with the Clemenses
in 1873
Right: 23 Rutland
Street

WEST END

10 RANDOLPH CRESCENT
Birthplace of writer
Naomi Mitchison (1897–1999)

I know I can handle words, the way other people handle colours or computers or horses.
Naomi Mitchison, *Saltire Self-Portraits*

Socialist, feminist, traveller, birth-control and anti-nuclear campaigner, Naomi Mitchison broke all the rules, wrote over 70 books and lived until she was 101. Her work included poetry, plays, travel writing, children's fiction, short stories and biography, but she will be best remembered for her historical fiction.

She was born on 1 November 1897, the daughter of physiologist John Scott Haldane and suffragist Kathleen Trotter, and was brought up in Oxford. She attended the (boys) Dragon School until she began to menstruate and her education was continued at home with a governess. In 1916, she married her brother's friend, Dick Mitchison. This was a marriage which was reputedly a happy one, but nonetheless an 'open' one. Dick became Labour MP for Kettering, Northamptonshire (1945–64) and was later Lord Mitchison. The couple had seven children.

Inspired by a diary she kept of her dreams and Gibbon's *Decline and Fall*, she wrote her first book, *The Conquered* (1923), set during Caesar's Gallic Wars and mirroring the 1920s situation in Ireland. Her epic historical novel *The Corn King and the Spring Queen* (1931) is set in the Greek city states of Athens and Sparta, and a visit to the Soviet Union in 1932 produced *We Have Been Warned* (1935), depicting a rape, a seduction, an abortion and contraception. She travelled extensively, and in 1963 the Bakgatha of Botswana made her their tribal adviser and 'mother'. During her life, her friends included Neil Gunn, W.H.

WEST END

Auden, Doris Lessing, Aldous Huxley, Stevie Smith and E.M. Forster. Mitchison was actively involved in Scottish politics and stood as Labour candidate for the Scottish Universities in 1935. In 1937, she bought Carradale, an estate on the Mull of Kintyre, where she was still living and writing 50 years later, commenting, 'so long as I can hold a pencil, let me go on.'

FURTHER READING: Naomi Mitchison published three volumes of autobiography: *Small Talk* (House of Lochar, 2000), *All Change Here* (Bodley Head Ltd, 1975) and *You May Well Ask* (Flamingo, 1986); and two volumes of diaries: *Vienna Diary* (1934), *Among You Taking Notes* (Weidenfeld & Nicolson, 2000); J. Calder, *The Nine Lives of Naomi Mitchison* (Virago, 1997).

Naomi Mitchison c. 1920

8 EGLINTON CRESCENT
Birthplace of Fred Urquhart (1912–95)
Novelist and short-story writer

Time ... something that cannot be measured by days or months or by years, for yesterday may not be so clear as a day twenty years ago, and something said five minutes ago can be forgotten, while words spoken when you were young are still ringing in your ears ...
Fred Urquhart, *Time Will Knit* (1938)

Time Will Knit was the first novel of Edinburgh writer Fred Urquhart, written when he was 26 years old. It tells the story of Mirren and Wattie Gillespie who live in the small, decayed fishing port of Harrisfield on the Forth and who, after 50 years, are about to be evicted from their crumbling cottage in 1929. Although the novel is set in fictional Harrisfield, it is clearly inspired by the Granton of Urquhart's childhood, which is situated to the north of Edinburgh on the Firth of Forth, about a mile west of Newhaven (Forthport in the book), and three miles from the city centre.

In 1919, Urquhart's family moved from his birthplace at 8 Eglinton Crescent in Edinburgh's west end to 37 West Cottages, Granton. Now demolished, the cottages were located opposite Granton Harbour, between the Middle and West Piers. The book was outspoken for its day and didn't flinch when discussing taboo subjects such as homosexuality, premarital sex, the dysfunctional Royal Family and the futility of the First World War, which takes the Gillespies' two sons:

> Medals! ... You got some satisfaction from seeing the flames lick the coloured red, white and blue ribbons into ashes. You felt as if it really were the men who had

started the war who were burning in hellfire. And you laughed as you watched them burn.

Fred Urquhart left school at 15 and worked at various jobs. As well as being employed as a labourer and a tailor's assistant, he did a seven-year stint as a bookseller's assistant at Cairns' Bookshop in Teviot Place. Later, he became a publisher's reader, London scout for Walt Disney and literary editor of *Tribune*. His first published story was 'The Daft Woman in Number Seven', published by Adelphi in 1936. Other novels include *The Ferret Was Abraham's Daughter* (1949), *Jezebel's Dust* (1951) and *Palace of Green Days* (1979). He also published 11 collections of short stories.

BOOK LOVERS' EDINBURGH

16 CHARLOTTE SQUARE
Former home of Sir Patrick Heron Watson, Conan Doyle's inspiration for Dr Watson

Nobody in Scotland is willing to die till they have seen Watson.
(Anon.)

Conan Doyle's inspiration for Sherlock Holmes' devoted sidekick, Dr Watson, was his former teacher, forensic expert Dr Patrick Heron Watson. A son of the manse, Watson was one of the four surviving sons of Revd Charles Watson, who had been a minister at Burntisland in Fife.

Dr Patrick Watson

His third son, Patrick, was born in Edinburgh in 1832, graduating in medicine at Edinburgh University in 1853. Shortly after the completion of his term as house surgeon at Edinburgh's Royal Infirmary he joined the Royal Army Medical Corps in 1855 for service in the Crimean War. Before embarking for action he bought himself a uniform, a lamp, a robe of lynx skin, a raccoon coat coming down to his ankles, fur boots and a revolver. On reaching Constantinople he was posted to the military hospital at Scutari. Writing home to his mother he recalled the grim conditions of a barrack hospital: 'The deaths in the Barrack Hospital amount to 50 a day. They are carted off, sewn up in blankets, in arabahs [Turkish carts, drawn by bullocks] and laid in layers in trenches; officers are distinguished only by having a white-wood coffin. My first view of this was an arabah upset in the mud with the bodies all in a heap.' During Watson's first month at the hospital, 300 out of 1,200 patients, one in every four, died, the majority of fever, dysentery or other infection, much originating within the hospital itself, his theatre of operations for the next five months. 'The nuns are far better than the nurses,' he wrote, 'and if I were ill I would rather have a nun to attend me. Some of the nurses have had fever and upon my word they are almost no loss. A bevy of good cooks would be a good deal more useful and not half so troublesome.' He was also displeased concerning 'the absurd puff about Miss Nightingale in *The Times* of 8 February, where it speaks about her angelic form. From what I have seen of her, which certainly has been in the distance, she is a very dowdy old maid, about whom the less romance the better.' Nine months later Watson was shipped home following attacks of typhus and dysentery.

In 1856 he returned to Edinburgh and became private assistant to James Miller, Professor of Surgery, whose daughter he later married, and in 1860 was appointed assistant surgeon in Edinburgh Royal Infirmary, becoming a full surgeon in 1863. In 1858 he became lecturer on surgery in the extramural school of medicine of the Royal Colleges of Medicine and Surgery, and it was while in this post, which he held for many years, that Conan Doyle would have had contact with him.

Although no friend of Florence Nightingale and the nurses of the Crimea, Watson was an early pioneer for the medical education of women and was one of the first to open his class of surgery in the extramural school to women students.

A fellow surgeon and contemporary of Watson, described him after his passing in 1907: 'His old house-surgeons will remember his military walk; correct attire; neat, plainly written notes; ready command of language peculiarly his own; his courteous manner; his independence of character. We will revere those memories for we loved the man.'

SEE ALSO: Joseph Bell, Conan Doyle.

NEW TOWN

3 ROSE STREET
The Abbotsford
Regular watering-hole of Hugh MacDiarmid (1892–1978) and the poets of the Scottish Renaissance

I'll hae nae hauf-way hoose, but aye be whaur Extremes meet
Hugh MacDiarmid, from *A Drunk Man Looks at the Thistle* (1926)

During the 1950s and early '60s, Hugh MacDiarmid was the centre of a group of Scottish Renaissance poets who met regularly in the city's pubs. Meeting initially in the Cafe Royal in West Register Street, they later moved along the road to the Abbotsford, then Milnes Bar and latterly the Oxford Bar in Young Street. All are still excellent howffs and little changed, apart from Milnes, which bears no resemblance today to its 'poet's pub' heyday. The

Abbotsford, named after Scott's mock-Baronial mansion in the Scottish Borders, was built between 1880 and 1910. It has steadfastly refused to opt for the fashionable tartan tat decor of many city-centre pubs and remains a bastion of traditional ales, malts and good pub grub – hence the attraction for MacDiarmid, Sydney Goodsir Smith, Robert Garioch, Norman MacCaig and many other poets of the Scottish Renaissance.

Regarded as the greatest of twentieth-century Scottish poets and, by many, the greatest of all poets in the Scots tradition, Hugh MacDiarmid's interpretation of the Scottish consciousness through his baiting and unsentimental verse helped Scotland recognise its true self. He became the catalyst of the Scottish Renaissance, which strove to detach itself from the romantic and nostalgic Scottish literature of the nineteenth century and establish Scottish writing as a contemporary force, and in so doing revitalised Scottish poetry.

MacDiarmid was born Christopher Murray Grieve on 11 August 1892, in Langholm, Dumfriesshire, 'the wonderful little Border burgh' just a few miles from England. The son of a postman, he attended Langholm Academy, and in 1908 he became a pupil-teacher at Broughton Higher Grade School in Edinburgh. For some years, he worked as a journalist for newspapers in Scotland and Wales. He became active in left-wing politics and in 1915 he joined the Royal Army Medical Corps, serving in Salonika, Italy and France. Invalided home with cerebral malaria, he married June Skinner in 1918. On demobilisation, he joined the staff of the *Montrose Review*, and started writing poetry that soon began to be noticed.

Between 1920 and 1922, he edited three volumes of *Northern Numbers*, and in August 1922 he founded the periodical *Scottish Chapbook*, which became a platform for talented Scots poets, including himself, now writing under the pseudonym Hugh MacDiarmid. The *Scottish*

Chapbook became dedicated to the furthering of a Scottish Renaissance, using Scots as a serious medium of poetic expression, liberating it from the Kailyard, comic verse and pseudo-Burnsian mawkishness. The 'golden lyrics' of *Sangschaw* (1925) and *Penny Wheep* (1926) were his first collections of mainly Scots poems. In 1926, he published his dramatic masterpiece *A Drunk Man Looks at the Thistle*, a meditation which defines and analyses the state of the Scottish nation. Next came *To Circumjack Cencrastus* (1930), an even longer poem-sequence.

He founded the Scottish Centre of PEN in 1927 and helped to found the National Party of Scotland in 1928. In 1934, he joined the Communist Party, but was expelled in 1938, and only rejoined in 1957 after the Russians invaded Hungary – a time when others were deserting the party. Grieve lived in Montrose until 1929, where he served as a Labour councillor. In 1929, he left for London to edit Compton Mackenzie's doomed radio magazine *Vox*. In 1932, he divorced his first wife and married Cornish girl Valda Trevlyn. Shortly afterwards, they moved to the island of Whalsay in Shetland, where they lived until 1941. During the war, he was a labourer on Clydeside and later entered the Merchant Service. In 1951, the Grieves, together with their only son, moved to Brownsbank Cottage, near Biggar, where, for the next ten years, they lived without water except from an outside pump, without electric light and without kitchen or bathroom. After this, conditions gradually improved, and MacDiarmid lived here until his death in 1978. Towards the end of his life, MacDiarmid evolved into a Scottish institution. His genius was recognised and rewarded, though never financially, and he is now rightly regarded as one of Scotland's greatest poets.

Other publications include the three *Hymns to Lenin* (1931, 1932, 1957), *Scots Unbound* (1932), *Stony Limits* (1934), and *A Kist of Whistles* (1947). His autobiography was published in *Lucky Poet* (1943) and *The Company I've Kept* (1966). His *Complete Poems* was published in 1976.

SEE ALSO: Sydney Goodsir Smith, Robert Garioch, Norman MacCaig, Oxford Bar.

FURTHER INFORMATION: Milnes Bar at 35 Hanover Street, the pub which held such an attraction to the poets of the Scottish Renaissance, along with others including Alan Bold, Stevie Smith, Dylan Thomas, W.H. Auden and George Mackay Brown, disappeared years ago. Modern refurbishment has totally eradicated the character and atmosphere which made it so appealing, and all that remains are a few portraits of poets hanging on its sanitised walls.

FURTHER READING: A. Bold, *Hugh MacDiarmid: A Biography* (Uni. of Massachusetts Press, 1990).

Sydney Goodsir Smith and Hugh MacDiarmid in The Abbotsford (© Michael Peto)

EAST PRINCES STREET GARDENS
The Scott Monument
A memorial to Sir Walter Scott
(1771-1832)

Following his death in 1832, there was a growing desire that something should be built in the city to commemorate Scott's enormous contribution to Scottish literature. J.G. Lockhart, Scott's biographer and son-in-law, proposed the erection of 'a huge Homeric Cairn on Arthur's Seat – a land and sea mark'. Many other suggestions were mooted, and eventually a competition was organised for the best-designed monument. Fifty-four plans were submitted, including twenty-two Gothic structures, fourteen Grecian temples, eleven statues, five pillars, an obelisk and a fountain.

The winning design was submitted by Biggar-born draughtsman and self-taught architect George Meikle Kemp (1795-1844), who drew up his plan in five days. Kemp probably thought his humble origins and lack of eminence might prejudice his chances of winning, and shrewdly submitted his design to the selecting committee under the pseudonym John Morvo, the medieval master-mason of Melrose Abbey, from which he admitted that the inspiration for his design 'was in all its details derived'. Tragically, Kemp died before the completion of the monument, when he drowned in mysterious circumstances in the Union Canal at Fountainbridge on the evening of 6 March 1844.

The 200-ft high monument, with two hundred and eighty-seven steps to its pinnacle, incorporating three Scottish monarchs, sixteen poets and sixty-four of Scott's characters into its design, was officially inaugurated fourteen years after Scott's death, on 15 August 1846. The twice-life-size statue of Scott at its base was sculpted by Sir

NEW TOWN

John Steell (1804–1901) in white Carrara marble, which skilfully camouflages the seagull guano deposited daily on his noble brow. Charles Dickens disliked the structure, commenting in 1847 that he was 'sorry to report the Scott Monument a failure. It is like the spire of a Gothic church taken off and stuck in the ground.' John Ruskin was of a similar view in 1873: 'The wise people of Edinburgh built a small vulgar Gothic steeple on the ground, and called it the Scott Monument.'

SEE ALSO: Birthplace of W.S., childhood home of W.S., townhouse of W.S., Lasswade Cottage, Parliament Hall, Greyfriars Kirkyard, St John's Kirkyard, The Heart of Midlothian, Holyrood Park, The Writers' Museum, High School, Old College, Sciennes Hill House, Assembly Rooms, J.G. Lockhart, Portobello Sands, Canongate Kirkyard, Dr John Brown.

FURTHER INFORMATION: George Kemp is buried in St Cuthbert's Curchyard at the West End of Princes Street, in the plot behind the former Mission Hall.

George Meikle Kemp's Gothic extravagance to Walter Scott. It is the largest monument to any writer, living or dead, anywhere in the world

61 PRINCES STREET
John Menzies' first bookshop

> *There was a young lady called Menzies*
> *Who asked, 'Do you know what this thenzies?'*
> *Her aunt with a gasp*
> *Replied, 'It's a wasp,*
> *And you're holding the end where the stenzies.'*
> (Menzies is pronounced Ming-iss, with
> the primary stress on the first syllable.)

John Menzies was a name synonymous with the book trade in Edinburgh for over 150 years. Born in 1808, he was educated at the old High School and, between 1823 and 1830, he was an apprentice with Sutherland the booksellers on Regent Road. Here, he worked a 14-hour day, an 84-hour week and, during the one hour he was granted for lunch, he was not expected to stop work while eating it. After his seven-year apprenticeship, he worked as a bookseller's assistant in London for a couple of years before returning to Edinburgh in 1833 following the death of his father. With fourteen pounds in his pocket, a stepmother and two sisters to support, life didn't promise to be a bowl of cherries.

The safest route would have been to gain regular employment, but instead he took a gamble and rented No. 61, a shop at the corner of Princes Street and Hanover Street (since renumbered) at the centre of the city's bookselling trade, where he became involved in all aspects of the business, most notably as a wholesale distributor of books to the trade. He also began publishing books and engravings, and selling *The Scotsman* newspaper – uniquely for his day, as newspapers were normally obtained by subscription from their publishers. It wasn't long until he prospered, and in 1837 he hired his first employees.

By the mid-1800s, the railways covered most of Scotland and passengers were buying books and magazines for their journeys. In 1857, Menzies began acquiring bookstalls on stations, and in 1862, outbidding previous leaseholder William Henry (W.H.) Smith, he offered an annual rent of £180 a year for the Waverley Station bookstall, giving him the right to sell 'books, pamphlets and newspapers' on the understanding that he would 'not sell any book objectionable in its moral character or tendency'.

In 1845, he married Rossie Marr, a Leith merchant's daughter, with whom he had two sons and three daughters. His sons carried on the dynasty, which grew into a sizeable empire with its largest branch at 107 Princes Street employing over a hundred assistants during the 1990s. Since it sold off its retail stores to WH Smith in 1999, John Menzies has ceased to be a familiar high-street name, but still thrives today as a major wholesaler and distributor of newspapers and magazines. John Menzies is buried in Warriston Cemetery.

FURTHER READING: L. Gardiner, *The Making of John Menzies* (Edinburgh Bartholomew, 1983).

John Menzies delivery van in 1910

32 CASTLE STREET
Birthplace of Kenneth Grahame
Children's writer and author of *The Wind in the Willows*

The Mole was bewitched, entranced, fascinated. By the side of the river he trotted as one trots, when very small, by the side of a man who holds one spellbound by exciting stories; and when tired at last, he sat on the bank, while the river still chattered on to him, a babbling procession of the best stories in the world, sent from the heart of the earth to be told at last to the insatiable sea.
Kenneth Grahame, *The Wind in the Willows*

Since it was first published in 1908, *The Wind in the Willows* has appeared in over 100 editions and the riverside adventures of Rat, Mole, Badger and Toad now constitute an established children's classic, ranking Kenneth Grahame alongside Edward Lear and Lewis Carroll.
Born on the morning of 8 March 1859 at 32 Castle Street, Kenneth Grahame had in attendance none other than Queen Victoria's 'beloved professor of chloroform fame', Dr James Simpson. His father was James Cunningham Grahame, an Edinburgh lawyer, and his mother was Bessie Inglis from Lasswade. Kenneth was the third of four children in what was initially a happy and loving family home. In 1860, his father was appointed sheriff-substitute of Argyllshire at Inverary and the family moved to the Highlands. In 1864, after Bessie gave birth to Roland, her fourth child, she contracted scarlet fever and died. Her last words were, 'It's all been so lovely.' As a consequence of Bessie's death, Kenneth's father sent all his children to be reared by their maternal grandmother at Cookham Dene, Oxfordshire. From this time onwards, James Grahame's life fell apart through alcoholism and a broken

Kenneth Grahame in the 1890s

heart. He resigned his post in 1867 and went to live in France for the next 20 years, where he died alone.

Schooled in Oxford, and denied the chance of a university education because of the financial cost, Kenneth began his career, albeit reluctantly, as a gentleman-clerk at the Bank of England, in London's Threadneedle Street, on 1 January 1879. Around this time, he began to jot down quotations, anecdotes, poems and prose in an old bank ledger, and London editors first began to publish his essays and articles in 1887. His first known published work was a country essay entitled 'By a Northern Furrow' which appeared in the *St James's Gazette*. He also contributed to Henry Harland's *The Yellow Book* and various publications edited by W.E. Henley. His first book was a collection of essays and tales, *Pagan Papers* (1893), and he followed this with *The Golden Age* (1895) and *Dream Days* (1898) – collections of classic essays about Victorian childhood.

In 1898, aged 39, he was promoted to the post of secretary

of the Bank of England – one of the youngest on record – by which time his literary works had become so popular that he was a household name. In 1899, he married Elspeth Thompson and the following year she gave birth to their only child, Alistair, nicknamed 'Mouse'. Unfortunately, he was born semi-blind due to a congenital cataract of the right eye. *The Wind in the Willows* began as bedtime stories for Mouse around 1904 and later continued as a series of letters to him from spring to autumn of 1907. The story depicts themes close to Grahame's heart: vanishing rural landscapes and the shrinking boundaries of country life provoked by advancing agricultural mechanisation, the railways and the motor car. Grahame based his tale on the stretch of the Thames which runs from Marlow to Pangbourne concentrated around Cookham Dene, where he had spent the golden days of his childhood. Publishers were sceptical of the finished manuscript. However, after many rejections, it was eventually published by Methuen, who offered no advance but agreed to 'excellent rising royalties'. The reviews on publication were lukewarm, as this example from the *Times Literary Supplement* of 22 October 1908 demonstrates:

> *The Wind in the Willows* (Methuen 6s.) is a book with hardly a smile in it, through which we wander in a haze of perplexity, uninterested by the story itself and at a loss to understand its deeper purpose … For ourselves, we lay *The Wind in the Willows* reverently aside.

Fortunately, the reading public made sense of it, as did novelist Arnold Bennett, who summed the book up perfectly: 'The book is an urbane exercise in irony at the expense of the English character and of mankind. It is entirely successful.'

Tragedy struck the Grahames on the night of Friday, 7 May 1920 when Alistair, then an undergraduate at

Christchurch, was struck by a train and killed. His body had been decapitated and suicide was suspected, although never proven.

After a short stroll on Tuesday, 5 July 1932, Kenneth Grahame retired to bed with Walter Scott's *The Talisman*. Around 6 a.m. the following morning, he suffered a cerebral haemorrhage from which he never regained consciousness. He is buried in Holywell Churchyard, Oxford. Over the grave is carved an inscription composed by his novelist cousin, Anthony Hope: 'To the beautiful memory of Kenneth Grahame, husband of Elspeth and father of Alistair, who passed the River on 6 July 1932, leaving childhood and literature through him the more blest for all time.'

SEE ALSO: W.E. Henley.

FURTHER READING: P. Green, *Beyond the Wild Wood: The World of Kenneth Grahame* (Webb & Bower, 1982).

E.H. Shepard's illustration of Ratty and Mole on the river from the 1931 edition of *The Wind in the Willows*

39 NORTH CASTLE STREET
Townhouse of Sir Walter Scott (1771–1832)

That d—d Sir Walter Scott, that everybody makes such a work about! ... I wish I had him to ferry over Loch Lomond: I should be after sinking the boat, if I drowned myself into the bargain; for ever since he wrote his Lady of the Lake, as they call it, everybody goes to that filthy hole Loch Katrine, then comes round by Luss, and I have had only two gentlemen to guide all this blessed season.
Loch Lomond ferryman, after publication of Scott's *The Lady of the Lake* in 1810

Walter Scott married French émigrée Charlotte Carpenter on Christmas Eve 1797 and the couple took temporary lodgings on the second floor of 108 George Street for a few weeks before moving into 10 Castle Street, which was soon exchanged for 39 North Castle Street, where they lived until 1826. Scott, now in his late 20s, was beginning to settle down in life. The income from his Bar earnings, his wife's allowances, his father's estate (his father died in 1799) and his newly appointed post as sheriff-deputy of Selkirkshire was bringing in around £1,000 a year. In 1796, he published his translation of Gottfried Burger's *The Chase*, and *William and Helen*, the first publication to bear his name. His writing hobby was now absorbing him more and more, and law was becoming a chore, but there was never any question of devoting his life entirely to the Muses. His father's advice – that literature was a good staff but a bad crutch – was wise counsel not forgotten.

His wanderings in the Border country inspired him to start collecting the region's ancient and rapidly disappearing ballads, which he believed would soon be lost forever if not properly recorded. With the assistance of Border wordsmiths John Leyden and James Hogg, *The Minstrelsy of the Scottish Border* appeared in 1802–3, printed in Kelso by Scott's old schoolfriend James Ballantyne.

Between 1799 and 1805, Charlotte gave birth to two sons and two daughters. In the autumn of 1804, the family moved to Ashiestiel, near Clovenfords, the sheriff being bound by statute to reside for part of the year in the Borders. North Castle Street was kept on as a winter residence. It was at Ashiestiel that Scott wrote the works which turned him into a celebrated poet: *The Lay of the Last Minstrel* (1805), *Marmion* (1808) and *The Lady of the Lake* (1810).

In 1806, he became principal clerk to the Court of Session in Edinburgh, which meant he no longer needed to practise as an advocate. In 1809, he became a secret partner in James Ballantyne's printing business, a rash move for which he would later pay dearly.

Byron was beginning to eclipse Scott as a poet, and, wisely, Scott turned his talents to novel writing. *Waverley*, his first novel, was published by Constable anonymously on 7 July 1814, and was staggeringly successful, much to Scott's surprise. The impact the novel had on the literary world at that time is difficult to take in today, but it was a literary phenomenon which caused a sensation around the world. With one book, Scott had established the form of the modern historical novel, a genre which did not exist before, and, perhaps more importantly, he gave the novel prestige. In the early nineteenth century, the novel was an extremely questionable form of literature, and far beneath the dignity of a clerk of the Court of Session. Scott knew the legal establishment would not have approved so, rather than jeopardise his career, he published anonymously.

After the success of *Waverley*, Scott turned into a virtual novel-writing machine, producing some of his best work over the next five years, all without giving up the day job and all published anonymously, including *Guy Mannering* (written in six weeks in 1815), *The Antiquary* (1816), *Old Mortality* (1816), *Rob Roy* (1818), *The Heart of Midlothian* (1818), *The Bride of Lammermoor* (1819) and *Ivanhoe* (1820).

In 1811, he bought a small farm near Melrose called Cartley (nicknamed Clarty Hole) which he renamed Abbotsford, and began building himself what can only be described as a fake castle. In 1823, Maria Edgeworth visited Abbotsford and afterwards wrote, 'All the work is so solid you would never guess it was by a castle-building romance writer and poet.'

Scott was created a baronet in 1820 and did not publicly admit authorship of his novels until 1827. In 1826, disaster struck when he became insolvent after the failure of his printer, James Ballantyne, and his publisher Archibald Constable. As a partner of Ballantyne's, he was liable for debts of over £100,000. His wife Charlotte died the same year.

Most men would have buckled under this enormous burden, but all Scott asked of his creditors was time to write his way out of debt. After his death six years later in 1832, he had paid off a substantial proportion of his debts, which his family settled in full by selling off the copyrights to his novels. He died at Abbotsford and his remains were laid by the side of those of his wife in the sepulchre of his ancestors in the ruins of Dryburgh Abbey. Lockhart quotes a fitting epitaph from *The Iliad*: 'There lay he, mighty and mightily fallen, having done with his chivalry.'

NEW TOWN

SEE ALSO: Birthplace of W.S., childhood home of W.S., Lasswade Cottage, The Heart of Midlothian, Greyfriars Kirkyard, Scott Monument, Holyrood Park, St John's Churchyard, The Writers' Museum, High School, Old College, Sciennes Hill House, Assembly Rooms, James Hogg, J.G. Lockhart, Portobello Sands, Archibald Constable, Canongate Kirkyard.

FURTHER INFORMATION: 39 North Castle Street is not open to the public. James Ballantyne's printing office – Old Paul's Work – was in old Leith Wynd, now the lower end of Cranston Street, off the Canongate.

39 North Castle Street, townhouse of Sir Walter Scott

60 GEORGE STREET
Lodgings of Percy Bysshe Shelley
English lyric poet and writer

Lift not the painted veil which those who live
Call Life ...
Percy Bysshe Shelley, 'Sonnet' (1824)

Portrait of Shelley by by Alfred Clint (1829)

One of the major English Romantics, Shelley was born in Horsham in Sussex in 1792, and educated at Eton and Oxford, from where he was expelled in 1810 for contributing to a pamphlet called 'The Necessity of Atheism'. The summer of the same year, he eloped to Edinburgh with 16-year-old Harriet Westbrook, the daughter of a coffee-house proprietor, and they were married at the home of Revd Joseph Robertson at 225 Canongate on 28 August. They stayed for five weeks in the city in a two-storey flat (a third storey was added later) at 60 George Street, the ground floor of which is now a shop.

Novelist and poet Thomas Love Peacock (1785–1866), a close friend of Shelley's, described Harriet as 'fond of her husband, and accommodated herself in every way to his tastes. If they mixed in society, she adorned it; if they lived in retirement, she was satisfied; if they travelled, she enjoyed the change of scene.' Shelley and Harriet had two children, but their marriage collapsed in 1814 when Shelley fell in love with 16-year-old Mary Wollstonecraft Godwin, whom he described as 'a dream from heaven'. In December of 1816, Harriet drowned herself in the Serpentine, and in the same month Shelley and Mary were married. After Harriet's death, her family brought a petition before the courts which effectively deprived Shelley of the custody of his children, making them wards of the court.

An eccentric and a nomad, Shelley, when not writing masterpieces like *Prometheus Unbound* (1820), spent his short life dodging creditors, speaking in public or writing on subjects such as political reform, democracy and vegetarianism. The pressure of creditors and being ostracised socially eventually drove him abroad. In 1818, the Shelleys left England for good and settled in Italy, where Shelley was drowned when the schooner *Ariel* sank in a violent summer squall off the coast near Livorno in August 1822. Mary returned to England in 1823 with her son Percy. She lived until the age of 53 and is best remembered not for marrying Percy Shelley, but for her first, ground-breaking novel, *Frankenstein* (1818).

FURTHER READING: R. Holmes, *Shelley: The Pursuit* (Weidenfeld & Nicolson, 1974); T.L. Peacock, *Memoirs of Shelley* (Hart-Davis, 1970).

54 GEORGE STREET
The Assembly Rooms
Where Sir Walter Scott
first publicly admitted the authorship
of the Waverley novels

> *The novel was not the form of literature in the best repute, and a Clerk of Court, who had hopes of the Bench, and whose name had so far only been associated with the responsible roles of poet, critic and antiquary, might well seek an incognito when he appeared in the character of a popular entertainer.*
> John Buchan, *Sir Walter Scott* (1932)

Many literary legends have given readings in the Assembly Rooms, including Charles Dickens and William Thackeray, but probably its most memorable literary event happened at a Theatrical Fund dinner on 23 February 1827, when Sir Walter Scott, after 13 years of the public's postulation and conjecture, finally admitted that he was the author of the Waverley novels. It had long been an open secret, and when Lord Meadowbank, who had been asked to propose a toast, took him aside, he asked him if the time had not come to own up to their parentage. Scott smiled, and said, 'Do just as you like – only don't say much about so old a story.' (Lockhart's *Life*.) When Meadowbank made his announcement, the 300 diners stood up on their chairs and tables, and their applause was said to be deafening. Scott, known as 'The Wizard of the North', replied, 'The wand is broken and the book buried.'

Scott desired anonymity initially because the novel at that time was judged to be of low moral and artistic status, and he didn't want to jeopardise his reputation. But there was also another reason. What a lark it must have been to have written successive bestsellers signed simply, 'By the author of *Waverley*', while critics and the public were kept guessing year after year. It was also slightly fashionable to publish anonymously, but it's more likely he just loved playing at being a literary Scarlet Pimpernel.

SEE ALSO: Birthplace of W.S., childhood home of W.S., townhouse of W.S., Lasswade Cottage, Parliament Hall, Greyfriars Kirkyard, St John's Churchyard, The Heart of Midlothian, Holyrood Park, The Writers' Museum, Old College, Sciennes Hill House, Scott Monument, High School, J.G. Lockhart, Portobello Sands.

FURTHER INFORMATION: Scott's novels sold in enormous numbers in the USA, but largely in pirated editions. A copy of *Quentin Durward* was received by an American printer in 1823 and within 28 hours pirate copies had been printed and bound and were ready for sale.
The Assembly Rooms, designed by John Henderson, was built in 1782–7 by public subscription, and its chandeliers and mirrored walls have played host to dinners, balls, conferences and concerts for over 200 years. The arcaded Doric portico overhanging the pavement was added in 1818.

The Assembly Rooms

BOOK LOVERS' EDINBURGH

45 GEORGE STREET
Offices of *Blackwood's Magazine* from 1830 to 1972

Ever since the days of John Keats, to be bludgeoned by Blackwood has been the hallmark of an author of ideas.
Thomas Hardy, 1907

> BLACKWOOD'S
> Edinburgh
> MAGAZINE.
> VOL. I.
> APRIL—SEPTEMBER, 1817.

Blackwood's Magazine, the monthly periodical known affectionately as '*The Maga*', was launched by Edinburgh bookseller and publisher William Blackwood (1776–1834) from his bookshop at 17 Princes Street in 1817 as a Tory rival to the Whig-dominated *Edinburgh Review*. It began as the *Edinburgh Monthly Magazine*, but within six months it changed its title to *Blackwood's Edinburgh Magazine*, and from 1906 onwards became *Blackwood's Magazine*.

The witty satirical journalism of its early editors John Wilson and John Gibson Lockhart set the tone of *The Maga* as it praised and pilloried leading literary figures of the day. Depending on your point of view, you either rolled about in hysterics or contacted your lawyer. 'How I have longed for their utter extinction!' wrote Gerard Manley Hopkins in 1863.

NEW TOWN

Many of the literary greats of the nineteenth and early twentieth century were published in *Blackwood's*, notably Sir Walter Scott, Anthony Trollope, Joseph Conrad, James Hogg, Thomas De Quincey, John Galt, Susan Ferrier, Henry James, Oscar Wilde, Elizabeth Barrett Browning, R.D. Blackmore, John Buchan, Walter de la Mare, J.B. Priestley, Neil Munro and Hugh MacDiarmid. The talents of the unknown George Eliot were not lost on *Blackwood's*, who serialised her first fictional work, *The Sad Fortunes of Amos Barton*, in 1857, and went on to publish all her works except *Romola*.

Blackwood's failed, however, to detect genius when they rejected a short story entitled 'The Haunted Grange of Goresthorpe' submitted by an 18-year-old Edinburgh medical student in 1877. The story was filed by *Blackwood's* and was never returned to the student because he failed to supply a stamped addressed envelope. It lay forgotten until the Blackwood archives were presented to the National Library of Scotland in 1942. The story was written by Arthur Conan Doyle, and although the names are different, the characters in the tale are clearly blueprints of Sherlock Holmes and Dr Watson.

The magazine ceased publication in December 1980 after more than 180 years, a victim of changing taste and style, an ageing readership and falling advertising revenue.

SEE ALSO: William Blackwood, John Wilson, J.G. Lockhart, John Buchan, James Hogg, Thomas De Quincey, Sir Walter Scott, Susan Ferrier, Oscar Wilde, John Galt, Neil Munro, Hugh MacDiarmid.

FURTHER INFORMATION: The Blackwood archives can be consulted at the National Library of Scotland, George IV Bridge.

FURTHER READING: F.D. Tredrey, *The House of Blackwood, 1804–1954* (W. Blackwood & Sons, 1954); M. Oliphant, *Annals of a Publishing House* (W. Blackwood & Sons, 1897).

84 GEORGE STREET
Former Headquarters of the Commissioners of Northern Lights and offices of Thomas Stevenson (1818-87), engineer father of Robert Louis Stevenson. Where the 'redrawn' map of Treasure Island was born

> *Fifteen men on a dead man's chest*
> *Yo-ho-ho, and a bottle of rum!*
> *Drink and the devil had done for the rest –*
> *Yo-ho-ho, and a bottle of rum!*
> from *Treasure Island*, Chapter 3

Robert Louis Stevenson's *Treasure Island* (1883) is today one of the great classics of children's literature with the lovable rogue Long John Silver, and the crew of the Hispaniola, part of the popular consciousness. He wrote the first 15 chapters while holidaying in Braemar in the summer of 1881, and finished the story in Davos, in eastern Switzerland. The weather at Braemar was wet and miserable, and to entertain his 12-year-old stepson Lloyd, he began drawing treasure maps and writing the story that would become *Treasure Island*:

> '[Lloyd] had no thought of literature; it was the art of Raphael that received his fleeting suffrages; and with the aid of pen and ink and a shilling box of water colours, he had soon turned one of the rooms into a picture gallery. My more immediate duty towards the gallery was to be showman; but I would sometimes unbend a little, join the artist (so to speak) at the easel, and pass the afternoon with him in a generous emulation, making coloured drawings. On one of these occasions,

I made the map of an island; it was elaborately and (I thought) beautifully coloured; the shape of it took my fancy beyond expression; it contained harbours that pleased me like sonnets; and with the unconsciousness of the predestined, I ticketed my performance 'Treasure Island.' ...

Somewhat in this way, as I paused upon my map of 'Treasure Island,' the future character of the book began to appear ...

On a chill September morning, by the cheek of a brisk fire, and the rain drumming on the window, I began The Sea Cook, for that was the original title. I have begun (and finished) a number of other books, but I cannot remember to have sat down to one of them with more complacency ...

Fifteen days I stuck to it, and turned out fifteen chapters; and then, in the early paragraphs of the sixteenth, ignominiously lost hold .... down I sat one morning [in Davos] to the unfinished tale; and behold! It flowed from me like small talk; and in a second tide of delighted industry, and again at a rate of a chapter a day, I finished Treasure Island ...

But the adventures of Treasure Island are not yet quite at an end. I had written it up to the map. The map was the chief part of my plot ... The time came when it was decided to republish, and I sent in my manuscript, and the map along with it, to Messrs. Cassell [who first published the story as a book in 1883]. The proofs came, they were corrected, but I heard nothing of the map. I wrote and asked; was told it had never been received, and sat aghast. It is one thing to draw a map at random, set a scale in one corner of it at a venture, and write up a story to the measurements. It is quite another to have to examine the whole book, make an inventory of all the allusions contained in it, and with a pair of compasses, painfully design a map to suit the data. I did it; and the map was drawn again in my father's office, with embellishments of blowing whales and sailing ships, and my father himself brought into service a knack he had of various writing, and elaborately FORGED the signature of Captain Flint, and the sailing directions of Billy Bones. But somehow it was never Treasure Island to me.

From 'My First Book: Treasure Island'. First published in *The Idler*, August 1894.

'Treasure Island' was first serialised in the children's magazine *Young Folks* from 1881 to 1882 under the pseudonym, Captain George North. As a magazine story, it didn't make much of an impact. Stevenson's wife Fanny didn't like the story, describing it as 'tedious', and was not keen on it being published as a novel. Fortunately for literary history, Louis was keen to publish and was staggered to be paid 'a hundred jingling, tingling, gold-minted quid' for it when it was published by Cassell in 1883 with the inclusion of the redrawn map.

Left: Thomas Stevenson, father of Robert Louis Stevenson
Right: The redrawn map of Treasure Island

SEE ALSO: Robert Louis Stevenson, New Calton Cemetery, E.H. Henley.

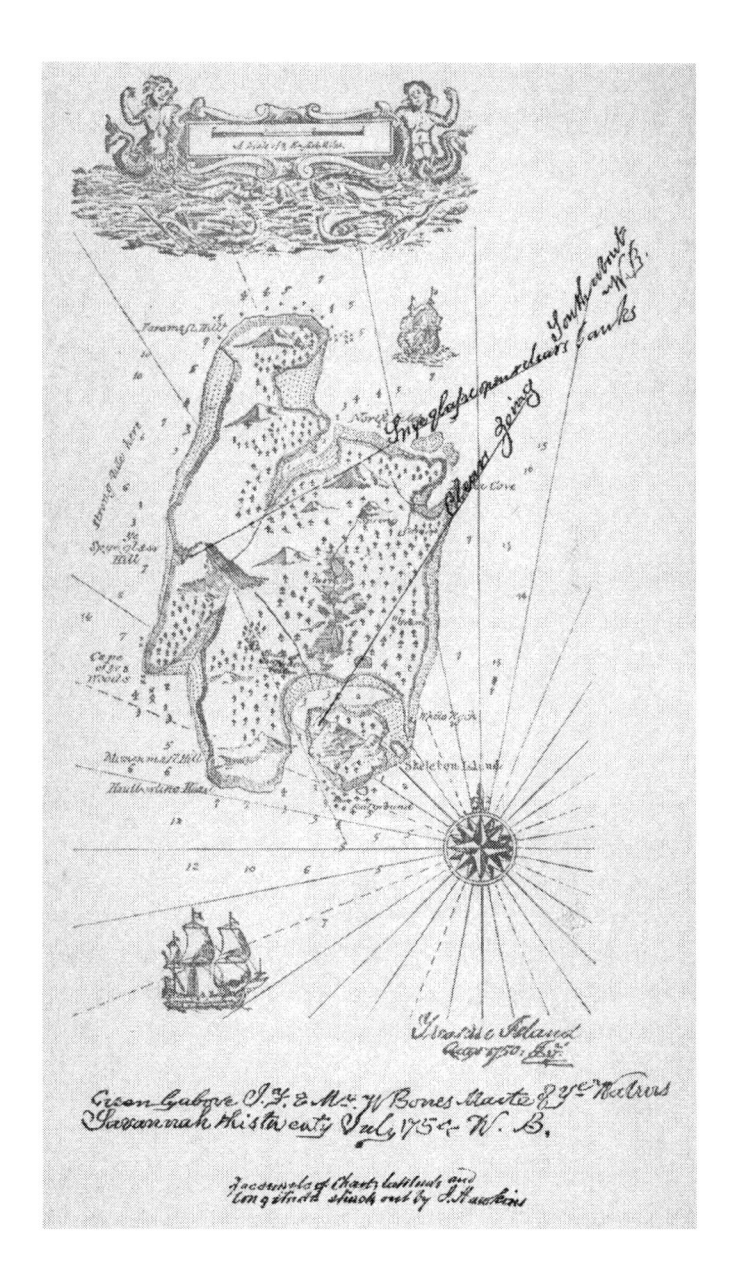

'The map was drawn again in my father's office, with embellishments of blowing whales and sailing ships ... '

CORNER OF ST COLME AND NORTH CHARLOTTE STREET
The Catherine Sinclair Monument

All play of imagination is now carefully discouraged, and books written for young persons are generally a mere record of dry facts.
Catherine Sinclair, from the preface of *Holiday House* (1839)

At the western end of Queen Street stands the Catherine Sinclair Monument, an imperious Gothic memorial designed by architect David Bryce (1803–76) for novelist and philanthropist Catherine Sinclair (1800–64), best known for her classic children's novel *Holiday House*.
Born in Edinburgh, she was the fourth daughter of agrarian reformer Sir John Sinclair, and at the age of 14 she became her father's secretary until his death in 1835. After her father's demise, she started writing and evolved into a prolific writer of travel, biography, children's books, novels and essays. Unlike most Victorian children's books, which guaranteed a predictably moralising tale, Sinclair's *Holiday House* attempted to reverse the trend, and was an enormous success with young readers. Apart from writing, she also immersed herself in philanthropic works, namely setting up workers' canteens, funding street fountains and benches, and founding a Volunteer Brigade for boys in Leith. She is buried close by at St John's Churchyard at the west end of Princes Street.

FURTHER INFORMATION: Catherine Sinclair is often credited as being the first person to guess the identity of the author of *Waverley*, published anonymously by Sir Walter Scott in 1814. This seems unlikely, as it became an open secret at the time, and a fairly well known one, although Scott only 'officially' admitted authorship in 1827.

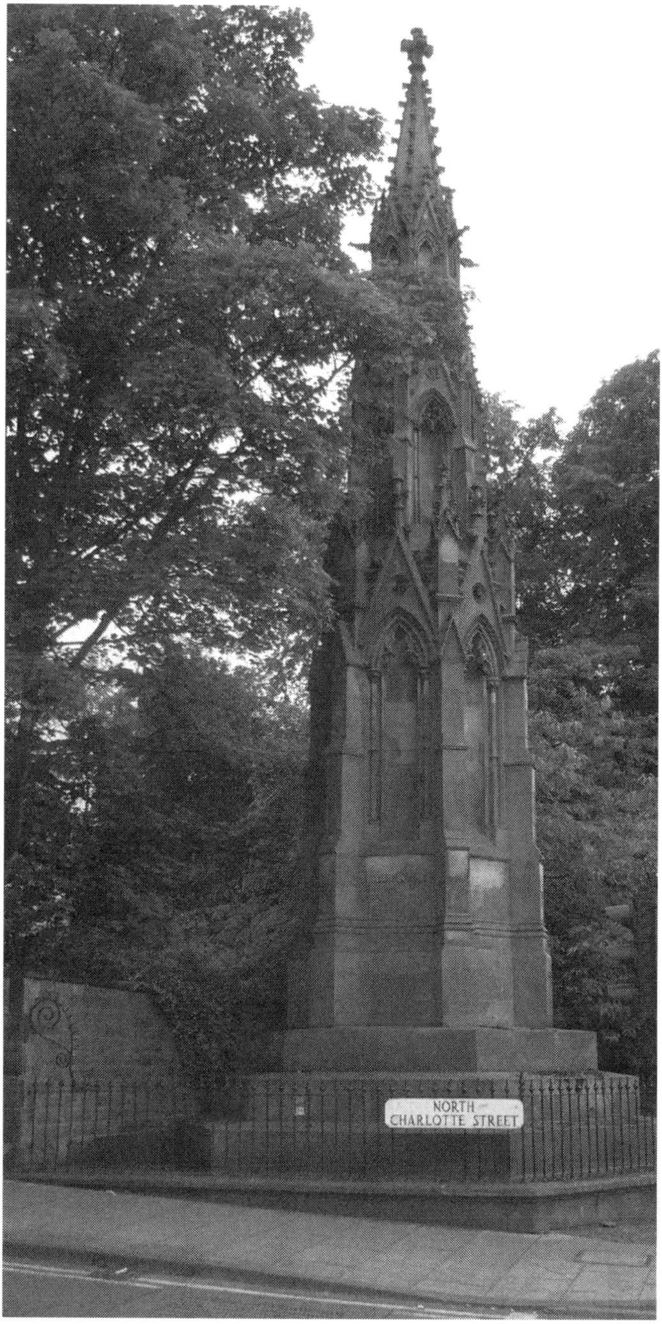
NORTH
CHARLOTTE STREET

8 YOUNG STREET
The Oxford Bar

Wullie Roose's Coxfork in Bung Strait
Sydney Goodsir Smith, *Carotid Cornucopius* (1947)

Today this pub is synonymous with Ian Rankin and Inspector Rebus, who both regularly drink here. The Oxford Bar has always been a popular watering hole for Scottish writers and artists, especially those of the Scottish Renaissance, who frequented it when it was run by the late and legendary Willie Ross. Ian Rankin gave a colourful description of Ross in *Guardian Unlimited* in October 2002:

> He left in 1979, just before I started drinking there ... You weren't allowed to hit on women because no women were allowed in. There was no women's toilet. If you were English, you weren't allowed in. If you were a student, you weren't allowed in. If you asked for food, like a packet of crisps, he dragged you outside, pointed at the sign and said, 'Does that say bar or fucking restaurant?' Some people have got great stories about him. He sounds like a terrible man to me, but a character, and you need characters.

Although Willie Ross is now part of the pub's history, there is no shortage of colourful characters at the Oxford Bar and, as one local commented, 'It's the only pub I know with an emergency entrance.'

SEE ALSO: The Abbotsford, Milnes Bar, Sandy Bell's. Ian Rankin, Sydney Goodsir Smith, Hugh MacDiarmid, Robert Garioch, Norman MacCaig.

NEW TOWN

17 HERIOT ROW
Former home of
Robert Louis Stevenson (1850–94)

For we are very lucky with a lamp before the door,
And Leerie stops to light it as he lights so many more;
And O! before you hurry by with ladder and with light,
O Leerie, see a little child and nod to him tonight!
RLS, from 'The Lamplighter',
A Child's Garden of Verses (1885)

Thomas Stevenson, engineer to the Northern Lighthouse Board, was prospering, and his new house reflected it. The Stevensons moved to Heriot Row in 1857, a Georgian street in Edinburgh's New Town which today still exudes affluence and pedigree. Built between 1802 and 1806, this large terraced house overlooking Queen Street Gardens is spacious enough to billet a boy-scout troop. For the three Stevensons and a couple of servants, it must have seemed positively Brobdingnagian. Looking at No. 17 from the street, Louis's bedroom was situated on the top floor on the far right, overlooking the gardens. These were the windows from which the sickly Louis would have observed Leerie, 'The Lamplighter', and heard the coarse cries of the carters as they wound their way up from Stockbridge to the town.

Thomas Stevenson had hoped that his son would follow in his footsteps and become an engineer, but Louis gave up his engineering studies in favour of law, passing his Bar exams in 1875. Louis the advocate, however, was never a serious proposition. What he really wanted to be was a writer, an artist and a free spirit. In appearance and lifestyle, he was already halfway there, wandering around the Old Town in his famous velvet jacket, carousing with the city's underbelly and sowing his wild oats. And, like all good bohemians, he doubted the existence of God (which infuriated his father), became seriously depressed, wrote and abandoned novels, fell in love with an older woman and yearned to travel.

In France in 1876, he met his future wife, Fanny Osbourne, and in the same year he canoed through Belgium and France with his friend Walter Simpson, a journey which inspired the creation of his first book, *An Inland Voyage* (1878). In 1878, he tramped across the Cévennes with his obstreperous donkey Modestine, which resulted in *Travels with a Donkey* (1879). He travelled to California in pursuit of Fanny in 1879, a trip which nearly killed him. The literary outcome of this was *The Silverado Squatters* (1883). After marrying Fanny, who was ten years his senior, Stevenson and his new wife returned to Britain in 1884 and settled in Bournemouth for three years. His short stories, essays and travel writings were now appearing regularly in magazines and in 1883 he published *Treasure Island*, his first full-length work of fiction. *The Strange Case of Dr Jekyll and Mr Hyde* (1886) and *Kidnapped* (1886) followed, establishing his reputation as a master storyteller.

Following his father's death in May 1887, he returned home for the funeral. However, he was too ill on the day of the service to attend. This was to be his last visit to Heriot Row before departing for the South Seas in 1888.

Flora Masson recalled his departure from Edinburgh in *I Can Remember Robert Louis Stevenson* (1922):

> An open cab, with a man and a woman in it, seated side by side, and leaning back – the rest of the cab piled high with rather untidy luggage – came slowly towards us …
> As it passed us, out on the broad roadway … a slender, loose garbed figure stood up in the cab and waved a wide-brimmed hat.
> 'Good-bye!' he called to us. 'Good-bye!'

BOOK LOVERS' EDINBURGH

Searching for the climate that he hoped would prolong his life, Stevenson eventually settled in Samoa. In his exile, he still wrote prodigiously, notably *Island Nights Entertainments* (1893) and his unfinished masterpiece *Weir of Hermiston* (1896). Not even an island paradise, however, could prolong his life. He died of a brain haemorrhage shortly after 8 p.m. on 3 December 1894 and is buried on the summit of Mount Vea in Samoa.

Left: RLS aged 29
Right: 17 Heriot Row

SEE ALSO: Howard Place, Inverleith Terrace, Pilrig House, Colinton Manse, Swanston Cottage, Baxter's Place, Glencorse Kirk, Rutherford's Howff, New Calton Cemetery, Old Calton Burial Ground, St Giles, Hawes Inn, Rullion Green, W.E. Henley, Alison Cunningham, Deacon Brodie, The Writers' Museum, *Kidnapped* Statue, George Mackenzie, Martyrs' Monument, Edinburgh Castle, Old College, Parliament Hall, Holyrood Park, Royal College of Surgeons' Museum, R.M. Ballantyne, RLS Memorial.

FURTHER INFORMATION: The 'Stevenson House' is not open to the public, but it does operate as a bed & breakfast and hospitality venue.

FURTHER READING: RLS, *Edinburgh: Picturesque Notes* (Pallas Athene, 2003); R. Masson (ed.), *I Can Remember Robert Louis Stevenson* (1922); E.B. Simpson, *Robert Louis Stevenson's Edinburgh Days* (Kessinger, 2005).

NEW TOWN

4 NELSON STREET
Former home of Robert Garioch (1909–81)
Satirical poet and translator

> *But truth it is, our couthie city*
> *has cruddit in twa parts a bittie*
> Robert Garioch, from 'To Robert Fergusson' (1950)

Garioch's poem 'To Robert Fergusson' was addressed to a poet with whom he felt a special kinship. Both wrote in Scots and had a passion for Edinburgh – the city that 'speaks twa tongues' – which they observed and celebrated throughout their lives, memorialising the city, warts and all, in their own 'coorse and grittie' verse.
Born Robert Garioch Sutherland on 9 May 1909, he was educated at the Royal High School and Edinburgh University. During the Second World War, he was a POW for four years, an experience he recounted in his only prose work, *Two Men and a Blanket*, written in 1945 but not published until 1975. A shy, retiring man, he spent most of his life as a schoolmaster, teaching in Scotland and London. Although Garioch wrote comic verse, it would be wrong to dismiss him as a comic lightweight, for his poetry has great depth, and had he not chosen to write mainly in Lallans (a distinctive Scottish literary form of English, based on standard older Scots), there is no doubt he would have had a wider audience. Scottish literature is, nonetheless, much the richer for it. Whether in the informal style of 'Fi'baw in the Street' and 'Heard in the Cougate', or the formal language of poems like 'The Muir' and 'The Wire', his poetry has universal appeal. He undertook Scots versions of George Buchanan's Latin tragedies, *Jephthah and The Baptist*, and also produced translations from the Roman sonnets of Guiseppe Belli. His first book of poetry, *17 poems for 6d*: *in Gaelic*,

Lowland Scots and English (1940), was published jointly with Gaelic poet Sorley Maclean (1911–96). His last individual volume was *Doktor Faust in Rose Street* (1973) and his long-awaited *Complete Poetical Works* was published in 1983. He died on 26 April 1981, aged 71.

Poet Donald Campbell recalled in 1981 that 'if I learned anything at all from Robert Garioch, it was to do the work as well as I could do it and not worry too much about either the applause of success or the obscurity of failure.'

SEE ALSO: Robert Fergusson, Old College.

4 Nelson Street

3 ABERCROMBY PLACE
Birthplace of Marie Stopes (1880–1958) Birth-control pioneer and author of *Married Love* (1918)

Marie Stopes in her laboratory 1904

Condemned by the Catholic Church and denounced as a worse enemy of the Empire than Hitler or Goebbels, Marie Stopes' pioneering work on sex education and birth control freed countless women from the anguish of sexual ignorance and accidental pregnancy. She wrote over 70 books, including volumes of plays, novels and poetry, but it is her works on parenthood, birth control and sexual fulfilment within marriage, notably *Married Love*, for which she will be remembered. *Married Love* was written by Stopes during the First World War after her first unhappy and unconsummated marriage, and discusses frankly the then sacred mystery of mating, arguing that marriage should be an equal relationship between husband and wife. It caused an outcry on publication and was declared obscene in the USA, where it was promptly banned. Despite the controversy, the book was an immediate success, selling two thousand copies in two weeks. By the end of the year, it had been reprinted six times and it was later translated into fifteen languages.

Marie Charlotte Carmichael Stopes was the daughter of English engineer, architect and fossil collector Henry Stopes and Edinburgh native Charlotte Carmichael, daughter of landscape painter J.F. Carmichael. In 1898, she won a science scholarship to University College, London, and in 1901 achieved a double first in botany and geology. In 1904, she was awarded a doctorate in Munich for her work on fossilised plants. She also became a passionate supporter of the women's suffrage campaign. In 1911, her marriage to Reginald Gates was a union which proved to be both antagonistic and sexless. Gates was impotent and Stopes was so sexually ignorant it took her three years to comprehend the fact. The marriage was annulled in 1916 and Stopes began writing *Married Love*, stating in the preface to the first English edition that in 'my first marriage I paid such a terrible price for sex-ignorance that I feel that knowledge gained at such a cost should be placed at the service of humanity'.

She first became interested in birth control after a meeting in London with American campaigner and former nurse Margaret Sanger, who fled America after being charged with publishing an 'obscene and lewd' birth-control article. In 1918, Stopes wrote her contraception guide, *Wise Parenthood*, and in 1921 she founded the Society for Constructive Birth Control.

Her second husband was aircraft manufacturer Humphrey Roe, and with his help and money she opened the Mothers' Clinic in Holloway, North London – Britain's first birth-control clinic – on 17 March 1921, offering a free service to women. A small network of clinics soon followed and today the Marie Stopes International Global Partnership works in 37 countries.

25 DRUMMOND PLACE
Former home of
Sydney Goodsir Smith (1915–75)
Poet, dramatist, novelist and critic

A most lovable, unpretentious and compassionate man who, as poet, translator, literary critic, art critic, dramatist, and editor displayed a record of versatility hardly any of his contemporaries come near equalling.
Hugh MacDiarmid

Although born in Wellington, New Zealand, it was 'the auld toon o' Edinburgh' that was Sydney Goodsir Smith's spiritual home. He wrote about what he saw in the city, often fused with the common speech of his favourite Edinburgh howffs, in lively and humorous Lallan lyrics. Regarded as one of Scotland's leading literary scholars and a major figure in the Scottish Renaissance, he was also a well-known broadcaster, dramatist, novelist and critic, but he will be best remembered as a poet who invoked and upheld the spoken tradition of Scottish verse in the essence of Dunbar and Fergusson. His greatest achievement was *Under the Eildon Tree* (1948), now acknowledged as one of the masterpieces of Scottish poetry.

He arrived in Edinburgh in 1927 when his father became

professor of forensic medicine at Edinburgh University. He studied medicine at Edinburgh University, but abandoned it to read history at Oriel College, Oxford. He started writing poetry in Scots in the 1930s and during the Second World War taught English to Polish troops. Writing poetry in a language which is not one's native tongue can be problematic for an audience. Stanley Roger Green attempted to explain this enigma in his 1975 'Appreciation' of Smith:

> At first, like most people who knew him, I was puzzled by the apparent paradoxes in his nature. A life-long socialist with aristocratic tastes: a New Zealander educated mainly in England who became one of our greatest modern patriots: a man with a gentlemanly 'English' accent who carried Lallans to heights of virtuosity which few have emulated ... Only when I came to know him better did I realise that here was one of those outstanding people who are too richly varied, too kaleidoscopic in character to be constrained by ordinary definitions, and that analysis of such a person is almost an impertinence.

Smith's interests and talents were wide-ranging. As a playwright, he wrote the verse play *The Wallace* in 1960. As a novelist, he penned *Carotid Cornucopius* in 1947, in which Carotid, the Caird o' the Cannon Gait, visits the well-known watering holes of 'Sunday Balls in Fairest Redd' (Sandy Bell's on Forrest Road), 'the Abbotsfork in Low Street' (The Abbotsford on Rose Street), 'Doddie Mullun's' (Milnes Bar) and 'Wullie Roose's Coxfork in Bung Strait' (the Oxford Bar on Young Street). Hugh MacDiarmid described *Carotid Cornucopius* as 'doing for Edinburgh no less successfully what Joyce did for Dublin in *Ulysses*'. His first collection of poetry was *Skail Wind*, published in 1941. Other works include *The Deevil's Waltz* (1946), *So*

BOOK LOVERS' EDINBURGH

Late Into the Night (1952), *Figs and Thistles* (1959), *Kynd Kittock's Land* (1965) and *Gowdspink in Reekie* (1974). Sydney Goodsir Smith lived for many years in 'Schloss Schimdt' at 50 Craigmillar Park and in later life at 25 Drummond Place. He died a relatively young man, aged 59, in 1975 and is buried in Dean Cemetery. Scottish poet Tom Scott attended his funeral and recorded his last farewell in the *Scotia Review*, April 1975:

> On the Sunday, after the funeral at which strong men grat and some less strong were feart to greet, I went to the cemetery to spend a last half hour with him. The roses were already frost-bitten, and on impulse I cut one off, took it home, kept it in a whisky bottle till it faded, then buried the calyx deep in our rose-bed here. Silly, but I FELT so relieved.

SEE ALSO: Sandy Bell's, The Abbotsford, Oxford Bar, Milnes Bar.

FURTHER READING: H. MacDiarmid, *Sydney Goodsir Smith* (Hamilton, 1963); E. Gold, *Sydney Goodsir Smith's* Under the Eildon Tree: An Essay (Akros, 1975).

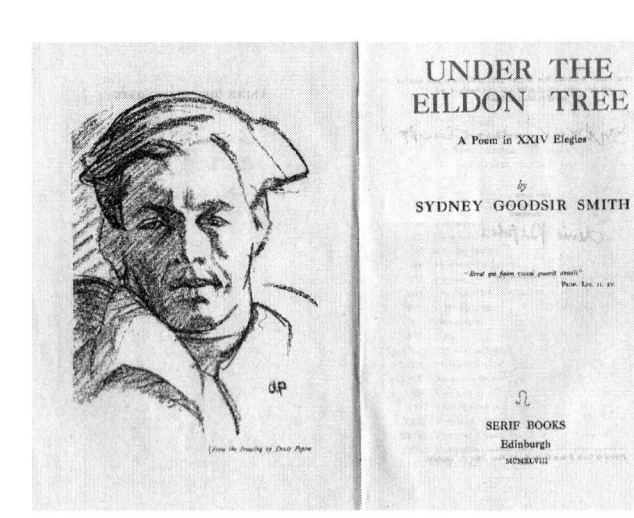

Left: First edition of Goodsir Smith's *Under the Eildon Tree* (1948) with frontispiece drawing of the author by Denis Peploe
Right: 25 Drummond Place

NEW TOWN

31 DRUMMOND PLACE
Home of Compton Mackenzie (1883-1972)
Novelist, journalist, biographer and poet

Many romantic pages have been written about the sunken Spanish galleon in the bay of Tobermory. That 4,000-ton steamship on the rocks off Little Todday provided more practical romance in three and a half hours than the Tobermory galleon has provided in three and a half centuries. Doubloons, ducats, and ducatoons, moidores, pieces of eight, sequins, guineas, rose and angel nobles, what are these to vaunt above the liquid gold carried by the Cabinet Minister?
Compton Mackenzie, *Whisky Galore* (1946)

Mackenzie based *Whisky Galore* on actual events which occurred in 1941 when the 4,000-ton cargo ship SS *Politician* ran aground in treacherous seas in the Sound of Eriskay, off the coast of Barra. Her cargo included pianos, bicycles, Jamaican banknotes and 22,000 cases of whisky. Mackenzie was commander of the Home Guard on Barra at the time, and got his fair share of the 'liquid gold', unlike the pompous Captain Waggett in his novel. When working on the final draft for the script of the 1949 Ealing Studios film adaptation, Mackenzie grumbled, 'Another of my books gone west.'
Producer Monja Danischewsky seemed of the same opinion, commenting, 'Well, I don't know ... all I can see is a lot of elderly Scotsmen sitting by the fire and saying "och aye".' History has proved them both wrong. The film became an Ealing classic and the novel is now ranked amongst the great Highland comedies.
For a successful writer, praised by Henry James and acknowledged as a major influence on Scott Fitzgerald,

NEW TOWN

Compton MacKenzie in Drummond Place

Compton Mackenzie is today curiously neglected. His main desire was to entertain his readers, and his portraits of couthy Highlanders are uproarious subtle parodies that never patronise.

He was born in West Hartlepool in 1883, the son of actor Edward Compton, and was educated at St Paul's School and Magdalen College, Oxford. He studied for the English Bar, but abandoned law in 1907 to write his first play, *The Gentleman in Grey*. His first novel, *The Passionate Elopement,* was published in 1911. *Carnival* (1912) followed, but it was the publication of *Sinister Street* (1913) which won him acclaim. During the First World War, he was recruited into the British Secret Service in Greece, an experience he later recounted in *Greek Memories* (1932). The book was immediately withdrawn, however, and all remaining copies destroyed. Mackenzie was charged with breaching the Official Secrets Act and fined £100.

After the war, he returned to novel writing, producing *Rich Relations* (1921) and two novels about lesbian love, *Vestal Fire* (1927) and *Extraordinary Women* (1928). Between 1937 and 1945, he published the sextet *The Four Winds of Love*, and between 1963 and 1971 he produced his massive ten-volume autobiography, *My Life and Times.*

Mackenzie was a staunch nationalist and a founder member of the Scottish National Party. He was also literary critic of the *Daily Mail* during the 1930s and was the founder-editor of *Gramophone* magazine in 1923, now the oldest surviving classical music review magazine in the world. He lived for a period in Capri after the war and in 1934 built a house on the island of Barra. He was knighted in 1952.

He died in Edinburgh on 30 November 1972 and is buried at Eoligarry on Barra. During his burial service, piper Calum Johnston, an old friend of Mackenzie, collapsed and died after playing a lament.

FURTHER READING: A. Linklater, *Compton Mackenzie: A Life* (Chatto & Windus, 1987).

Left: Birlinn's 2012 edition of *Whisky Galore*
Right: 31 Drummond Place

NEW TOWN

BOOK LOVERS' EDINBURGH

SCOTLAND STREET
Setting for Alexander McCall Smith's 'daily novel', *44 Scotland Street*

Scotland Street is an unassuming New Town street which does not quite possess the class of Heriot Row or Abercromby Place. Nevertheless, it is the setting for one of Edinburgh's most famous fictional addresses: No. 44 Scotland Street (the street exists but No. 44 does not). This celebrity status is due to Alexander McCall Smith's daily novel of the same name which appeared in *The Scotsman* during 2004. To write weekly instalments of a novel for the press is a daunting enough prospect, but to write daily ones is a feat only a novel-writing machine like McCall Smith – who can polish off 3,000 words before lunch – can tackle. 'In the last three weeks,' he told *The Scotsman* in May 2004, 'I've written episodes at Palm Springs in the Californian desert, in Hollywood and New York, and on the plane between Las Vegas and Virginia. I wrote two the other day, coming up on the train from London.'

Alexander McCall Smith was born in Bulawayo, Southern Rhodesia (now Zimbabwe), and was educated there and in Scotland, where he became professor of medical law at Edinburgh University. He also helped set up a new law school at the University of Botswana, is an international authority on genetics, and advisor to UNESCO and the UK government on bioethics. How he has found the time to write more than 50 books over the past 20 years is anybody's guess.

Although he's written specialist academic titles, children's books and short-story collections, it was his 1998 detective novel, *The No. 1 Ladies' Detective Agency*, which introduced his heroine Mma Ramotswe, Botswana's finest – and only – female detective, which shot him to literary super-stardom. More than four million copies of the books in the series have been sold in the English-speaking world, and they have been translated into 26 other languages from Catalan to Estonian. He also created Isabel Dalhousie, a respectable lady detective who inhabits genteel Merchiston, in *The Sunday Philosophy Club*, in which a young man plunges to his death from the gods in Edinburgh's Usher Hall.

When not on gruelling American book tours, McCall Smith lives in Edinburgh with his wife and two daughters. He plays the bassoon with 'The Really Terrible Orchestra', but dislikes 'the very high notes'. And by the way, not only is No. 44 Scotland Street fictitious, but its residents are too, so if you're after the blood of Bruce, the vain surveyor, you'll have to vent your wrath on someone else.

Left: McCall Smith in the New Town
Right: Scotland Street

14 CUMBERLAND STREET
Former student lodgings of J.M. Barrie. Novelist and dramatist

Oh, for an hour of Herod.
Anthony Hope's comment after watching a performance of *Peter Pan*.

J.M. Barrie by Herbert Rose Barraud, 1892

Chiefly remembered today as the creator of Peter Pan, James Matthew Barrie rose from humble origins to become one of the most praised and successful dramatists of his day. Wealth and fame, however, failed to bring him happiness, and he spent much of his life trying to win the love denied him as a child. His generosity could be overwhelming, his affection intense and possessive. Small in stature, shy, secretive and with unpredictable moods, Barrie was an odd and complex genius.

He was born on 9 May 1860 in Kirriemuir, the ninth child of Margaret Ogilvy and David Barrie, a hand-loom weaver. They had ten children in all: seven daughters and three sons. David, his mother's favourite son, died tragically in a skating accident aged fourteen, when James was six. His mother was 'always delicate from that hour', he recalled, and constantly thinking of her boy who was gone. She never recovered from her loss and throughout his childhood James tried desperately to replace him, yearning for his mother's love.

He attended Glasgow Academy, Dumfries Academy and the local school in Kirriemuir. When he was 18, he entered Edinburgh University, the fees for which were paid by his elder brother, Alec, with whom he shared lodgings at the top of a house at 14 Cumberland Street. His father sent him an allowance, which he supplemented by writing theatre reviews for the *Edinburgh Courant*. He lived frugally and kept pretty much to himself. A fellow student described him as 'a spare, short figure in a warm-looking Highland cloak'. In 1882, he received his degree and had his photograph taken in cap and gown, with 'hair straggling under the cap as tobacco may straggle over the side of a tin when there is difficulty in squeezing down the lid'. He was writing regularly by this time, but apart from a few articles written for the *Courant*, no one was interested in publishing his work. In 1883, more in desperation than as a career move, he started work as a leader writer for the *Nottingham Journal*, eventually moving to London in 1885, where he began freelancing. In 1888, he published the first of his Kailyard stories, *Auld Licht Idylls* (1888), followed by *A Window in Thrums* (1889) and *The Little Minister* (1891). His first play, *Richard Savage*, was performed in

London in 1891, and from this point onwards he wrote mainly for the theatre.

In 1894, he married 32-year-old actress Mary Ansell, who discovered on her wedding night that Barrie was impotent; consequently their marriage was never consummated. Barrie refused to discuss his problem or seek medical advice. Mary made the best of it, but effectively they ended up living separate lives, eventually divorcing in 1909.

Between 1901 and 1920, Barrie produced his most successful plays, including *Quality Street* (1901), *The Admirable Crichton* (1902), *Peter Pan* (1904), *What Every Woman Knows* (1906), *Dear Brutus* (1917) and *Mary Rose* (1920).

In 1897, he began a curious infatuation with Sylvia Llewelyn Davies and her young sons, to whom he became an oppressive and domineering guardian, lavishing gifts, holidays, money and counsel. Sylvia and her husband died young and Barrie unofficially adopted the five children; they became literally the 'Lost Boys'. One of them, Michael, photographed by Barrie in 1906, was the original inspiration for the Peter Pan statue in Kensington Gardens. Another of the boys, Peter, once described *Peter Pan* as 'that terrible masterpiece'.

The 'little Scotchman' died on 19 June 1937 and is buried in the town cemetery, Kirriemuir.

SEE ALSO: Old College, Rutherford's Howff, W.E. Henley.

FURTHER INFORMATION: J.M. Barrie also lived at 3 Great King Street and 20 Shandwick Place. His birthplace at 9 Brechin Road, Kirriemuir, is now a museum containing manuscripts, diaries, photographs and Barrie's own writing desk. The National Library of Scotland contains his university notebooks. Barrie bequeathed the perpetual rights of *Peter Pan* to the Great Ormond Street Hospital for Sick Children in London.

FURTHER READING: J. Dunbar, *J.M. Barrie, The Man Behind the Image* (Collins, 1970); C. Asquith, *Haply I May Remember* (1950), *Portrait of Barrie* (Barrie, 1954).

14 Cumberland Street

6 GLOUCESTER PLACE
Former home of John Wilson (1785–1854) Critic, novelist, essayist and editor of *Blackwood's Magazine*, who wrote under the pseudonym Christopher North

Damning wit and a mastery of the art of the spoof catapulted John Wilson to the centre stage of early-nineteenth-century literary Edinburgh when he became co-editor, along with John Gibson Lockhart, of *Blackwood's Edinburgh Magazine* in 1817.

Born in Paisley, the son of a wealthy gauze manufacturer, he was educated at Glasgow and Oxford, where he built up a reputation as a poet and an athlete. After graduating, he bought an estate in Windermere, where he befriended Wordsworth, Coleridge, Southey and De Quincey. Through an uncle's mismanagement, he lost his estate. He moved to Edinburgh, where he qualified as an advocate, but never practised. His writings were relatively successful, but it was his connection with *Blackwood's Edinburgh Magazine* which established the literary reputation for which he is remembered.

William Blackwood's '*Maga*', a direct challenge to the Whig-dominated *Edinburgh Review*, got off to a shaky start when it first appeared on 1 April 1817. After six monthly issues, it was clearly no match for the *Edinburgh Review* and looked like ending up a costly failure. Blackwood acted swiftly, sacking its editors and giving editorial control to Wilson and Lockhart. It was the appearance of the 'Translation from an Ancient Chaldee Manuscript' in the October 1817 issue – a biting satire on literary and political Edinburgh written in the language of the Old Testament, the first draft of which was reputedly written by James Hogg – which overnight transformed *Blackwood's Magazine* from a lethargic rag into a flagship of satirical journalism. Nobody was immune from the sting of Wilson's pen, not even his close circle of friends, and no subject was sacrosanct.

A few years later, together with James Hogg, Wilson (writing as Christopher North) created 'Noctes Ambrosianae' for *Blackwood's*: fictional dialogues of alcohol-fuelled evenings spent at Ambrose's Tavern in Gabriel's Road (now demolished, but stood on the site of New Register House at the east end of Princes Street).

In 1820, the Tory Town Council elected Wilson to the chair of moral philosophy at Edinburgh University. This was a subject on which he knew next to nothing, but such was the excellence of his oratory that his lectures proved a popular and instructive entertainment for generations of students.

He published a series of rural short stories, collectively entitled *Lights and Shadows of Scottish Life* (1822), and two novels, *The Trials of Margaret Lyndsay* (1823) and *The Foresters* (1825).

SEE ALSO: James Hogg, Sir Walter Scott, J.G. Lockhart, Thomas De Quincey, *Blackwood's Magazine*, *Edinburgh Review*, James Thin, Susan Ferrier.

STOCKBRIDGE

25 ANN STREET
Birthplace of R.M. Ballantyne (1825–94) Writer of adventure stories and author of *Coral Island*

One Sunday in 1866 after morning service outside St Cuthbert's Church in Edinburgh's West End, an admiring, thin, long-haired stranger of 16 years approached Ballantyne and invited him to dinner. Unfortunately, he had to decline due to another engagement, and a teenaged Robert Louis Stevenson lost his only chance of making acquaintance with his boyhood hero. Although they never met again, Stevenson acknowledged Ballantyne's influence on his own adventure stories.

Robert Michael Ballantyne was born in Edinburgh in 1825 at 25 Ann Street, Stockbridge, the son of a newspaper editor, and was educated at Edinburgh Academy (1835–7) and privately. Bad financial investments caused the family's fortunes to topple and Ballantyne's life changed dramatically. Between the ages of 16 and 22, he was employed in Canada by the Hudson Bay Company, trading with local American Indians in remote areas. He started writing about his adventures while stationed at the desolate outposts of the Company and, in 1848, *Hudson's Bay; Or, Every-Day Life in the Wilds of North America* was published. An autobiographical work, the book depicts his youth and adventures in Canada. From 1856, he devoted himself entirely to freelance writing and giving lectures.

Annoyed by a mistake he made in *Coral Island* (1858),

STOCKBRIDGE

Ballantyne subsequently travelled widely to gain first-hand knowledge and to thoroughly research the backgrounds of his embryonic stories. He spent three weeks on Bell Rock, near Arbroath, to write *The Lighthouse* (1865) and joined the London Fire Brigade to write *Fighting the Flames* (1867); for *Deep Down* (1868) he lived with the tin miners of St Just for over three months.

He became every schoolboy's hero and his lighthearted descriptions of the slaughter of fauna and natives in *Coral Island*, the book for which he will be best remembered, then passed without comment. His 'ripping yarns', although well written and meticulously researched, now belong to that other age when most of the world map was pink and the British Empire shone like an unquestioned beacon. Ballantyne's narrative skills remain nonetheless supreme. During his career, Ballantyne wrote over 80 books. In 1866, he married Jane Grant; they had four sons and two daughters. After 1883, the family lived in Harrow, Middlesex. Ballantyne died in Rome on 8 February 1894.

SEE ALSO: *Kidnapped* Statue, James Ballantyne.

R.M. Ballantyne by John Ballantyne. Oil on canvas c. 1855

COMELY BANK

21 COMELY BANK
Former home of historian and essayist Thomas Carlyle (1795–1881) and his wife, Jane Carlyle (1801–66)

It was very good of God to let Carlyle and Mrs Carlyle marry one another and so make only two people miserable instead of four.
Samuel Butler, letter to Miss Savage, 21 November 1884

Much has been made of Thomas Carlyle's melancholy and Jane Carlyle's frustration in the role of the 'Lion's wife' during their tempestuous 45-year relationship, but had they not met, the world would have been denied the bounteous correspondence of this high Victorian thinker and his ingenious, caustic wife, who between them wrote thousands of letters, of which over nine thousand still survive, describing everything from revolutionary Europe to dinner parties at Charles Dickens's house, which Jane recounted in 1849:

> The dinner was served up in the new fashion – not placed on the table at all – but handed round – only the des[s]ert on the table and quantities of artificial flowers, but such an overloaded des[s]ert! – pyramids of figs raisins oranges – ach!

Thomas Carlyle was born in Ecclefechan, Dumfriesshire, the son of a stonemason. He arrived in Edinburgh for the

COMELY BANK

Thomas and Jane Carlyle

first time in 1809, barely 14 years of age, to study at the University for a general Arts degree. He left in 1813, without taking his degree, and took up teaching at his old school in Annan. He returned to Edinburgh again in 1817 to begin theological training, but religious doubts and disaffection with the Church put an end to his intended career in divinity. Miserable and suffering from chronic dyspepsia, he commented, 'I was entirely unknown in Edinburgh circles ... a prey to nameless struggles and miseries.'

He first met 19-year-old Jane Welsh, the only child of Dr John Welsh and his wife, Grace, at her parents' home in Haddington in 1821. After a frenetic courtship, they married in October 1826. He was 31, careerless, possibly impotent and would not achieve fame until middle age. Their first home was at 21 Comely Bank, an unpretentious Georgian terraced house on the north-east edge of the New Town, described by Jane as 'quiet and light and dry', with 'a pretty tree before the door'.

Carlyle's early efforts at trying to make a living from his

pen included writing entries for *Brewster's Encyclopaedia*. He also tutored and began penning articles for the *Edinburgh Review*. As a writer and historian, he became influenced by German philosophy and literature, and in 1824 he published a translation of Goethe's *Wilhelm Meister*. In 1833–4, *Sartor Resartus*, his first major work on social philosophy, was published in instalments in *Fraser's* magazine. His best-known work remains his *History of the French Revolution* (three volumes, 1837), the first of which had to be rewritten after a servant accidentally burnt the draft. Described by Dickens as 'that wonderful book' – which he claimed in a letter in 1851 to be reading 'for the 500th time' – it was, no doubt, a major influence on his own *A Tale of Two Cities* (1859).

The Carlyles left Edinburgh in May 1828 to live at Jane's family farm at Craigenputtoch in Dumfriesshire in an attempt to reverse Thomas's declining health, moving to London in 1834, where they were to spend the rest of their lives. In 1841, when Thomas's phenomenal success as a historian and social prophet was at its height, the possibility of returning to Edinburgh loomed on the horizon. Jane swiftly discounted it, writing to her mother, 'No, no, we are done with Edinburgh. He owes it no gratitude for any recognition he ever found there. It is only now when London and the world have discovered his talent that they are fain to admit it. As for me, I would as soon go back to Craigenputtock as to that poor, proud, formal, "highly respectable" city.'

The Carlyles settled in Chelsea at 5 Cheyne Row (now renumbered 24) in June 1834, where they lived together for 32 years until Jane's death. In 1848, William Thackeray told his mother, 'Tom Carlyle lives in perfect dignity' in a little house in Chelsea, 'with a snuffy Scotch maid to open the door, and the best company in England ringing at it'.

Jane died on 23 April 1866, and is buried with her father in the nave of the old Abbey Kirk, Haddington. Thomas survived Jane by nearly 15 years, dying on 4 February 1881, aged 85, and is buried beside his parents in Ecclefechan churchyard. Although Thomas is the more renowned of the two – his reputation is secure as one of the great historians – Jane's talents were also formidable. Had she written in the novel form, she might well have achieved the fame of Eliot, Sand or Brontë. After her death, Thomas dated and annotated her letters, which he thought 'among the cleverest ever written'; in contrast to Dickens, who burned most of his, or George Eliot, who took her partner's letters to her grave, the letters of Mr and Mrs Carlyle are preserved for posterity, warts and all.

SEE ALSO: Old College, *Edinburgh Review*, National Library of Scotland, St Giles, James Boswell, James Thin.

FURTHER INFORMATION: The largest collection of letters, journals and related material is in the National Library of Scotland, George IV Bridge. The second largest collection is in the Houghton Library, Harvard University.

FURTHER READING: J.A. Froude, *Thomas Carlyle: A History of the First Forty Years of his Life* (Uni. Press of the Pacific, 2002); R. Ashton, *Thomas and Jane Carlyle: Portrait of a Marriage* (Pimlico, 2003), K. Chamberlain, *Jane Welsh Carlyle* (Duckworth, 2017). Collections of Jane's letters have been published by J.A. Froude (1883), L. Huxley (1924) and T. Scudder (1931).

21 Comely Bank. First home of the Carlyles

DEAN VILLAGE

DEAN PATH
Dean Cemetery

Grave of Dr Joseph Bell (1837–1911)
Sir Arthur Conan Doyle's inspiration for Sherlock Holmes

Doyle was always making notes. He seemed to want to copy down every word I said. Many times after the patient had departed my office, he would ask me to repeat my observations so that he would be certain he had them correctly.
Dr Joseph Bell

When Arthur Conan Doyle was a young unknown medical student in the late 1870s at Edinburgh University, his most memorable teacher was Dr Joseph Bell, whose talent for making lightning diagnoses, combined with his acute powers of observation, inspired Doyle in later life to use him as the model for the world's greatest consulting detective: Sherlock Holmes. Bell was a noted surgeon of the time, who practised at the Royal Infirmary and who also passed on his knowledge and skills through lectures to medical students. Besides studying under Bell, Doyle was also appointed as his clerk for a time – a duty which was regularly

A white-haired Joseph Bell

given to students – thereby allowing Doyle even more intimacy with the eminent physician. They only had contact with each other for a couple of years, but the impression was a lasting one which planted the seeds for the great sleuth in Doyle's imagination. In an interview published in *The Bookman* in May 1892, Doyle stated that:

> Sherlock Holmes was the literary embodiment of my memory of a professor of medicine at Edinburgh University, who would sit in the patients' waiting room, with a face like a Red Indian, and diagnose the people as they came in, before even they had opened their mouths. He would tell them their symptoms. He would give them details of their lives, and he would hardly ever make a mistake.

Bell later wrote to Doyle praising the stories and denied that he had been 'more than a minor influence on them'. Doyle replied:

> It is most certainly to you that I owe Sherlock Holmes although, in the stories, I have the advantage of being able to place him in all sorts of dramatic positions, I do not think that his analytical work is in the least an exaggeration of some of the effects which I have seen you produce in the outpatient ward.

Bell's dramatic and arrogant diagnosing style may have seemed like the inspired guesswork of a show-off lecturer to some, but in the 1870s there were no X-rays or scans to help make up a physician's mind. Everything rested on what they saw, what they felt, what they smelt and what they heard with their stethoscope.

Born the eldest of nine children in Edinburgh in 1837, Joseph Bell came from a medical family which spanned four generations. Educated at Edinburgh Academy and

The white marble cross marking Joseph Bell's grave

Edinburgh University, qualifying as an MD in 1859, he began his surgical career as a house surgeon at the Royal Infirmary in Lauriston Place. In 1887, he became the first chief surgeon at the fledgling department of surgery in the Royal Hospital for Sick Children in Sciennes Road. In 1863, he became a fellow of the Royal College of Surgeons of Edinburgh, becoming its president in 1887.

In 1865, he married Edith Murray, with whom he had three children. When Edith died of puerperal peritonitis in 1874, Dr Bell's black hair is said to have turned white almost overnight. Following his death on 4 October 1911, a staggering number of people attended his funeral, while thousands more lined the streets.

This turnout, however, was nothing to do with Sherlock Holmes. The tribute was for Joseph Bell. The following extract from the *British Medical Journal*'s obituary for Joseph Bell faithfully sums up the feeling of the time:

> Dr. Joseph Bell died at his country house, Mauricewood, Milton Bridge, Midlothian, on October 4th. His health broke down in February last, and although he rallied and was able to be out to enjoy a drive, he did not resume practice. A week or two ago serious heart symptoms recurred, and ended his life. Dr. Bell was a marked figure in Edinburgh. Nearly to the end of his life he retained his buoyant and even boyish disposition. He was bright, cheerful, and happy. He had many admiring friends. He was a kindly man, and unknown to all but a few, he did very many fine and helpful actions to those in trouble. Till his illness in February last he carried on a large family practice. He was a brilliant and impressive teacher. He missed nothing as a clinician. Among his pupils in the Edinburgh Royal Infirmary was Sir Arthur Conan Doyle, who, it is generally believed, took him as the prototype of the famous detective of the 'Sherlock Holmes' stories. Sir Arthur Conan Doyle says of his old teacher: 'Personally I can say very little of Dr. Joseph Bell, for I have never met him in his own house, and really only know him as my professor. As such I shall always see him very clearly, his stiff, bristling, iron-grey hair, his clear, half-humorous, half-critical grey eyes, his eager face, and swarthy skin. He had a very spare figure, as I remember him, and walked with a jerky energetic gait, his head carried high, and his arms swinging. He had a dry humour, and a remarkable command of the vernacular, into which he easily fell when addressing his patients. His skill as a surgeon and his charm as a lecturer are, of course, proverbial.'
> *British Medical Journal*, Oct. 14, 1911.

BOOK LOVERS' EDINBURGH

SEE ALSO: Arthur Conan Doyle, Joseph Bell

FURTHER INFORMATION: Joseph Bell's grave is marked by a white marble cross situated roughly midway along the northern wall bordering Ravelston Terrace.

Grave of Lord Cockburn (1779–1854)
Advocate, biographer and memorialist

> The exemption of Scotch claret from duty, which continued (I believe) till about 1780, made it till then the ordinary beverage. I have heard Henry Mackenzie and other old people say that, when a cargo of claret came to Leith, the common way of proclaiming its arrival was by sending a hogshead of it through the town on a cart, with a horn; and that anybody who wanted a sample, or drink under pretence of a sample, had only to go to the cart with a jug, which, without much nicety about its size, was filled for sixpence.
>
> Dinner hours and customs; from *Memorials of His Time*

Henry Cockburn is best remembered today for *Memorials of His Time* (1856), a rich and amusing memoir of a vanished Edinburgh, and his *Life of Jeffrey* (1852). The son of a lawyer, Henry Cockburn was educated at the old High School and Edinburgh University. As an advocate, he defended Thomas Burke's wife in the Burke and Hare trial of 1828, eventually becoming solicitor general for Scotland. A passionate Whig, he contributed legal and political articles to the *Edinburgh Review*, which fondly described him as 'rather below the middle height, firm, wiry and muscular, inured to active exercise of all kinds, a good swimmer, an accomplished skater and an intense lover of the breezes of heaven. He was the model of a high-bred Scotch gentleman.'

SEE ALSO: *Edinburgh Review.*

DEAN VILLAGE

Grave of Francis Jeffrey (1773–1850)
Judge, critic and editor of the *Edinburgh Review*

[You combine] the force and nature of Scott in his pathetic parts, without his occasional coarseness and wordiness, and the searching disclosure of inward agonies of Byron, without a trait of his wickedness.
Letter from Jeffrey to Charles Dickens, 1847

Francis Jeffrey, along with the Reverend Sydney Smith, Henry Brougham and Francis Horner, founded the *Edinburgh Review* in 1802, an enormously successful quarterly magazine which became renowned for its highly influential views and savage criticism. Jeffrey, who became its first editor, was also an advocate and an MP. In 1830, he was appointed lord advocate.

SEE ALSO: *Edinburgh Review.*

FURTHER READING: H. Cockburn, *Life of Jeffrey* (Lexden, 2004).

Tomb of Francis Jeffrey

CANONMILLS

8 HOWARD PLACE
Birthplace of Robert Louis Stevenson
Writer who became a legend in his lifetime

A fractious little fellow ... though decidedly pretty.
A description of the baby RLS by one of his mother's bridesmaids

Robert Lewis Balfour Stevenson was born on 13 November 1850 and was named after his grandfathers, Robert Stevenson and the Reverend Lewis Balfour. His parents, Thomas Stevenson and Margaret Balfour, married in 1848 and set up their first home at 8 Howard Place, a relatively new Georgian terrace situated just beyond the northern rim of the New Town. Their only child was christened by his grandfather at Howard Place, and the family nicknamed him 'Smout', after the Scots word for salmon fry.

The universal image of RLS is synonymous with that of chronic ill health, but for the first two of years of his life Smout was a healthy child, with no signs of the purgatory to come. Like many Victorians, his parents worried about the family's health, but for the time being Smout was in no danger. When he was 18 months old, his nurse, Alison Cunningham, entered his life. 'Cummy' was from Torryburn, in Fife, and her zealous devotion to her young charge, coupled with her strict Calvinism and 'blood-curdling tales of the Covenanters', had a profound and lasting influence on RLS for the rest of his life. It was Cummy to whom he dedicated *A Child's Garden of Verses* in 1885.

CANONMILLS

Howard Place was small, and a little too close for comfort to the dampness of the Water of Leith, which in those days conveyed sewage, secretions from local mills and their hovering stench towards the sea. Hence the move in 1853 to a house at 1 Inverleith Terrace, which, although just across the street, was a larger and, it was hoped, a healthier one.

SEE ALSO: Robert Louis Stevenson.

FURTHER INFORMATION: 8 Howard Place is not open to the public.

FURTHER READING: J.C. Furnas, *Voyage to Windward* (Faber, 1952); I. Bell, *Dreams of Exile: Robert Louis Stevenson - A Biography* (Mainstream, 1992).

8 Howard Place

INVERLEITH

9 INVERLEITH TERRACE
Childhood home of Robert Louis Stevenson

> *Whenever the moon and stars are set,*
> *Whenever the wind is high,*
> *All night long in the dark and wet,*
> *A man goes riding by.*
> *Late in the night when the fires are out,*
> *Why does he gallop and gallop about?*
> RLS recalling his fear of stormy nights
> at Inverleith Terrace, from 'Windy Nights',
> *A Child's Garden of Verses* (1885)

On 27 June 1853, when RLS was two years six months old, the Stevenson family moved from 8 Howard Place to 1 (now No. 9) Inverleith Terrace, conveniently situated just across the road. This larger three-storey house was, at first glance, more salubrious, but in reality it proved to be the opposite, and was draughty, damp and mildewed. Whether Inverleith Terrace was a catalyst for RLS's decline in health around this time is debatable, but it sounds likely. Both his parents had bronchial complaints, so his respiratory problems would probably have been inherited anyway, but a combination of 'one of the vilest climates under heaven', dampness, air pollution and chronic chest trouble doesn't bode well. Tuberculosis of the lungs is a diagnosis which is often put forward but cannot be confirmed, as there were no blood tests or X-rays available in the nineteenth century. RLS wrote of Inverleith Terrace in *Notes of Childhood* (1873):

> All this time, be it borne in mind, my health was of the most precarious description. Many winters I never crossed the threshold, but used to lie on my face on the nursery floor, chalking or painting in water-colours the pictures in the illustrated newspapers; or sit up in bed, with a little shawl pinned about my shoulders, to play with bricks or whatnot.

When he was well, his devoted nurse Cummy took him for walks to the Royal Botanic Gardens and nearby Warriston Cemetery. 'Do you remember, at Warriston, one autumn Sunday,' he wrote to Cummy in 1883, 'when the beech-nuts were on the ground, seeing Heaven open? I would like to make a rhyme of that, but cannot.' His spirits were lifted in October 1856 when cousin Bob, his uncle Alan's son, came to spend the winter. 'This visit of Bob's was altogether a great holiday in my life,' wrote RLS in *Memoirs of Himself* (1880). 'We lived together in a purely visionary state. We had countries; his was Nosingtonia, mine Encyclopaedia; where we ruled and made wars and inventions ... We were never weary of dressing up. We drew, we coloured our pictures; we painted and cut out figures for a pasteboard theatre; this last one of the dearest pleasures of my childhood.'

In 1856, the Stevensons moved to their new south-facing home at 17 Heriot Row in the middle of the New Town – a move that reflected Thomas Stevenson's thriving career and would, it was hoped, improve their young son's health.

SEE ALSO: Robert louis Stevenson.

FURTHER READING: R. Woodhead, *The Strange Case of R.L. Stevenson* (Luath Press, 2001).

COLINTON

87 COLINTON ROAD
Former home of Dorothy Dunnett
Historical novelist

A historical novel without humour, like passion without humour, is a very dull thing.
Dorothy Dunnett

Author of the Lymond Chronicles and the House of Niccolò series of historical novels, Dorothy Dunnett was a prolific writer whose meticulous research into the fifteenth and sixteenth centuries created a series of novels which attracted a worldwide readership.
Born Dorothy Halliday in 1923 in Dunfermline, Fife, she was educated at James Gillespie's High School for Girls in Bruntsfield, Edinburgh – the model for the Marcia Blaine School in the novel *The Prime of Miss Jean Brodie*. From 1940 to 1955, she worked with the Civil Service as a press officer and in 1946 she married the journalist Alastair Dunnett. Her writing career began in the late 1950s, but her first novel was rejected by five British publishers. Not unduly perturbed by this, her husband sent the manuscript to his American friend Lois Cole, the

agent who discovered *Gone with the Wind* by Margaret Mitchell. *The Game of Kings* was subsequently published by Putman in the USA in 1961, and its romantic hero, the sixteenth-century soldier of fortune Francis Crawford of Lymond, made the first of his many appearances. Five more volumes of the Lymond Chronicles followed over the next fifteen years, together with her Johnson Johnson detective novels. In 1986, she began a second historical series: the eight-volume House of Niccolò, set during the Renaissance. Dunnett was also an accomplished portrait painter and exhibited at the Royal Scottish Academy. In 1992, she was awarded the OBE for services to literature. Dorothy Dunnett lived for more than 40 years at Colinton Road and wrote most of her books there, writing in a converted garage at the back of the house. She died of cancer on 9 November 2001 in an Edinburgh hospice.

SEE ALSO: St Giles, Heart of Midlothian.

FURTHER READING: E. Morrison, *The Dorothy Dunnett Companion, Volumes I and II* (Vintage, 2001, 2002).

Left: Dorothy Dunnett
(© Olive Millward)
Right: *The Game of Kings*, first published in 1961

BOOK LOVERS' EDINBURGH

DELL ROAD
Colinton Manse
Former home of Robert Louis Stevenson's maternal grandparents and birthplace of his mother

> *For long ago, the truth to say,*
> *He has grown up and gone away,*
> *And it is but a child of air*
> *That lingers in the garden there.*
> RLS, from 'To Any Reader',
> *A Child's Garden of Verses* (1885)

Colinton Manse

Stevenson's 'rhymes' and 'jingles', as he called his poems in *A Child's Garden of Verses*, were written when he was in his early 30s. Some were written in the intervals of writing *Treasure Island*, at Braemar, and the rest were written in his sickbed at Hyères. Many of the poems are recollections of his childhood days spent with his grandparents at Colinton Manse, which he fondly recalls in *Memoirs of Himself* (1880):

> I have not space to tell of my pleasures at the manse. I have been happier since; for I think most people exaggerate the capacity for happiness of a child; but I have never again been happy in the same way. For indeed, it was scarce a happiness of this world, as we conceive

it when we are grown up, and was more akin to that of an animal than to that of a man. The sense of sunshine, of green leaves, and of singing of birds, seems never to have been so strong in me as in that place. The deodar upon the lawn, the laurel thickets, the mills, the river, the church bell, the sight of people ploughing, the Indian curiosities with which my uncles had stocked the house, the sharp contrast between this place and the city where I spent the other portion of my time, all these took hold of me, and still remain upon my memory.

Stevenson's grandfather, Lewis Balfour, was born in 1777, the third son of the laird of Pilrig, and was described by his grandson as 'the noblest looking old man I have ever seen ... one of the last, I suppose, to speak broad Scots and be a gentleman'. He entered the ministry in 1806 and his first parish was at Sorn, in Ayrshire, where he met and married minister's daughter Henrietta Scott Smith in 1808. The couple moved into Colinton Manse in 1823, and on 11 February 1828 Margaret Isabella Balfour (RLS's mother) was born. Maggie, 'the Minister's white-headed lassie', was the twelfth of thirteen children and the fourth and youngest daughter. After a chance meeting on a train, she was courted by engineer Thomas Stevenson, whom she married in 1848. He was 30 and she was 19. The newly-weds moved into 8 Howard Place at Canonmills, and on 13 November 1850 their son, and only child, Robert Lewis Balfour Stevenson was born.

The Balfour tomb, the last resting place of RLS's grandparents and family, including four of their children who died in infancy, can be seen at the north end of the churchyard near the church door. Robert Louis Stevenson and his wife Fanny are entombed on the summit of Mount Vea in Samoa, 1,300 feet above sea level, but RLS longed to be buried in Scotland, perhaps in Colinton Kirkyard, close to the manse and garden he loved so dearly.

BOOK LOVERS' EDINBURGH

SEE ALSO: Robert Louis Stevenson

FURTHER INFORMATION: Colinton Parish Church, Dell Road (at the foot of Spylaw Street), opened The Swing Cafe in 1998. The cafe is named after RLS's poem 'The Swing' in *A Child's Garden of Verse*s, and outside the east window stands the yew tree that RLS's original swing hung from. The 'dark brown' river in 'Where Go the Boats?' in *A Child's Garden of Verses* is the Water of Leith, which RLS would have accessed through the water door (now just a gap) behind the graveyard wall to the rear of the manse. In 2014 Colinton Conservation Trust inaugurated a Stevenson poetry trail that begins on Bridge Road at the top of the Long Steps and continues via a series of poetry panels to the Colinton Parish Church.

Left: Bronze statue of RLS as a boy with his Skye terrier, Coolin, outside the gates of Colinton Parish Church (opposite), unveiled in 2013.

COLINTON

SWANSTON

SWANSTON VILLAGE
Swanston Cottage
Summer retreat of the Stevenson family

The cottage was a little quaint place of many rough-cast gables and grey roofs. It had something of the air of a rambling infinitesimal cathedral, the body of it rising in the midst two storeys high, with a steep-pitched roof, and sending out upon all hands (as it were chapter-houses, chapels, and transepts) one-storeyed and dwarfish projections. To add to this appearance, it was grotesquely decorated with crockets and gargoyles, ravished from some mediaeval church. The place seemed hidden away, being not only concealed in the trees of the garden, but, on the side on which I approached it, buried as high as the eaves by the rising of the ground.
RLS's description of Swanston Cottage in *St Ives* (1897)

Swanston is the most romantic of Stevenson's Edinburgh haunts. A rural idyll, it is conveniently situated at Edinburgh's back door, only a two-hour walk from Heriot Row with the Pentland Hills on its doorstep. It was a place where Stevenson could lose himself walking in the hills and write undisturbed save for 'the whaup's wild cry on the breeze'. The steep slopes of Allermuir and Caerketton Hill rose before him with Glencorse, Rullion Green and the Covenanter's graves beyond. 'The hills are close by across a

The velvet-jacketed RLS with habitual gasper

valley,' he wrote in *Picturesque Notes*, 'Kirk Yetton, with its long, upright scars visible as far as Fife, and Allermuir, the tallest on this side, with wood and tilled field running high upon their borders, and haunches all moulded into glens and shelvings and variegated with heather and fern. The air comes briskly and sweetly off the hills.'

'The place in the dell' first entered his heart in 1867 when his father decided to rent Swanston Cottage as a summer retreat, an arrangement which lasted 14 years. Built in 1761, the cottage was given a second storey about 1835, and in 1867 the Stevensons built an extension on its west side. In 1871, the census records that Swanston village had

22 houses with 72 residents. Stevenson befriended many of them, including the farmers and shepherds, notably John Todd, the 'Roaring Shepherd', who features in his essay 'Pastoral', in *Memories and Portraits* (1887):

> In the ripeness of time, we grew to be a pair of friends, and when I lived alone in these parts in the winter, it was a settled thing for John to 'give me a cry' over the garden wall as he set forth upon his evening round, and for me to overtake and bear him company.

Stevenson used the hen-house at Swanston Cottage as the basis for his fictional place of refuge for the fugitive Monsieur le Vicomte de Saint-Yves during his daring escape from Edinburgh Castle in *St Ives*, his unfinished novel which was completed by Arthur Quiller-Couch in 1897.

Today, Edinburgh is steadily creeping towards Swanston like volcanic lava, and one day it will swallow it. They say a Scotsman never thinks of hills but he hears a whaup (a curlew), but if the wind is in the right direction at Swanston, the drone of the city bypass is more likely to reach your ears than a whaup. Stevenson was thankfully spared this pollution and, writing from his tropical exile in Samoa to S.R. Crockett, the Pentlands were set in aspic as his 'Hills of Dream':

> Be it granted me to behold you again in dying,
> Hills of home! and to hear the call,
> Hear about the graves of the martyrs the peewees crying,
> And hear no more at all.

SEE ALSO: Robert Louis Stevenson.

FURTHER INFORMATION: To get to Swanston, approach

it from Swanston Road, off Oxgangs Road. If coming from the city bypass, exit at Lothianburn for Oxgangs Road. Swanston Cottage is off to the right behind Swanston Farm. It is not open to the public. A bench near the gate at the south end of the village leading to the Pentlands is dedicated to the memory of Edwin Muir, who often visited Swanston and enjoyed its peace and tranquillity.

FURTHER READING: D.G. Moir, *Pentland Walks: Their Literary and Historical Associations* (Bartholomew, 1977); R.A. Hill, *Pure Air and Fresh Milk: Robert Louis Stevenson at Swanston* (privately printed, 1995).

Swanston Cottage, from a drawing by John Knight

PENTLAND HILLS

RULLION GREEN
Site of the Covenanters' first battle and inspiration for Stevenson's 'The Pentland Rising'

> *Those who sacrificed themselves for peace, the liberty, and the religion of their fellow-countrymen, lay bleaching in the field of death for long, and when at last they were buried by charity, the peasants dug up their bodies, desecrated their graves, and cast them once more upon the heath for the sorry value of their winding sheets!*
> Robert Louis Stevenson, 'The Pentland Rising' (1866)

The Pentland Rising and the Battle of Rullion Green in 1666 is a significant event in Covenanting history, as it was the first time that Covenanters had banded together as a force to be reckoned with to protest against the outlawing of their Presbyterian religion. On 28 November, 900 Covenanters were intercepted by 3,000 professional troops, who, after a bloody battle, left 50 Covenanters dead on the slopes of Turnhouse Hill overlooking the valley of the Glencorse Burn. Many of the wounded died in the hills and about 30 prisoners were hanged at the Mercat Cross in Edinburgh. After their execution, their right hands were cut off and nailed to the prison door at Lanark and their severed heads displayed in their home towns and villages: a severe lesson to others thinking of sacrificing themselves 'for peace, the liberty, and the religion of their fellow-countrymen'.

Stevenson grew up with tales of the Covenanters resounding in his ears and was surrounded by their bloody history during his summers at Swanston. In 1866, aged only 16, he wrote and published anonymously 'The Pentland Rising: a page of History, 1666'. This 16-page 'slim green pamphlet', of which only 100 copies were printed, is now a collector's item. His father, however, wasn't impressed, as his Aunt Jane Balfour recollected in 1866:

> I was at Heriot Row ... and Louis was busily altering 'The Pentland Rising' then to please his father. He had made a story of it, and by so doing, had, in his father's opinion, spoiled it. It was printed not long after in a small edition, and Mr Stevenson very soon bought all the copies in, as far as was possible.

This, his first published work, never seemed to find a fond corner in his memory and he described it in later life as 'an absurdity written by a schoolboy'. Maybe so, but Louis always loved a lost cause, and the Covenanters would surely have been honoured.

SEE ALSO: Robert Louis Stevenson.

FURTHER INFORMATION: Rullion Green lies about eight miles south of Edinburgh on the slopes of the Pentland Hills. Recommended map: OS Explorer 344. To visit Rullion Green, turn off the A720 city bypass at the Lothianburn Junction, heading south on the A702. Park at the Flotterstone Ranger and Visitor Centre about four miles further on. Walk along the pavement by the A702 for about 20 minutes, then turn right at Rullion Green Cottage into the hills. The Martyrs' Memorial is about half a kilometre from the A702 on the south-east slopes of Turnhouse Hill, and is marked on OS Explorer 344.

LEITH

2 WELLINGTON PLACE
Former Home of Irvine Welsh (1958–)
Author of *Trainspotting*

Somebody said, 'There's too many f***s and too many c***s in the book.' I says, 'Well, how many is enough and how much is too many?'
Irvine Welsh

Born in Leith and brought up in Muirhouse, Irvine Welsh became a household name in 1993 when his novel *Trainspotting*, about a group of heroin addicts living in Leith, exploded with the shock and impact of a thunderbolt and saw Welsh acknowledged as the voice of 1990s British youth culture. Danny Boyle's 1996 film reached an even wider audience, securing Welsh's place in Scotland's literary hall of fame – or infamy, depending on your taste. Today, the controversy and outrage has all but evaporated and *Trainspotting* sits comfortably on bookshop shelves beside the Waverley novels.

A controversial figure, who has a love–hate relationship with his native city, Welsh is never afraid of expressing his opinions in vernacular expletives. There have been many media 'claims' about Welsh's background. The word 'shrouded', for example, is often used when referring to his roots, but there's surely nothing sinister about a man who wants to keep his past from the muckrakers.

We attended the same secondary school – Ainslie Park in Pilton Avenue (now flats) – but we never met. Our

LEITH

Irvine Welsh

council estates were virtually next door to each other, and my Auntie Lizzie lived in sunny Leith, where her window looked directly onto the bleak stone wall of Leith Central Station, from which Welsh derived his title 'Trainspotting', an ironic reference to the fact that trains no longer stop there, Leith being a community ignored and forgotten at the time *Trainspotting* was written.

Welsh was reputedly born in 1958 and left school aged 16 to serve his time as an apprentice TV repair man. He later moved to London, where he had various jobs, got involved in the punk scene and ended up working in the offices of Hackney Council. He returned to Scotland and was employed as a training officer with Edinburgh City Council from 1986 to 1994, during which time he took computer studies at Heriot Watt University.

Trainspotting began appearing in 1991 in the London-based low-budget magazine *DOG* and also in Glasgow's

BOOK LOVERS' EDINBURGH

West Coast Magazine and *Scream, If You Want to Go Faster: New Writing Scotland No. 9*, edited by Hamish Whyte and Janice Galloway. Early drafts of *Trainspotting* also appeared in the first edition of the Edinburgh-based *Rebel Inc.* in April 1992, and in Duncan McLean's *Clocktower Booklet: A Parcel of Rogues*. It was McLean who recommended Welsh to Robin Robertson, editorial director of Secker & Warburg, who decided to publish *Trainspotting*. Following the book's success, Welsh gave up his day job and turned to full-time writing. Stories proliferate that he peaked with his debut and begot the craze for lad-lit, but he did reach a vast audience who understood where he was coming from and recognised a language they could tune into. Welsh continues to produce some startling work. *Porno* (2002) continues the story of the principal characters of *Trainspotting* ten years on, where Sick Boy is now a director of porno movies and Spud is writing a history of Leith, though still an addict. Other works include *The Acid House* (1994), *Marabou Stork Nightmares* (1995), *Ecstasy* (1996), *Filth* (1998),*Glue* (2001), *Skagboys* (2012), and *The Blade Artist* (2016).
According to Ron McKay of *The Observer* (4 February 1996), not everyone in Muirhouse is a fan:

> 'Ah ken that Irvine Welsh,' said the scarfaced barman in the Penny Farthing pub. 'He's a sad f**king case, he is. He's a f**king Hibee [supporter of the Hibernian football team] … ' One woman defended him stoutly, 'Ah don't care what they say, naebody's ever written aboot Muirhouse before,' but, asked whether she'd actually read any of his books, she said, 'Ah'll get roon tae them when they're on offer at Kwik Save.'

FURTHER INFORMATION: Muirhouse can be reached by a No. 37 bus outside Fraser's department store at the west end of Princes Street or by catching a northbound No. 27 bus in Hanover Street.

JUNCTION OF BERNARD STREET AND CONSTITUTION STREET
Statue of Robert Burns (1759–96)

This imposing bronze figure of Burns was erected by the Leith Burns Club in 1898 and sculpted by D.W. Stevenson. On each of the four faces of the plinth there is a bronze plaque bearing the following inscriptions respectively:

> South: The priest like father reads the sacred page. From scenes like those old Scotia's grandeur springs, that makes her loved at home, revered abroad.
> East: When Vulcan gies his bellows breath an' plowmen gather wi' their graith.
> West: In order on the clean hearth staine, the luggies three are ranged.
> North: I there wi' something did forgather that pat me in an eerie swither.

SEE ALSO: Burns Monument, Canongate Kilwinning Lodge, St Giles, William Smellie, William Creech, The Writers' Museum, Sciennes Hill House, Robert Fergusson, Clarinda, Henry Mackenzie, The Pear Tree.

PORTOBELLO

37 BELLFIELD STREET
Former home of J.G. Lockhart (1794–1854) Novelist, critic, essayist, and biographer and son-in-law of Sir Walter Scott

You can't know Burns unless you hate the Lockharts and all the estimable bourgeois and upper classes as he really did – the narrow gutted pigeons ... Oh, why doesn't Burns come to life again, and really salt them?
D.H. Lawrence, letter to Donald Carswell (1927), after reading Lockhart's *Life of Burns*.

John Gibson Lockhart is best remembered today for his biographies of Napoleon and Robert Burns, and his monumental seven-volume magnum opus on the life of his father-in-law, Sir Walter Scott. He was born at Cambusnethan in Lanarkshire, where his father was a Church of Scotland minister. He grew up in Glasgow, studying at the University and later at Oxford. In 1815, he moved to Edinburgh to practise as an advocate and in 1817, along with John Wilson, began editing the new monthly *Blackwood's Magazine*, where his powers of derision and parody gained him a reputation as a vicious critic. James Hogg, who joined forces with the two editors, described Lockhart as:

> a mischievous Oxford puppy, for whom I was terrified, dancing after the young ladies, and drawing caricatures of every one who came into contact with him ... I

dreaded his eye terribly; and it was not without reason, for he was very fond of playing tricks on me, but always in such a way, that it was impossible to lose temper with him.

Such was the hostility between *Blackwood's Magazine* and its competitor, the *London Magazine*, that Lockhart in 1821 challenged its editor John Scott to a duel in which Scott was fatally wounded by Lockhart's second (his assistant). In 1819, Blackwood published Lockhart's *Peter's Letters to His Kinfolk*, in which he lampooned leading Edinburgh figures.

Lockhart was a handsome young blade and demands for locks of his hair from young ladies were such that he once remarked that 'it threatened me with premature baldness'. He was also slightly deaf, which tended to make him appear stand-offish. In 1820, he married Sir Walter Scott's daughter, Sophia. They moved to London in 1825, where Lockhart edited the *Quarterly Review*. His pen name, The Scorpion – he 'who delighteth to sting the faces of men' – was a fitting nom de plume.

In 1827, the Lockharts occupied 37 Melville Street (now Bellfield Street), Portobello, a two-storey house on the east side of the street which was next to the grounds of Melville House (now the site of Vernon Villas). This visit appears to have been primarily for the sake of their children's health, and especially for their ailing eldest child. On 9 June 1827, Scott noted in his journal:

> When I came home from Court, I found that John Lockhart and Sophia were arrived by the steamboat at Portobello, where they have a small lodging. I went down with a bottle of champagne and a flask of maraschino, and made buirdly cheer with them for the rest of the day.

Here Scott regularly visited his grandchildren, who Lockhart tells us were 'a source of constant refreshment to him ... for every other day he came down and dined with them, and strolled about afterwards on the beach'.

Lockhart wrote four novels – *Valerius* (1821), *Adam Blair* (1822), *Reginald Dalton* (1823) and *Matthew Wald* (1824) – about which George Saintsbury commented in his *Essays in Literary Criticism*, 'Lockhart had every faculty for writing novels, except the faculty of novel writing.' Be that as it may, no one can deny that Lockhart's magnum opus, *The Life of Sir Walter Scott* (seven volumes, 1837–8), is an outstanding work of biography, arguably second only to Boswell's *Life of Samuel Johnson*.

He died at Abbotsford, Scott's former home in the Scottish Borders, which Sophia had inherited, on 25 November 1854, and is buried at nearby Dryburgh Abbey, at Sir Walter's feet.

SEE ALSO: *Blackwood's Magazine*, Sir Walter Scott, John Wilson, James Hogg.

FURTHER INFORMATION: Lockhart lived at various addresses in Edinburgh, including 23 Maitland Street and 25 Northumberland Street.

Bellfield Street

PORTOBELLO SANDS
Where Walter Scott rode with the 'soor dooks'

It was not a duty with him, or a necessity, or a pastime, but an absolute passion, indulgence in which gratified his feudal tastes for war ...
Lord Cockburn on Scott's military zeal in *Memorials of his Time* (1856)

The Battle of Puerto Bello took place off the Panama coast in 1739, and George Hamilton, a sailor who fought in it, built himself a cottage on a stretch of coast on the Firth of Forth which he named the Portobello Hut. Over the years, Portobello and its picturesque beach grew into a favourite resort.

During the Napoleonic Wars, Portobello Sands was used by the Volunteer Cavalry Regiment, known as the Edinburgh Light Horse, for exercising and practising drills. Prevented from joining the infantry because of his lameness, Walter Scott joined this new cavalry corps in 1797, the headquarters of which were at Musselburgh, and became its quartermaster. The 'soor dooks', as the regiment was nicknamed for its members' surly demeanour, became his passion and he could often be seen galloping through the surf of Portobello Sands on his black horse, or practising with his sabre at charging a turnip stuck on top of a staff, bellowing, 'Cut them down, the villains, cut them down!'

Once, in Paris, the Tsar of Russia asked him in what battles he'd been engaged. 'In some slight actions,' he replied, 'such as the battle of the Cross Causeway and the affair of Moredoun Mill.'

SEE ALSO: Sir Walter Scott.

CORSTORPHINE

CORSTORPHINE ROAD
Statue of David Balfour and Alan Breck Heroes in Robert Louis Stevenson's *Kidnapped*

> *We came the by-way over the hill of Corstorphine; and when we got near to the place called Rest-and-be-Thankful, and looked down on Corstorphine bogs and over to the city and the castle on the hill, we both stopped, for we both knew without a word said that we had come to where our ways parted.*
> The parting of David Balfour and Alan Breck in *Kidnapped* (1886)

Stevenson began writing his tale of the Forty-five Rebellion, begun 'partly as a lark, partly as a potboiler', in March 1885 at Skerryvore, his house in Bournemouth. Breck and Balfour represent a Scotland divided: Breck the romantic Highlander and follower of the Young Pretender, Charles Edward Stuart, known as Bonnie Prince Charlie; Balfour the steadfast Lowlander faithful to the Hanoverian cause. In bringing these two protagonists together, Stevenson created his first and best Scottish historical novel.

Three years in the making and sculpted in bronze by Alexander Stoddart, this 15-ft statue was unveiled by another Scots exile, Sean Connery, in 2004. Commissioned by Scottish & Newcastle brewers, the sculpture is situated at Corstorphine Road and Western Corner.

CORSTORPHINE

SEE ALSO: Robert Louis Stevenson, Old Calton Burial Ground, Hawes Inn, Pilrig House, RLS Club, R.M. Ballantyne.

FURTHER INFORMATION: It's ironic that Robert Louis Stevenson was known to be no great lover of statues. He was once asked to contribute towards a statue for his boyhood hero, R.M. Ballantyne, to which he responded thus: 'Mr Ballantyne would, I am sure, be vastly more gratified if we added to the prosperity of his wife and family than if we erected to him the tallest monument in Rome.'
The viewpoint of 'Rest and be Thankful' is on the Ravelston side of Corstorphine Hill and can be accessed from Ravelston Dykes Road.

SEE ALSO: R.M. Ballantyne.

FURTHER READING: I. Nimmo, *Walking With Murder: On the Kidnapped Trail* (Birlinn, 2005).

TURNHOUSE

TURNHOUSE ROAD
RAF Turnhouse
Former headquarters of No. 603 (City of Edinburgh) Squadron – legendary squadron of Richard Hillary (1919–43), Battle of Britain fighter pilot and author of *The Last Enemy*

> *The fighter pilot's emotions are those of the duellist – cool, precise, impersonal. He is privileged to kill well. For if one must either kill or be killed, as now one must, it should, I feel, be done with dignity. Death should be given the setting it deserves; it should never be a pettiness; and for the fighter pilot it never can be.*
> Richard Hillary, *The Last Enemy*

When Richard Hillary's bestselling book *The Last Enemy* was published in 1942, it joined the ranks of the classic literature of the Second World War. It is not just another tale of combat reminiscences; it is a book which has given future generations a real understanding of what life was like for 'The Few' who died during the Battle of Britain.
Born in Sydney, Australia, in 1919, he was sent to boarding school in England in 1927. He later attended Shrewsbury and entered Trinity College, Oxford, in 1937, where he joined the University Air Squadron. When war broke out, he joined the RAF Volunteer Reserve, which led in July 1940, after initial training, to a posting to 'B' Flight of No.

TURNHOUSE

Richard Hillary

603 (City of Edinburgh) Fighter Squadron, then based at Montrose.

On 16 October 1939, 603 Squadron shot down the first enemy aircraft over the UK and by November 1940 it had shot down its 100th. Shortly after Hillary joined them, the squadron headed south to RAF Hornchurch and into the cauldron of the Battle of Britain. After a week of relentless combat, he was hit during an aerial attack at 25,000 feet. Bailing out of his blazing Spitfire, he was plucked out of the sea by the Margate Lifeboat. Suffering from horrific burns to his face and hands, his life hung in the balance. Miraculously, he survived and he later underwent extensive plastic-surgery treatment.

During his lengthy convalescence, he visited the USA in 1941 on a propaganda tour, as did many of the British war-wounded, to try to persuade Americans to join the war effort, but ironically his mutilated face and claw-like hands were thought to convey too much of the horror of war and most of his tour was cancelled. It was at this time, during a three-month period in New York, that he wrote his book, published first in America under the title *Falling Through Space*. In June 1942, it was published in Great Britain by Macmillan as *The Last Enemy* and within a few weeks it had sold out of its run of 15,000 copies. The book was more than just an account of a fighter pilot's experience of war. His biographer, Lovat Dickson, described it as the story of 'a spoilt young man who had gone into the war pour le sport, who had mocked at everything, not least at himself and his own class, and came in the end humbly to accept humanity'.

He returned to operational flying in November 1942 and was posted to a night fighter squadron at RAF Charterhall in the Scottish Borders. On 8 January 1943, Richard Hillary finally met his last enemy ('The last enemy that shall be destroyed is death' – I Corinthians XV.26) when his converted bomber crashed during a night-training exercise shortly after take-off, killing Hillary and a crew member. Had he lived, his career as a writer would have been assured, because Richard Hillary was a writer who was a fighter pilot, not a fighter pilot who could write, and although his life was short, *The Last Enemy* – his only book – turned him into a legend.

FURTHER INFORMATION: In 2001, a memorial was erected in memory of Hillary and all who died at Charterhall during the Second World War. There were 85 deaths. Charterhall is situated in the Borders, east of Greenlaw on the B6460.

Sadly, much of RAF Turnhouse has now disappeared and what remains is in a sad state of disrepair. Edinburgh Airport was built on the south side of the airfield, opposite the original site,

TURNHOUSE

which was, in the early days of 603 Squadron, a small grass airfield. The first hard runway was not built until late 1939 and early 1940. The RAF badges have disappeared from the main gates, although the gates themselves still exist and the concrete gate pillars are still adorned with the RAF eagles, simply because they are part of the concrete moulding. The air-traffic-control tower still exists, although it has been modernised. An air-freight ferry depot has based itself in this location. One of the original hangars is still standing, although many buildings, including the officers' mess, have been demolished. The wartime operations room (bunker) is still where it was during the Second World War. Richard Hillary and friends would frequently visit the Maybury, a nearby art-deco watering-hole on Maybury Road, now a casino.

FURTHER READING: D. Ross, *Richard Hillary* (Grub Street, 2003); L. Dickson, *Richard Hillary* (Macmillan, 1950); A. Koestler, 'The Birth of a Myth', first published in *Horizon*, April 1943 (reprinted in his book of essays *The Yogi and the Commissar*, 1945); E. Linklater, 'Richard Hillary', an essay in *Art of Adventure* (Macmillan, 1947).

Edinburgh Airport's Spitfire memorial. The replica is in the colours of the original 603 (City of Edinburgh) Fighter Squadron Royal Auxiliary Air Force, sited on the main approach road to the airport.

LASSWADE

CHURCH ROAD
Lasswade Old Kirkyard
Grave of poet William Drummond of Hawthornden (1585–1649)

I long to kiss the image of my death.
William Drummond, from the sonnet 'Sleep, Silence Child' (1614)

In an age of confrontation and dispute, the poet William Drummond was no radical, but a royalist who desired peace and the seclusion of his idyllic castle 'far from the madding worldling's hoarse discords', to compose his mournful and highly stylised poetry. Born at Hawthornden Castle in the parish of Lasswade, he was educated at Edinburgh University and studied law in France, returning to his estate on the death of his father *c.*1610. He is best remembered today for his meeting with Ben Jonson, who visited him at Hawthornden for Christmas in 1618, when they reputedly greeted each other in rhyme: 'Welcome, welcome, royal Ben,' – 'Thank ee, thank ee, Hawthornden.' Jonson thought that Drummond's poetry 'smelled too much of the schools', and Drummond recorded their spirited dialogue in his book *Conversations of Ben Jonson and William Drummond*.

He is best known for his pastoral lament *Teares on the Death of Moeliades* (1613); *Poems, Amorous, Funereall, Divine, Pastorall in Sonnets, Songs, Sextains, Madrigals* (1614); and *Flowers of Sion and Cypresse Grove* (1623).

He also wrote the *History of Scotland 1423–1524* and a *History of the Five Jameses*, posthumously published in 1655.

Melancholic to the end, Drummond wrote his own epitaph, which reads:

> Here Damon lies, whose song did sometimes grace
> The wandering Esk; may roses shade the place.

FURTHER INFORMATION: William Drummond's grave is situated in what was a small arched aisle in the remains of the old parish church, but no stone marks the exact spot. A memorial was erected to him here in 1893. Hawthornden Castle lies on the banks of the River North Esk about a mile east of Roslin. It is not open to the public.

FURTHER READING: F.R. Fogle, *A Critical Study of William Drummond of Hawthornden* (1952).

Plaque to William Drummond above the door of his burial vault dating from its restoration in 1892

WADINGBURN ROAD
Barony House, formerly Lasswade Cottage
Summer house of Sir Walter Scott
and family

And it was amidst these delicious solitudes that he did produce the pieces which laid the imperishable foundations of all his fame …
J.G. Lockhart, *Memoirs of the Life of Sir Walter Scott, Bart.* (1839)

Walter and Charlotte Scott rented Lasswade Cottage on the western edge of Lasswade village (the 'Gandercleugh' in *Tales of my Landlord*) every summer from 1798 to 1804. Lockhart describes its picturesque charm in his *Life*:

> It is a small house, but with one room of good dimensions, which Mrs Scott's taste set off to advantage at very humble cost – a paddock or two – and a garden (commanding a most beautiful view) in which Scott delighted to train his flowers and creepers. Never, I have heard him say, was he prouder of his handiwork than when he had completed the fashioning of a rustic archway, now overgrown with hoary ivy, by way of ornament to the entrance from the Edinburgh road. In this retreat they spent some happy summers, receiving the visits of their few chosen friends from the neighbouring city, and wandering at will amidst some of the most romantic scenery that Scotland can boast.

In the summer of 1798, Walter Scott was beginning to feel settled in life: a steady income, a new wife of six months and a pen that wouldn't stop writing. The Scotts' townhouse was at 39 North Castle Street, bang in the city centre – wonderful if you need to be at the pulse of things, but not so good if you want peace to write. Lasswade Cottage, therefore, was the perfect retreat – a rural idyll only six miles from Edinburgh.

Scott wrote his translation of Goethe's *Götz von Berlichingen* here, the first substantial publication to bear his name, and also his ballad 'The Gray Brother' and the opening stanzas of the poem which made him famous, *The Lay of the Last Minstrel*.

Visiting literati included James Hogg (the 'Ettrick Shepherd'), and William and Dorothy Wordsworth during their tour of Scotland in 1803. His near neighbours were Henry Mackenzie, the Duke of Buccleuch and Lord Melville. Life was sweet and fame was just around the corner.

SEE ALSO: Sir Walter Scott.

FURTHER INFORMATION: Barony House is not open to the public. In c.1781 it was extended from an existing eighteenth-century cottage by the addition of a thatched, bowed drawing room and tree-trunk porch. In 1865, it was converted into a dower house with unbecoming baronial dormers and crowstepped gables. Lasswade lies on the River North Esk, six miles south-west of Edinburgh, between Dalkeith and Loanhead.

Drawing of a young Walter Scott and his dog

GLENCORSE

KIRK BRAE
Glencorse Old Kirk
Favourite haunt and inspiration of Robert Louis Stevenson (1850–94)

Built in 1699, with a steep slate roof and a wooden steeple, this little kirk and kirkyard was one of Robert Louis Stevenson's favourite haunts. When he stayed at Swanston Cottage, Stevenson would go to services there with his father and listen to old Mr Torrance preach ('over eighty and a relic of times forgotten, with his black thread gloves and mild old foolish face'). Glencorse is also the church featured in his prose poem 'Sunday Thoughts':

> A plague o' these Sundays! How the church bells ring up the sleeping past! I cannot go into sermon: memories ache too hard; and so I hide out under the blue heavens, beside the small kirk whelmed in leaves. Tittering country girls see me as I go past from where they sit in the pews, and through the open door comes the loud psalm and the fervent solitary voice of the preacher.

The grave-robbing scene in his 1884 'crawler' 'The Body Snatcher' was set in the old kirkyard:

> The coffin was exhumed and broken open; the body inserted in the dripping sack and carried between them to the gig; one mounted to keep it in its place, and the other, taking the horse by the mouth, groped along by

wall and bush until they reached the wider road by the Fisher's Tryst.

He also placed scenes from *Weir of Hermiston* (1896) here and it is highly likely that one of the tombstones ignited the inspiration for his Napoleonic prisoner-of-war novel, *St Ives* (1897): 'Ici repose Charles Cotier de Dunkerque. Mort le 8 Janvier 1807.' 'I suppose he died prisoner in the military prison hard by,' noted Stevenson.

He remembered Glencorse with affection and missed it dearly, lamenting from his tropical Samoan paradise that he 'shall never take that walk by the Fisher's Tryst and Glencorse; I shall never see Auld Reekie; I shall never set my foot again upon heather. Here I am until I die, and here will I be buried.'

SEE ALSO: Robert Louis Stevenson.

FURTHER INFORMATION: Unfortunately, Glencorse Old Kirk is on private land and is not open to the public. For many years, the kirk was a roofless ruin, but recent restoration has returned it to its former glory. RLS's description of the location 'where the road crosses the burn' in his letter to S.R. Crockett refers to a spot about half a mile westward from the gates of Glencorse House, where the public road crosses Glencorse Burn, and is on a double bend. Glencorse Kirk is signposted in Milton Bridge, opposite the Fisher's Tryst pub on the A701. This signpost refers to the new Glencorse Kirk, but the old kirk and 'where the road crosses the burn' are on the same road.

Glencorse Old Kirk

PENICUIK

PEEBLES ROAD
Penicuik South Church
Former church of novelist S.R. Crockett (1860–1914)

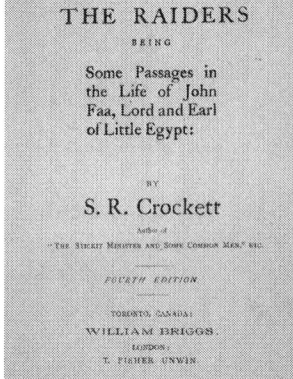

Left: S.R. Crockett and the frontispiece of the fourth edition of *The Raiders*
Right: Penicuik South Church

Born the illegitimate son of a dairymaid at the farm of Little Duchrae, Balmaghie, Kircudbrightshire in 1860, Samuel Rutherford Crockett was a leading exponent of the Kailyard school, which typified a sentimental and romantic image of Scottish rural life. Written in a cosy vernacular, his books were frequently bestsellers, but are little read today. Educated at the Free Church School at Castle Douglas, he won a bursary to Edinburgh University, where legend has it he lived on meals of oatmeal, penny rolls and milk. In 1886, he was appointed Free Church minister at Penicuik. With the success of *The Stickit Minister*, published in 1893, he abandoned the ministry in 1895 and became a full-time writer. *The Raiders* and *The*

PENICUIK

Lilac Sunbonnet followed in 1894, and 40-odd novels later he had accrued vast fame and fortune.

Crockett lived at Bank House in Penicuik Estate on the banks of the River Esk. The former Free Church (now Penicuik South Church) is still standing on the Peebles Road at Alder Bank. Crockett moved to Torwood Villa, near Peebles, in 1906, and died suddenly in Tarascon in France in 1914.

SEE ALSO: Swanston, Old College, W.E. Henley, Glencorse Kirk.

MILTON BRIDGE
Mauricewood, country retreat of Joseph Bell and where he died in 1911

[Sherlock Holmes] *has definitely retired from London and betaken himself to study and bee-farming on the Sussex Downs, notoriety has become hateful to him, and he has peremptorily requested that his wishes in this matter should be strictly observed.*
Arthur Conan Doyle, from 'The Adventure of the Second Stain', *The Return of Sherlock Holmes* (1905)

In 1894 Joseph Bell purchased Mauricewood, a modest Victorian mansion with a small estate, on the northern fringes of Penicuik, at the foot of the Pentland Hills. By the time he was almost 60 in 1896 he was seriously contemplating retirement. He still had one of the largest practices in the city. He was chief surgeon of the Royal Hospital for Sick Children, did charitable work for the Royal Hospital for Incurables, and had recently been elected to the post of University of Edinburgh assessor. Few would have criticised him for wanting to wind down from such a workload, and where better to do it than at Mauricewood, then an idyllic country retreat on the edge of Edinburgh? 'He loved to romp here with his grandchildren; to welcome his friends,' commented his granddaughter in 1943, 'Such were its delights, his garden might have been the island valley of Avilon.' And so, immersed in his flower garden, often surrounded by his grandchildren, who nicknamed him 'Gigs' because of his fondness for the horse-drawn carriage, Joe Bell withdrew slowly, but never completely, from the world of medicine.
He died on 4 October, 1911, at Mauricewood, aged 73, from a combination of heart disease, uraemia and albuminuria.

His final days were recorded in the *Edinburgh Medical Journal* for October, 1911, by his friend and colleague, Dr. John Playfair:

> During all the weeks and months of illness, never a murmur nor fretful word was heard from him, and his cheerfulness, even after a bad night was remarkable. I shall never forget, at the morning visit, and in response to my knock at his bedroom door, the loud and cheery come in, or come in, dear boy, so glad to see you. Then he gave me, with many humorous touches, a description of his night ... All orders and suggestions were gratefully and readily accepted and carried out with unfailing punctuality – this, too, although he was no ardent believer in the power of medicine. He realized that the best he could ever hope for would be a life of quiet invalidism. He accepted the outlook with perfect resignation and composure ... When he began to feel the end might be drawing near, he calmly and quietly asked us what we thought his prospects of life now were, requesting us to state our opinions plainly and frankly and to keep nothing back. A strong, simple Christian faith sustained him, not only then but through some of life's severest afflictions, and enabled him with a rare and lofty courage unshrinkingly to contemplate and prepare for the inevitable.

SEE ALSO: Conan Doyle, Joseph Bell.

Joseph Bell with his grandchildren

ROSLIN

ROSSLYN CHAPEL
Medieval treasure house and muse of Sir Walter Scott, William Wordsworth, Dan Brown and others

There are twenty of Roslin's barons bold
Lie buried within that proud chapelle;
Each one the holy vault doth hold –
But the sea holds lovely Rosabelle!

And each St. Clair was buried there,
With candle, with book, and with knell;
But the Kelpy rung, and the Mermaid sung,
The dirge of lovely Rosabelle.

Sir Walter Scott,
from *The Lay of the Last Minstrel* (1805)

When Dan Brown's bestselling novel *The Da Vinci Code* was published by Doubleday in 2003, it rivaled the sales of Harry Potter. With well over 60 million copies in print and translated into over 40 languages, it is said to be the ninth-bestselling book of all time. *The Da Vinci Code* well and truly captivated millions. Many swallowed the premise of the

The first U.S. edition, April 2003

book, but many did not, and a stream of titles debunking *The Da Vinci Code* have surfaced in recent years, accusing Dan Brown of distorting and fabricating history.

The novel is based on the contentious assumption that there is a conspiracy within the Roman Catholic Church to cover up the true facts about Jesus, especially concerning the Holy Grail and the role of Mary Magdalene. To keep itself in power, the Vatican must perpetuate the conspiracy. All clues lead the novel's two main characters, Sophie and Langdon, to Rosslyn Chapel, where they discover the location and the secret of the Holy Grail.

Rosslyn Chapel, however, didn't need *The Da Vinci Code* to make it famous; it was already was. For centuries it has been known for its remarkable peculiarities of architectural style, the richness of its ornaments and the conjecture over the chapel's so-called hidden 'treasures', ranging from the head of Christ to parchments revealing his bloodline. The name Rosslyn is derived from two words: 'Ross', meaning steep cliff; and 'Lyn', meaning fast-flowing water. The chapel was originally named the Collegiate Chapel of St Matthew and was built in the mid-fifteenth century by the St Clair family, a Scottish noble family descended from Norman knights who had strong connections with the Knights Templar and Scottish Freemasonry. Many foreign masons were said to be involved in its construction, a fact often used to explain some of the chapel's exuberant excesses. Built around fourteen pillars, the interior forms an arcade of twelve arches on three sides of the nave. The three pillars at the east end of the chapel are named, from north to south, the Master Pillar, the Journeyman Pillar and the Apprentice Pillar.

The Apprentice Pillar in the south-east corner is adorned with an elaborate relief of spiralling flowers and foliage, with ornaments of Abraham offering up Isaac and dragons at its base. The story from which the pillar gets its name is a well-known Rosslyn tale. The master-mason working on

Left: William Wordsworth
Right: Rosslyn Chapel

the pillar's elaborate plans was said to be unable to fathom them and journeyed to Rome to view a similar pillar. On his return he discovered that his apprentice had overcome the problems and finished the work. Overcome with jealousy and rage, he killed the apprentice with a blow from his hammer and was sentenced to death for his crime.

Sir Walter Scott mentions Rosslyn Chapel in his poem *The Lay of the Last Minstrel*, and the ceiling of the library at Abbotsford, his historic home near Melrose, is a detailed representation of Rosslyn Chapel interior.

Early visitors to the chapel included William and Dorothy Wordsworth in 1803. Dorothy thought the architecture 'quite beautiful', and William recorded his feelings in a sonnet written during a storm at a nearby inn, titled 'Composed in Rosslyn Chapel':

> The wind is now thy organist; a clank
> (We know not whence) ministers for a bell

ROSLIN

To mark some change of service. As the swell
Of music reached its height, and even when sank
The notes, in prelude, Roslin! to a blank
Of silence, how it thrilled thy sumptuous roof,
Pillars, and arches, not in vain time-proof,
Though Christian rites be wanting! From what bank
Came those live herbs? by what hand were they sown
Where dew falls not, where rain-drops seem unknown?
Yet in the Temple they a friendly niche
Share with their sculptured fellows, that, green-grown,
Copy their beauty more and more, and preach,
Though mute, of all things blending into one.

SEE ALSO: Sir Walter Scott.

FURTHER INFORMATION: Rosslyn Chapel is six miles south of Edinburgh. The easiest way to get there is to take a No. 37 bus from North Bridge heading south towards Newington. For the chapel disembark at The Original Rosslyn Hotel.

SOUTH QUEENSFERRY

NEWHALLS ROAD
The Hawes Inn
Sixteenth-century inn featured in Robert Louis Stevenson's *Kidnapped*

The romantic setting of the Hawes Inn first appealed to Sir Walter Scott, who had Lovel and Jonathan Oldbuck dining there in *The Antiquary* in 1816, but it was Robert Louis Stevenson who secured its immortality when he wove it into the plot of *Kidnapped* (1886), his tale of the Jacobite rising of 1745 and its sad aftermath. 'There it stands,' he wrote, 'apart from the town, beside the pier, in a climate of its own, half inland, half marine – in front, the ferry bubbling with the tide and the guardship swinging to her anchor; behind, the old garden with the trees.'

Although altered and extended over the years, the Hawes Inn still retains some of the backdrop, and perhaps a little of the spirit, in which old Ebenezer arranged the kidnap of his nephew David Balfour with the assistance of Captain

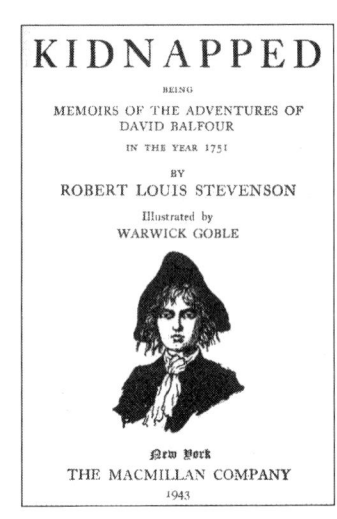

Left: Cover of Macmillan's 1943 edition of *Kidnapped*
Right: The Hawes Inn

SOUTH QUEENSFERRY

Hoseason in 'a small room, with a bed in it, and heated like an oven by a great fire of coal'. The unsuspecting David Balfour later boards the brig *Covenant*, moored at South Queensferry, where he is kidnapped and destined to be sold as a slave in the Carolinas.

Stevenson was a regular visitor to Queensferry in his youth, rambling along the shores of Cramond and canoeing in the Forth with Walter Simpson, his companion in *An Inland Voyage*. Since 1890, the Hawes Inn has been dwarfed by the adjacent Forth Railway Bridge, a spectacular feat of Victorian engineering that Stevenson never saw. The ferry disappeared in the early 1960s with the opening of the Forth Road Bridge.

SEE ALSO: Robert Louis Stevenson.

FURTHER INFORMATION: In *Catriona* (1893), the sequel to *Kidnapped*, David Balfour is imprisoned on the Bass Rock, opposite North Berwick, about 20 miles east of Edinburgh. Stevenson visited North Berwick for holidays as a young boy and set his essay 'The Lantern-Bearers' (1887) there.

FURTHER READING: I. Nimmo, *Walking With Murder: On the Kidnapped Trail* (Birlinn, 2005).

APPENDICES

LIBRARIES

George IV Bridge
National Library of Scotland and Central Library

Left: Poster for a Muriel Spark exhibition at the NLS during her centenary year, 2018
Right: The carved stone lintel over the entrance of the Central Library

The NLS is Scotland's largest library and is the world centre for the study of Scotland and the Scots. It also ranks among the largest libraries in the UK, housing 8,000,000 printed books, 120,000 volumes of manuscripts, 2,000,000 maps and over 20,000 newspaper and magazine titles. The online catalogue records 3,500,000 items for public access. The NLS developed from the Advocate's Library of 1682, the legal section of which is still housed in its original premises at Parliament Square. In 1925, its entire contents, apart from its legal section, were removed to the NLS. The library has the right to receive free of charge a copy of every book published in the United Kingdom and Ireland, based on the Legal Deposit Libraries Act 2003,

APPENDICES

and before that the Copyright Act 1911. This right has enabled the library to build extensive general collections on all subjects, though it has a special responsibility for the acquisition and preservation of material of Scottish interest. NLS is one of only five libraries in the UK today with copyright status. Since 1925, the NLS has also been collecting literary manuscripts, working papers and correspondence of writers such as Robert Burns, Sir Walter Scott, Edwin Muir, Sydney Goodsir Smith, A.J. Cronin, Lewis Grassic Gibbon, Neil Gunn, Muriel Spark, Hugh MacDiarmid, Naomi Mitchison, Alasdair Gray, Eric Linklater, Sir Arthur Conan Doyle, and Robert Louis Stevenson. The NLS also holds frequent public exhibitions of its collections and has a small gift shop and cafe.

Across the street from the National Library, at 7–9 George IV Bridge, stands the Central Library, Edinburgh's main lending library. Visited by half a million people annually, the library was founded by the Scots philanthropist Andrew Carnegie (1835–1919). Opened in 1890, and built in the French François I style, its foundations are rooted several storeys below George IV Bridge in the Cowgate. As well as being a general lending library, it houses important collections of Scottish and Edinburgh-related material. Collections in the Scottish Library hold extensive information about the city and Scotland.

BOOK LOVERS' EDINBURGH

5 Crichton's Close
Scottish Poetry Library

No' wan in fifty kens a wurd Burns wrote
But misapplied is a'body's property,
And gin there was his like alive the day
They'd be the last a kennin' haund to gie –
Hugh MacDiarmid, from 'A Drunk Man Looks at the Thistle' (1926)

With its mono-pitch roof slung over a steel frame, and walls of oak and glass, the award-winning building by architect Malcolm Fraser is deceptively simple, relaxing and, most of all, welcoming. Scottish artists were commissioned to contribute pieces, including Liz Ogilvie's glass-panelled balustrade inscribed with lines from Scottish poems, a tapestry by Ian Hamilton Finlay and a 'carpet of leaves' by Mary Bourne. As if this wasn't enough pleasure, the building also houses a collection of 30,000 items, many of which are available to borrow. Here you will find the poetry of Scotland in three languages – English, Scots and Gaelic.

APPENDICES

SELECTED BOOKSHOPS

McNaughtan's Bookshop, 3a–4a Haddington Place
(Second-hand and antiquarian)
Andrew Pringle Booksellers, 68 West Port
(Rare and antiquarian books and prints)
Armchair Books, 72–74 West Port
(General second-hand and antiquarian)
Aurora Books, 6 Tanfield
(General second-hand and antiquarian)
Barnardo's Bookshop, 45 Clerk Street
(Charity bookshop)
Blackwell's Bookshop, 53–62 South Bridge
(The city's largest bookshop)
Grant & Shaw, 10 Leslie Place
(Rare and antiquarian books)
Main Point Books, 77 Bread Street
(General second-hand)
Oxfam Bookshops, (Charity bookshops)
210 Morningside Road
116 Nicolson Street
25 Raeburn Place

BOOK LOVERS' EDINBURGH

Peter Bell Books, 68 West Port
(History, philosophy and Scottish)
Southside Books, 58 South Bridge
(New and second-hand)
The Edinburgh Bookshop, 219 Bruntsfield Place
(Children's book specialist)
Shelter Bookshop, 104 Raeburn Place
(Charity bookshop)
Till's Bookshop, 1 Hope Park Crescent
(General second-hand)
Citadel Books, 41 Montrose Terrace
(New and second-hand)
Lighthouse – Edinburgh's Radical Bookshop,
43–45 West Nicolson Street
(Politics, history, fiction, travel, children's)
Waterstones, (UK's largest book retailer)
6 Lady Road; 31B Fort Kinnaird
98/99 Ocean Terminal; 128 Princes Street
Transreal Fiction, 46 Candlemaker Row
(Science fiction and fantasy)
Golden Hare Books, 68 St Stephen Street
(Non-fiction, fiction, and children's books)
Old Town Bookshop, 8 Victoria Street
(Second-hand and antiquarian)

EDINBURGH INTERNATIONAL BOOK FESTIVAL

By the time Susie finally pronounced herself ready to set off for Charlotte Square Gardens and the tented village of the Book Festival, the clouds had scattered, bathing them in warm sunshine as they climbed the steep hill of Charlotte Street. This time, Cat was determined to subscribe to the pathetic fallacy. The sun shone; therefore only good things could happen to her.

Val McDermid, *Northanger Abbey* (2014)

Established in 1983 as a biennial festival, and becoming an annual celebration in 1997, this event is now the largest of its kind in the world. A mere 30 writers were hosted at the first festival, but today it holds hundreds of events, including debates, discussions, workshops and book signings, and has a lively children's programme. Located in Charlotte Square Gardens during August, when the Edinburgh International Festival and its satellite festivals are in full swing, the Book Festival becomes a place of sanctuary to recharge, reflect, relax and even read – an island in the stream when Edinburgh becomes culturally unhinged.

SEE ALSO: International Writers' Conference, J.K. Rowling.

BOOK LOVERS' EDINBURGH

EDINBURGH REMEMBERED

A dirty, cold, wet, run-down slum; a city of dull, black tenements and crass concrete housing schemes which were populated by scruffs, but the town still somehow being run by snobs. **Irvine Welsh**, Marabou Stork Nightmares (1995)

There is no street in Europe more spectacular than Princes Street; it is absolutely operatic. **Henry James**

It is quite lovely, bits of it. **Oscar Wilde**

This accursed, stinking, reeky mass of stones and lime and dung. **Thomas Carlyle**, letter to his brother John, February (1821)

Edinburgh is looking at its best, which is I think the best in the world, for it must be about the most romantic city on earth. But it strikes cold on me nowadays, for the familiar faces have long been gone and there are only buildings left. **J.M. Barrie**, 1909

But Edinburgh pays cruelly for her high seat in one of the vilest climates under heaven. She is liable to be beaten upon by all the winds that blow, to be drenched with rain, to be buried in cold sea fogs out of the east, and powdered with the snow as it comes flying southward from the Highland hills. The weather is raw and boisterous in winter, shifty and ungenial in summer, and a downright meteorological purgatory in the spring. The delicate die early, and I, as a survivor, among bleak winds and plumping rain, have sometimes been tempted to envy them their fate. **Robert Louis Stevenson**, Edinburgh: Picturesque Notes (1878)

What a wonderful City Edinburgh is! What alternation of Height & Depth! – a city looked at in the polish'd back of a Brobdingnag Spoon, held lengthways – so enormously stretched-up are the Houses. **Samuel Taylor Coleridge**

APPENDICES

The city stands upon two hills, and the bottom between them; and, with all its defects, may very well pass for the capital of a moderate kingdom. **Tobias Smollett**, *The Expedition of Humphry Clinker* (1771)

Tho' many cities have more people in them, yet, I believe, this may be said with truth that in no city in the world do so many people live in so little room as at Edinburgh. **Daniel Defoe**

It seems like a city built on precipices, a perilous city. Great roads rush down hill like rivers in spate. Great buildings rush up like rockets. **G.K. Chesterton**, 1905

Arrived at Edinburgh a little before sunset. As we approached, the Castle rock resembling that of Stirling – in the same manner appearing to rise from a plain of cultivated ground, the Firth of Forth being on the other side, and not visible … The Old Town, with its irregular houses, stage above stage, seen as we saw it, in the obscurity of a rainy day, hardly resembles the work of men. It is more like a piling up of rocks and I cannot attempt to describe what we saw so imperfectly, but must say that, high as my expectations had been raised, the city of Edinburgh far surpassed all expectations. **Dorothy Wordsworth**, *Recollections of a Tour Made in Scotland*: AD. 1803 (1874)

Edinburgh alone is splendid in its situation and buildings and would have even a more imposing and delightful effect if Arthur's Seat were crowned with thick woods and if the Pentland Hills could be converted into green pastures, if the Scotch people were French and Leith Walk planted with vineyards. **William Hazlitt**, 1826

I do wonder that so brave a prince as King James should be born in so stinking a town as Edinburgh in lousy Scotland. **Sir Anthony Weldon**, *A Perfect Guide to the People and Country of Scotland* (1617)

BOOK LOVERS' EDINBURGH

Well may Edinburgh be called Auld Reekie! The houses stand so one above another that none of the smoke wastes itself upon the desert air before the inhabitants have derived all the advantages of its odour and its smuts. You might smoke bacon by hanging it out of the window. **Robert Southey**, 1819

Edinburgh is a mad god's dream. **Hugh MacDiarmid**, *The Complete Poems* (1978)

I am not sorry to have seen the most picturesque (at a distance) and nastiest (when near) of all capital cities. **Thomas Gray**, 1765

It is the peculiar boast of Edinburgh, the circumstances on which its marvellous beauty so essentially depends, that its architecture is its landscape; that nature has done everything, has laid every foundation, and disposed of every line of its rocks and its hills, as if she had designed it for the display of architecture. **Edinburgh Review**, 1838

It would make a good prison in England. **Dr Samuel Johnson** on Edinburgh Castle

A setting for an opera nobody performs nowadays an opera called 'Scottish History'. **Alasdair Gray**, *Janine* (1984)

Six, seven, eight storeys high were the houses; storey piled above storey, as children build with cards. **Charles Dickens**

This (the Royal Mile) is, perhaps, the largest, longest, and finest street for buildings and number of inhabitants not in Britain only, but in the World. **Daniel Defoe**, *A Tour Through the Whole Island of Great Britain* (1724–27)

Glasgow plays the part of Chicago to Edinburgh's Boston. Glasgow is a city of the glad hand and the smack on the back; Edinburgh is a city of silence until birth or brains open the social circle. **H.V. Morton**

APPENDICES

What horrible alleys on each side of the High Street, especially downwards like passes of quarries of dark stone. I ventured down one, and hastened back to escape from the spitting of two children who were leaning out of an upper window. **Dorothy Wordsworth**, 1822

When I was lately in Scotland I went to visit some poor inhabitants of the Old Town of Edinburgh. In a close wynd – a most picturesque place – (picturesque and typhus synonymous) I saw more poverty and sickness than I ever saw before. In one wretched dwelling I saw a poor sick child cradled in an egg-box, which his mother had begged from a shop and that little wan child with his fevered face, his wasted hand and his bright watchful eyes, I have ever before my sight. I can still see him and seem to hear him say, 'Why am I lying here, shut in from the light of day and from the play of other children?' **Charles Dickens**, 1858

No smells were ever equal to Scotch smells. It is the School of Physic; walk the streets and you would imagine that every medical man had been administering cathartics to every man, woman and child in town. Yet the place is uncommonly beautiful and I am in constant balance between admiration and trepidation. **Sydney Smith**, 1798

The wynds down which an English eye may look but into which no English nose would willingly venture for stinks older than the Union are found there. **Robert Southey**, 1819

The main side streets are narrow, filthy and with six storey houses; one has to think of the great buildings in the dirty towns of Italy; poverty and misery seem to peep out of the open hatches which normally serve as windows. **Hans Christian Andersen**, 1847

Enchanting. It will make a delightful summer capital when we invade Britain. **Dr Joseph Goebbels**, 1938

BOOK LOVERS' EDINBURGH

As far as I am acquainted with modern architecture, I am aware of no streets which, in simplicity and manliness of style, or general breadth and brightness of effect, equal those of the New Town of Edinburgh. **John Ruskin**, Letters on Architecture and Painting (1854)

Beneath, the Old Town reared its dark brow, and the New one stretched its golden lines, while, all around, the varied charms of nature lay scattered in that profusion, which nature's hand alone can bestow. **Susan Ferrier**, Marriage (1818)

As long as sixteen or seventeen years ago, the first great public recognition and encouragement I ever received was bestowed on me in this generous and magnificent city – in this city so distinguished in literature and the arts ... coming back to Edinburgh is to me like coming home. **Charles Dickens**, 1858

The cook was too filthy an object to be described; only another English gentleman whispered me and said, he believed, if the fellow was to be thrown against a wall, he would stick to it. **Edmund Burt**, on an Edinburgh eating-house, Letters from the North of Scotland (1728–37)

Athenians, indeed! where is your theatre? who among you has written a comedy? ... you know nothing that the Athenians thought worth knowing, and dare not show your faces before the civilised world in the practice of any one art in which they were excellent. **Thomas Love Peacock**, on the pretensions of Edinburgh as the 'Athens of the North', in Crochet Castle (1831)

Fareweel, Edinburgh, where happy we hae been,
Fareweel, Edinburgh, Caledonia's Queen!
Auld Reekie, fare-ye-weel, and Reekie New beside,
Ye're like a chieftain grim and gray, wi' a bonny bride.
Baroness Carolina Nairne, *'Fareweel Edinburgh'*

Thanks to: Chris Foster, Kit Foster, Rob Hain, Harry Winslow, Ainslie Thin, Bob and Pat Watt, Elaine Greig, Alison Knight and the staff of the Writers' Museum, Stewart Conn, Val McDermid, the staff of Napier University Library, Quintin Jardine, Ali Bowden and the staff of Edinburgh UNESCO City of Literature, the staff of the Scottish Poetry Library, Christopher Reekie, Noël Donoghue, Walter Elliot, Tom and Lis Bryan, Charlie Woolley, Kath McDonald, Jennie Renton, Lucy Foster and the staff of St Giles Cafe & Bar.

INDEX

Abbey Strand 112–113
Abbotsford (bar) 248–251, 287
Abbotsford (house) 36, 262, 336
Abden House 186–187
Abercromby Place 284, 294
Aberdeen Breviary 46
Acheson House 104–107
Act of Union 38
Adam, Robert 146
'Address to a Haggis' 26
Advocate's Close 50–51
Advocates Library 72
Aeneid, The 31, 46
Ainslie, Bob 27
Albany Street 202
Ambrose's Tavern 301
An Inland Voyage 29, 279, 359
Anchor Close 30, 66, 68
Andersen, Hans Christian 369
Anderson, Rowland 147
Ann Street 237, 302
Annals of a Publishing House 45
Annand, David 91
Antigua Street 225
Antiquary, The 30, 358
Arden Street 190
Arendt, Hannah 174
Argyle Park Terrace 221
Aristophanes 11
Armour, Jean 30, 102, 165
Arnold, Matthew 142

Arthur's Seat 25, 114–115, 187, 252
Assembly Rooms 266–267
Atkinson, Eleanor 56–59
Auchinleck, Lord 17
Auden, W.H. 242–243, 251
Austen, Jane 95, 200–202, 229, 234

Balfour, James 230
Balfour, Lewis 230–231, 314, 320–321
Balfour, Margaret (RLS's mother) 125, 231, 314, 321
Ballantyne, James 97–98, 261–263
Ballantyne, John 98–99
Ballantyne, R.M. 302–303, 339
Bank Street 22, 27, 42
Barbour, John 28
Barker, Pat 213
Barnes, Julian 209
Barrie, J.M. 33, 145–146, 149–150, 154–155, 296–299, 366
Baudelaire, Charles 235
Baxter's Close 24, 27, 28
Baxter's Place 222
Bedlam Asylum 92–93
Bedlam Theatre 45, 92
Bell, Andrew 67
Bell, Dr Joseph 130, 131, 132, 136–139, 145, 163, 219, 308–312, 352–353

INDEX

Bellfield Street 334
Bentham, Jeremy 20
Blackfriars Wynd 46
Blackfriars' Monastery 139
Blacklock, Thomas 164–165
Blackmore, R.D. 269
Blackwood, William 45, 118–120, 268–269
Blackwood's Magazine 45, 52, 54, 118–119, 186–187, 236, 268–269, 300–301, 334–335
Blair, Hugh 89
Blunden, Edmund 215
Bob Skinner 50–51
Bonnie Prince Charlie 110, 202, 338
Bookshops (selected) 363–364
Borrow, George 8–11
Boswell, James 16–20, 27, 40, 43, 80–81, 336
Boyd's Entry 80–81
Boyd's Inn 80
Breck, Alan 117
Bride of Lammermoor, The 48, 62, 262
Brodie's Close 34–35
Brooke, Rupert 215
Brougham, Henry 166, 313
Brown, Dan 354–355
Brown, Dr John 238–241
Brown, George Mackay 199, 251
Brown, James and George 182
Browning, Elizabeth Barrett 269
Brunton, Mary 95–96
Bruntsfield Place 194
Buccleuch Parish Church 34
Buccleuch Place 166, 168–169

Buchan, John 97–98, 111, 146, 186–187, 193, 266, 269
Buchanan, George 60, 282
Burgh Muir 46
Burke and Hare 160–163
Burns, Robert 12, 24, 28, 30, 33, 43, 44, 52, 65–69, 86–87, 90, 93, 95–96, 100–103, 122, 124–125, 164–165, 188–189, 333–334
Burroughs, William 175, 177
Burt, Edmund 370
Butler, Samuel 304
Byron, Lord 31, 52, 119, 166, 168, 261, 313

Cafe Royal 248
Calder, John 177
Caledonian Hunt 26
Calton Hill 9, 96, 99, 102, 122–125
Calton Jail 37
Campbell, Mary 165
Candlemaker Row 52
Canongate 22, 34, 80–107, 123, 263, 265
Canongate Kilwinning Lodge of Freemasons 86–87
Canongate Kirkyard 25, 88–103, 106, 123
Captains Bar 157
Carlyle, Jane Welsh 180, 304–307
Carlyle, Thomas 18, 43, 141, 144, 146, 166–167, 180, 304–307, 366
Carpenter, Charlotte 62, 185, 260–262
Carroll, Lewis 256
Carrubber's Close 14
Carswell, Catherine 24

Castle Hill 12, 14
Castle Street 185, 256, 260
Castlereagh, Lord 31
Catriona 230, 359
Central Library 361
Chambers Street 78, 238
Chambers, Robert 47–48
Chambers, William 47–48
Chambers' Encyclopedia 48
Chambers' Journal 48
Charles I, King 57, 70, 106
Charles II, King 47
Charles Street 170–173
Charlotte Square 246
Charlotte Square Gardens 365
Chepman, Walter 46
Chessels Court 34
Chesterton, G.K. 367
Child's Garden of Verses, A 29, 208, 278, 314, 316, 320, 322
Christison, Professor Sir Robert 129
Chronicles of Carlingford 45
Church Road 344
City Cross 13
Clarinda 30, 100–103
Clerk Street 237
Clinton Road 200–203
Clow, Jennie 102
Cockburn Street 66, 229
Cockburn, Lord Henry 120–121, 312, 337
Coleridge, Samuel Taylor 235, 300, 366
Colinton Manse 71, 231, 320–321
Colinton Parish Church 322–323
Colinton Road 210, 318–319
College of Justice 39

College Wynd 78
Colvin, Sidney 38
Comely Bank 228, 304–307
Comiston Place 209
Confessions of an English Opium-Eater 235–237
Conn, Stewart 93–94
Conrad, Joseph 154, 269
Constable, Archibald 98, 118–121, 166, 261–262
Coral Island 302–303
Cornhill Magazine 153, 160
Corstorphine Hill 339
Corstorphine Road 338–339
Court of Session 14, 38
Covenanters 69–72, 324, 328–329
Cowgate 32, 43, 46, 206
Craig's Close 229
Craiglockhart War Hospital 210–215
Cranston Street 263
Crawford of Lymond, Francis 37, 43
Creech, William 26, 65–66, 69
Crichton, Sir William 9–10
Crochallan Fencibles 27, 30, 66–68
Crockett, S.R. 145, 155, 326, 349–351
Cromwell, Oliver 57
Cumberland Street 296–299
Cunningham, Alison 'Cummy' 29, 34, 45, 70, 208–209, 314, 317

Da Vinci Code, The 354–355
Daiches, Alan 170–171
Dalrymple, James and Janet 48

INDEX

Darnley, Lord 60, 109, 112, 146
Darwin, Charles 20, 146
David Hume Tower 22
David I, King 112
Davies, Tom 17
Dawney Douglas's Tavern 67–68
de la Mare, Walter 269
De Quincey, Thomas 112–113, 115, 141, 235–237, 269, 300
Deacon Brodie 30, 34–35,
Deacon Brodie's Tavern 35
Dean Cemetery 288, 308–313
Dean Path 308–313
Defoe, Daniel 367–368
Dell Road 320–323
Dickens, Charles 142, 220, 253, 266, 304, 306–307, 313, 368–370
Disorderly Knights, The 43
Doctor Watson 129, 219, 246, 269
Douglas 82
Douglas, Gavin 31, 33, 46
Douglas, Lord Alfred 206
Doyle, Charles (ACD's father) 111, 216–217, 219–221
Doyle, Sir Arthur Conan 33, 106, 111, 115, 126–132, 136, 145, 149–150, 153, 163, 180–181, 216–221, 269, 308–309, 352
Dr Knox 160–163
Drummond Place 286–293
Drummond Street 32, 144, 148, 152, 163
Drummond, William 344–345
Drunk Man Looks at the Thistle, A 248, 250

Dryburgh Abbey 262, 336
Dunbar, William 14, 109, 286
Duncan, Andrew 93
Dundas Street 198
Dunnett, Dorothy 37, 43, 318–319
Duras, Marguerite 172
Durrell, Lawrence 175–176

Earl of Douglas 9–10
Earl of Glencairn 25–26
Earl of Hertford 112
Earl of Hopetoun 13
East Morningside House 200–203
East Princes Street Gardens 252–253
Edgeworth, Maria 262
Edinburgh Book Lovers' Tour 31–33
Edinburgh Castle 8–11, 15, 25, 46, 51, 97, 234, 326
Edinburgh Festival 176
Edinburgh Fringe Festival 173
Edinburgh International Book Festival 158, 365
Edinburgh International Conference Centre 51
Edinburgh Review 119–120, 122, 166–169, 186, 268, 300, 306, 312–313, 368
Edinburgh University 20, 22, 66, 68, 76, 82, 94, 96, 122, 126, 128, 144–149, 171, 173, 180, 184, 186–187, 190, 193, 194–195, 197, 198, 230, 240, 246, 282, 287, 294, 297, 301, 305, 308, 310, 312, 344, 352
Edinburgh, Museum of 107

375

Edinburgh: Picturesque Notes 40, 71–73
Eglinton Crescent 244
Eliot, George 269, 307
Elizabeth I, Queen 110
Ellroy, James 190
Encyclopaedia Britannica 67, 121
Essays Moral and Political 21
Evergreen, The 12, 14
Expedition of Humphry Clinker, The 84–85, 108

Faculty of Advocates 21, 168
Falcon Avenue 204–205
Ferguson, Adam 67
Fergusson, Robert 12, 25, 30, 45, 63, 67, 90–95, 282, 286
Ferrier, Susan 45, 119, 200–203, 234–235, 269, 370
Fettes Avenue 51
Fettes Row 45
First World War 11, 210–215
Flodden Wall 63, 65, 66
Forres Street 237
Forrest Road 45, 74, 92, 287
Forster, E.M. 243
Foster, Allan 31–33
Frankenstein 265
Franklin, Benjamin 89, 122
Fraser's magazine 18, 306
Fried, Erich 175

Gaboriau, Emile 219
Galt, John 15, 119, 269
Game of Kings, The 37, 319
Garioch, Robert 22, 146, 249, 282–283
Garrick, David 82
Gayfield Square 226–228

Geddes, Jenny 43
Gentle Shepherd, The 14
George IV Bridge 225, 228, 269, 307
George Square 22, 32, 78, 178–185, 221
George Street 185, 201, 225, 232, 240, 260, 264–273
George Watson's Ladies College 178
Glencorse Old Kirk 348–349
Gloucester Place 300–301
Godwin, Mary Wollstonecraft 265
Goebbels, Dr Joseph 369
Goethe, Johann Wolfgang von 347
Goldsmith, Oliver 146
Graham, James 46
Grahame, Kenneth 256–259
Grange Cemetery 192
Grange Road 192
Grant, Anne 15
Grassmarket 24, 37, 64, 192
Graves, Robert 213, 215
Gray, Alasdair 368
Gray, John 204–207
Gray, Sir William 28, 30
Gray, Thomas 368
Great King Street 237, 298
Greyfriars Bobby 57–58
Greyfriars Kirkyard 14, 32, 37, 56–73, 96, 157
Greyfriars Place 56
Grindlay Street 196
Gunn, Neil 242
Guthrie Street 78
Guy Mannering 56, 262

Hailes, Lord 89
Hall, Anthony 147

INDEX

Hanover Street 97, 251, 254
Hardy, Thomas 154, 268
Harrow Inn 52, 55
Harry Potter and the Philosopher's Stone 158–159
Hawes Inn 358–359
Haynes, Jim 170–173
Hazlitt, William 167, 367
Heart of Midlothian (motif) 37
Heart of Midlothian (prison) 36–37
Heart of Midlothian, The 37, 63–65, 115, 262
Hebrides 16, 40, 80
Henderson, Hamish 74–77
Henley, W.E. 29, 34, 117, 152–155, 204
Henryson, Robert 14
Heriot Row 34, 38, 125, 153, 278–281, 294, 317
High School Yards 134–139
High School, old 134–136, 139, 163, 184, 224, 254, 312
High Street 14, 21, 22, 40, 46, 66, 68
Hillary, Richard 340–343
Hispaniola 148, 150
History of the French Revolution 306
Hogg, James 43, 52–55, 87, 185, 261, 269, 301, 334–335, 347
Holyrood 108–115
Holyrood Abbey 88, 108–113
Holyrood Abbey Sanctuary 112–113, 115, 236
Holyrood Palace 25, 88, 108–113, 202, 217
Holyrood Park 112–115, 193
Home, John 82–83, 89
Hope, Anthony 296

Hopkins, Gerard Manley 268
Horner, Francis 166, 313
Howard Place 314–316, 321
Hume, David 20–23, 42, 43, 89, 116–117, 146, 164, 230
Huxley, Aldous 243

I Can Remember Robert Louis Stevenson 279
Ibsen, Henrik 179
Impregnable Women, The 11
Infirmary Street 126, 163, 184
International Writers' Conference 174–177
Inverleith Terrace 315–317
Invictus 152–153

Jack's Land 22
Jacob, Violet 28
James Court 16, 80
James Gillespie's High School for Girls 194–195, 318
James II, King 9–10
James IV, King 109
James V, King 39, 109
James VI (I, of England), King 9, 60
James VII (II, of England), King 88
James, Henry 154, 179, 269, 366
Jardine, Quintin 50–51
Jefferson, Thomas 122
Jeffrey, Francis 145, 166–169, 240, 313
Johnson, Samuel 16–20, 40, 43, 80–81, 89, 144, 368
Jonson, Ben 344
Journal of a Tour to the Hebrides 43, 80

Kailyard School 145, 155, 250
Kant, Immanuel 20
Kay, Christina 195–197
Keats, John 168, 268
Kemp, George Meikle
    252–253
Kidnapped 117, 279,
    338–339, 358–359
King's Stables Road 237
Kipling, Rudyard 154
Kirk o' Field 146
Knox, John 40, 42, 197

La Flèche 20
Lady Chatterley's Lover
    170–173
Lady of the Lake, The 61,
    260–261
Lady Stair's Close 24, 27, 28,
    31, 35, 68, 201
Lady Stair's House 28
Lane, Allen 172
Larkin, Philip 170
Lasswade Old Kirkyard
    344–345
Last Enemy, The 340, 342
Lavengro 10
Lawnmarket 42, 80, 173, 201
Lawrence, D.H. 334
Lay of the Last Minstrel 121,
    261, 347, 354, 356
Leamington Terrace 198–199
Lear, Edward 256
Lehmann, Rosamond 175
Lessing, Doris 243
Leyden, John 261
Life of Robert Burns, The 24
Life of Samuel Johnson 16, 18,
    19, 336
Life of Sir Walter Scott, The
    97–98, 336

Lingard, Joan 112, 176
Linklater, Eric 11
Lister, Joseph 129, 133, 136,
    139, 145, 152
Littlejohn, Sir Henry 129
Livingston, Sir Alexander
    9–10
Lockhart, John Gibson
    97–99, 115, 119, 134–135,
    232, 252, 262, 266, 268, 300,
    334–336, 346
Lomax, Alan 75
London 14, 17, 18, 22, 27, 35
London Magazine 236, 335
Long John Silver 152, 154,
    270
Lost World, The 115
Lothian Road 202, 234–237
Luckenbooths 13, 40, 65
Lysistrata 11

Macaulay, Lord 16, 18
MacCaig, Norman 146,
    198–199, 249
MacDiarmid, Hugh 145, 149,
    174–175, 198–199, 248–251,
    269, 286–287, 368
MacFarquhar, Colin 67
MacIntyre, Duncan Ban
    59–60
Mackenzie, Compton
    290–293
Mackenzie, Henry 26, 67–69,
    146, 183, 312, 347
Mackenzie, Sir George 70–73
MacKinnon, Gillies 213
Maclaren, Ian 155
Maclean, Sorley 28, 199, 283
Magnus Merriman 11
Mailer, Norman 175, 177
Makars' Court 28

INDEX

Man of Feeling, The 68
Marchhall Crescent 186–187
Marmion 121, 167, 261
Marriage 202
Married Love 284–285
Martyrs' Monument 69–71
Mary, Queen of Scots 8–9, 11, 57, 60, 109–110, 146
Masson, Flora 279
Masson, Professor 145
Masson, Rosaline 150
Mauchline 24
McCall Smith, Alexander 33, 229
McCarthy, Mary 174–175, 177
McDermid, Val 226–229, 365
McEwan Hall 174–177
McGonagall, William 31, 33, 156
McLehose, Agnes 100–103
McLehose, James 101
McLevy, James 104–107
Melrose Abbey 252
Memorials of His Time 312, 337
Menzies, John 254–255
Merry Muses of Caledonia, The 68
Mill, James 96
Miller, Henry 175, 177
Miller, James 137
Milnes Bar 248, 251, 287
Milton Bridge 352–353
Minstrelsy of the Scottish Border, The 53, 97, 261
Minto House Hospital 238
Mitchison, Naomi 242–243
Monboddo, Lord 66
Montgomerie, Margaret 17
Moore, Thomas 168
Moray Place 123

Morgan, Edwin 175
Morningside Cemetery 208
Morningside Drive 208
Morton, H.V. 368
Mount Vernon Cemetery 207
Muir, Edwin 43
Munro, Neil 269
Myllar, Androw 46

Nabokov, Vladimir 196
Napier University 210
Napoleon 202–203
National Covenant 43, 46, 57
National Library of Scotland 39, 72, 94, 120–121, 197, 225, 269, 298, 307, 360–361
Naysmith, Alexander 25, 66
Nelson Street 282–283
Nelson, Thomas 186, 192–193
New Calton Burial Ground 124–125
Newbattle Terrace 202
Newman, John Henry 142
Nicolson Street 100, 158, 160–163
Nicolson's 158–159
Niddry Street 14, 90
Niddry's Wynd 14, 90
Nightingale, Florence 127, 247
Ninewells 20
No. 1 Ladies' Detective Agency, The 295
North Castle Street 30, 185, 260–263
North Charlotte Street 274–275
North, Christopher (see Wilson, John) 52, 54, 141, 300–301

Old Calton Burial Ground 22, 37, 116–121
Old College 78, 128, 144–147
Old Playhouse Close 82–83
Old Tolbooth Prison 34, 36–37, 40, 64, 66
Oliphant, Margaret 8, 45
o' Phaup, Will 53
Orwell, Sonia 177
Osbourne, Lloyd 29
Owen, Wilfred 210, 213–215
Oxford Bar 191, 248, 276, 287

Paoli, Pasquale 17
Parker, Dorothy 229
Parliament Hall 38–39, 51, 185
Parliament Hall (Edinburgh Castle) 9
Parliament House 118
Parliament Square 32, 38, 119
Peacock, Thomas Love 265, 370
PEN, Scottish International 176, 250
Penguin Books 171–173
Penicuik South Church 350–351
Pentland Hills 324, 326, 328–329
Peter Pan 155, 296, 298
Philp, George 93
Picardy Place 216–218, 221
Picture of Dorian Gray, The 204
Pilgrims of the Sun, The 54
Pilrig House 230–231
Pilrig Street 230
Playfair, William 123, 146, 163, 167
Playhouse Theatre 82–83

Poe, Edgar Allan 219, 235
Poems, Chiefly in the Scottish Dialect 24
Political Discourses 22
Porteous, Captain John 37, 63–65
Portobello Sands 337
Potterrow 100–101
Potterrow Port 32
Priestley, J.B. 269
Prime of Miss Jean Brodie, The 40, 42, 194–196, 318
Primrose, Viscountess 28
Princes Street 119, 138, 229, 232–233, 237, 252–255, 301
Private Memoirs and Confessions of a Justified Sinner, The 53, 114
Professor Challenger 129
Prometheus Unbound 265
Protestant Reformation 42

Quarterly Review 168, 335
Queen Street Gardens 278
Queen's Wake, The 53
Queensberry, Duke of 37
Quiller-Couch, Arthur 326

Raffalovich, André 206
Ramsay Garden 12
Ramsay Lodge 15
Ramsay, Allan (artist) 14
Ramsay, Allan (poet) 12–15, 25
Randolph Crescent 242
Rankin, Ian 33, 114, 190–191, 276
Ravelston Dykes Road 339
Rebus, Inspector 190–191, 276
Redgauntlet 62

INDEX

Regeneration 213
Regent Road 37, 124, 254
Reid, Thomas 96
Reynolds, Sir Joshua 19
Rhino head sculpture 170, 172–173
Richmond, John 24
Riddel's Land 21
Riddle's Court 20–23
Rivers, W.H.R. 213
Rizzio, David 109, 111
Robbe-Grillet, Alain 172
Robertson's Close 126
Roget, Peter Mark 146
Rokeby 62
Rose Street 248, 287
Ross, Willie 276
Rosslyn Chapel 354–357
Round the Red Lamp 126
Rousseau, Jean-Jacques 17, 22
Rowling, J.K. 33, 158–159
Royal Botanic Gardens 51, 209, 317
Royal College of Surgeons of Edinburgh 160–163
Royal Edinburgh Hospital 94
Royal High School 94, 198, 282
Royal Infirmary (Infirmary Street) 32, 126–131, 133, 136–139, 180, 246–247
Royal Infirmary (Lauriston Place) 133, 310
Royal Scottish Academy 319
Ruskin, John 240, 253, 370
Rutherford, Anne 62, 78, 183, 232–233
Rutherford, Professor 129
Rutherford's Bar 32, 144, 148–151
Rutland Street 238–241

Saint-Gaudens, Augustus 44
Salinger, J.D. 196
Salisbury Crags 114–115
Saltire Society 22
Samoa 29, 44–45, 280
Sandy Bell's 74–77, 287
Sarraute, Nathalie 172
Sartor Resartus 306
Sassoon, Siegfried 210–211, 213–215
School of Scottish Studies 76
Sciennes Hill House 188–189
Sciennes House Place 188–189
Scotland Street 294–295
Scots Musical Museum 27
Scott Monument 115, 252–253
Scott, Sir Walter 10, 28, 30, 32, 33, 36, 38–39, 43, 48, 53, 56, 61–65, 69, 78–79, 96–99, 110, 115, 121–122, 134–135, 144–145, 167–168, 180, 182–185, 188–189, 202, 232–234, 252–253, 259–263, 249, 266–267, 269, 274, 313, 334–337, 346–347, 354, 356–357, 358
Scott, Tom 288
Scott, Walter (sen.) 62–63, 78, 182, 232
Scottish Borders 20, 27, 52, 53, 55, 62, 97, 182, 185, 229, 249, 261, 342
Scottish Chapbook 249–250
Scottish National Portrait Gallery 94
Scottish Parliament 38
Scottish Pastorals 53
Scottish Poetry Library 362
Scottish Renaissance

381

248–251, 276, 286
Self-Control 95–96
Shandwick Place 298
Shaw, George Bernard 178, 205
Shelley, Mary 202
Shelley, Percy Bysshe 264–265
Sherlock Holmes 106, 129, 130, 145, 163, 216–221, 269, 308–309, 311, 352
Silverado Squatters, The 279
Simpson, James Young 136, 238, 256
Sinclair, Catherine 274–275
Singh, Khushwant 175–176
Skinner's Rules 50
Smellie, William 27, 66–68
Smith, Adam 67, 88–90, 122
Smith, Alexander McCall 294–295
Smith, Geida 30
Smith, Henrietta Scott 231, 321
Smith, Reverend Sydney 166, 313, 369
Smith, Stevie 243, 251
Smith, Sydney Goodsir 74, 199, 249, 276, 286–289
Smith, W.H. 254–255
Smollett, Tobias 84–85, 108, 234, 367
South Bridge 119, 148, 150, 180
South Clerk Street 199
South College Street 156–157
South Learmonth Gardens 228
Southern Bar 199
Southey, Robert 235, 300, 368–369
Spark, Muriel 52, 40, 42, 175, 194–197
Speculative Society 66, 144, 185
Spence, James 137
Spender, Stephen 174–175
Spoon Cafe 158–159
St Andrew Square 22
St Colme Street 274
St David Street 22
St Giles' Cathedral 13, 36, 40–49, 50, 94
St Ives 10, 324, 326, 349
St John Street 84–87
St John's Church 138, 232–233
St. Cuthbert's Church & Churchyard 202, 234–237, 253, 302
St. Mary's Street 81
St. Patrick's Church 206
St. Peter's Church 204
Stair, Lady 28, 30
Steell, Sir John 252–253
Stephen, Leslie 153
Stevenson, Alan 223
Stevenson, Fanny (RLS's wife) 272, 279, 321
Stevenson, Jean (RLS's grandmother) 125
Stevenson, Margaret (see Balfour, Margaret)
Stevenson, Robert (RLS's grandfather) 125, 222–225, 314
Stevenson, Robert Louis 10, 28, 32, 33, 34–35, 38–39, 40, 43, 44–45, 47, 52, 70–73, 84, 115, 117, 125, 144, 148–151, 153–155, 160, 208–209, 222–225, 230–231, 238, 270–273, 278–281, 302, 314–317, 320–323, 338–339,

INDEX

348–349, 366
Stevenson, Thomas (RLS's father) 125, 222–225, 270–273, 278, 314, 317, 321, 329
Stewart, Alec 75
Stewart, Dugald 26, 96–97, 122–123, 144, 167, 188
Stirling Castle 8
Stirling University 198
Stopes, Marie 284–285
Strand, The 219–220
Strange Case of Dr Jekyll and Mr Hyde, The 35, 279
Stuart-Belsches, Williamina 61
Study in Scarlet, A 129, 219
Surgeon's Square 162–163
Surgeons' Hall Museums 160–163
Surgical Hospital, (new) 128, 131, 152–155
Surgical Hospital, (old) 128, 136–139, 145
Swanston Cottage 324–327, 348
Swanston Village 71, 209
Syme, Dr James 136–139

Tales of a Grandfather 10
Tea-Table Miscellany, The 14
Teviot Place 174, 245
Thackeray, William 141, 240, 266, 306
The Hydra 213, 215
The New Yorker 196
The Paperback 170–173
The Scots Magazine 53, 120
The Scotsman 158, 175–176, 254, 294
The Vaults (Edinburgh Castle) 10
Theatre Royal 82
Thin, James 140–142
Thirty-Nine Steps, The 186–187, 193
Thomas, Dylan 251
Traditions of Edinburgh 48
Trainspotting 330–332
Travels with a Donkey 29, 279
Traverse Theatre 173
Treasure Island 117, 150, 154, 270–273, 279, 320
Treatise of Human Nature, A 21, 117
Trocchi, Alexander 175
Trollope, Anthony 269
Trollope, Joanna 229
Tron Kirk 43, 92
Turnhouse Road 340
Twain, Mark 240

Under the Eildon Tree 286, 288
Union Canal 252
Union Street 225
Updike, John 196
Urquhart, Fred 244–245
Utrecht 17

Vicomte de Saint-Yves 10
Voltaire 17–18, 89

Wadingburn Road 346–347
War Poets Collection 215
Warrender Park Crescent 194
Warriston Cemetery 209, 255, 317
Water of Leith 315, 322
Waterloo Place 22, 37, 116–121

Watson, Roderick 199
Watson, Sir Patrick Heron 130, 246–247
Watt, Bob 93
Waverley 30, 37–38, 69, 110, 261–262, 266–267, 274
Wealth of Nations, The 88–89
Weir of Hermiston 184, 280, 349
Weldon, Sir Anthony 367
Wellington Place 330
Wells, H.G. 154, 178–179
Welsh, Irvine 330–332, 366
West Nicolson House 164
West Register Street 248
West, Rebecca 175, 178–179
Westbrook, Harriet 264–265
Whisky Galore 290, 292
Whitehouse Terrace 207
Wilde, Oscar 204–207, 269, 366
Williamson, Peter 117–118

Wilson, Edmund 16
Wilson, John (see North, Christopher) 52, 54, 55, 235, 268, 300–301
Wind in the Willows, The 256–259
Wodrow, Reverend Robert 13
Woolf, Virginia 153
Wordsworth, Dorothy 347, 367, 369
Wordsworth, William 166, 235–236, 300, 347, 354, 356–357
Writers' Museum 28–31, 32, 33, 35, 68

Yeats, W.B. 154
Yevtushenko, Yevgeny 172
Young Street 248, 276, 287
Young, Douglas 199

Made in the USA
Lexington, KY
07 June 2018